T0275489

Computer and Information Science

Computer and Information Science

Edited by
Jensen Hunter

Larsen & Keller
www.larsen-keller.com

Computer and Information Science
Edited by Jensen Hunter
ISBN: 978-1-63549-150-0 (Hardback)

© 2017 Larsen & Keller

⊟ Larsen & Keller

Published by Larsen and Keller Education,
5 Penn Plaza,
19th Floor,
New York, NY 10001, USA

Cataloging-in-Publication Data

Computer and information science / edited by Jensen Hunter.
     p. cm.
Includes bibliographical references and index.
ISBN 978-1-63549-150-0
1. Computer science. 2. Information science. 3. Information technology.
4. Information storage and retrieval systems. I. Hunter, Jensen.
QA76 .C66 2017
004--dc23

The publisher's policy is to use permanent paper from mills that operate a sustainable forestry policy. Furthermore, the publisher ensures that the text paper and cover boards used have met acceptable environmental accreditation standards.

Printed and bound in the United States of America.

For more information regarding Larsen and Keller Education and its products, please visit the publisher's website www.larsen-keller.com

Table of Contents

Preface

This book elucidates new techniques and their applications in a multidisciplinary approach. It talks in detail about the various uses and methods of information and computer science. Information and computer sciences brings together both information technology and computer science to improve machines, computer architecture, logic circuits, computer algorithms, etc. The aim of this book is to provide this complex subject in an easy to understand and student-friendly manner. The topics included in this text on information and computer science are of utmost significance and bound to provide incredible insights to readers. Those in search of information to further their knowledge will be greatly assisted by the book.

To facilitate a deeper understanding of the contents of this book a short introduction of every chapter is written below:

Chapter 1- Computer science is the study and engineering that forms the basis for the design and the use of computers. The fields concerned with computer science can be divided into theoretical and practical disciplines. The chapter on computer science offers an insightful focus, keeping in mind the complex subject matter.

Chapter 2- Processes and techniques are the basics of a subject; this chapter makes it easy for the reader to understand the techniques dealt within the information systems. The system used for reporting and data analysis is known as data warehouse while an expert system is a system that follows the decision-making ability of a human expert. This chapter also delves in the concepts of decision support system, executive information system and transaction processing system.

Chapter 3- Algorithms perform calculations and data processes whereas data processing collects information of data to produce meaningful information. Computing, algorithm, data processing and information technology are the important aspects of information and computer science. This chapter helps the reader to understand and to elucidate the crucial theories of computer science.

Chapter 4- Informatics concerns itself with information and computer information systems. Informatics has many branches, such as computer science, information technology and statistics. This chapter on informatics offers an insightful focus, keeping in mind the complex subject matter.

Chapter 5- The intelligence exhibited by machines is called artificial intelligence, a machine is considered to be intelligent if it is a flexible agent that perceives its environment and maximizing its possibilities of achieving a goal. It also gives a brief detail on robotics and systems development life cycle. The aspects elucidated in this chapter are of vital importance to the field of information and computer science.

I would like to share the credit of this book with my editorial team who worked tirelessly on this book. I owe the completion of this book to the never-ending support of my family, who supported me throughout the project.

Editor

Introduction to Information and Computer Science

Computer science is the study and engineering that forms the basis for the design and the use of computers. The fields concerned with computer science can be divided into theoretical and practical disciplines. The chapter on computer science offers an insightful focus, keeping in mind the complex subject matter.

Information and Computer Science

Information and Computer Science (ICS) or Computer and Information Science (CIS) (plural forms, i.e. Sciences, may also be used) is a field that emphasizes both computing and informatics, upholding the strong association between the fields of information sciences and computer sciences and treating computers as a tool rather than a field.

A lab in which CIS is studied.

Information science is one with a long history, unlike the – relatively – very young field of computer science, and is primarily concerned with gathering, storing, disseminating, sharing and protecting any and all forms of information. It is a broad field, covering a myriad of different areas but is often referenced alongside computer science because of the incredibly useful nature of computers and computer programs in helping those studying and doing research in the field – particularly in helping to analyse data and in spotting patterns too broad for a human to intuitively perceive. While information science is sometimes confused with information theory the two have vastly different subject matter. Information theory focuses on one particular mathematical concept of information while information science is focused on all aspects of the processes and techniques of information.

Computer science, on the other hand, is less focused on information and its different states, but more, in a very broad sense, on the use of computers – both in theory and practice – to design and implement algorithms in order to aid the processing of information during the different states described above. It has strong foundations in the field of mathematics, as the very first recognised practitioners of the field were renowned mathematicians such as Alan Turing.

Information Science and computing began to converge in the 1950s and 1960s, as information scientists started to realize the many ways computers would improve information storage and retrieval.

Terminology

Due to the distinction between computers and computing, some research groups refer to "computing" or "Datalogy". The French refer to computer science as *informatique*. The term "information and communications technology", or ICT, refers to how humans communicate with using machines and computers, making a distinction from "information and computer science", which is how computers use and gain information.

Informatics is also distinct from "computer science," which encompasses the study of logic and low-level computing issues.

Education

Universities may confer degrees of ICS and CIS, not to be confused with a more specific Bachelor of Computer Science or respective graduate Computer Science degrees.

The QS World University Rankings is one of the most widely recognised and distinguished university comparisons. They ranked the top 10 universities for Computer Science and Information Systems in 2015. They are:

- Massachusetts Institute of Technology(MIT)
- Stanford University
- University of Oxford
- Carnegie Mellon University
- Harvard University
- University of California, Berkeley(UCB)

- University of Cambridge

- The Hong Kong University of Science and Technology

- ETH Zurich – Swiss Federal Institute of Technology

- Princeton University

A Computer Information Science degree gives students both network and computing knowledge which is needed to design, develop, and assist information systems which helps to solve business problems and to support business problems and to support business operations and decision making at a managerial level also.

Areas of Information and Computer Science

Due the nature of this field, many topics are also shared with Computer Science and Information Systems fields.

The discipline of Information and Computer Science spans a vast range of areas from basic Computer Science theory (Algorithms and Computational Logic) to in depth analysis of data manipulation and use within technology.

Programming Theory

The process of taking a given algorithm and encoding it into a language that can be understood and executed by a computer. There are many different types of programming languages and various different types of computers, however, they all have the same goal: to turn algorithms into machine code.

Popular programming languages used within the academic study of CIS include, but are not limited to;

- Java

- Python

- C#

- C++

- Perl

- Ruby

- Pascal

- Swift

- Visual Basic

Information and Information Systems

The academic study of software and hardware systems that process large quantities and data, support large scale data management and how data can be used. This is where the field is unique from the standard study of Computer Science. The area of information systems focuses on the networks of hardware and software that are required to process, manipulate and distribute such data.

Computer Systems and Organisations

The process of analysing computer architecture and various logic circuits. This involves looking at low level computer processes at bit level computation. This is an in-depth look into the hardware processing of a computational system, involving looking at the basic structure of a computer and designing such systems. This can also involve evaluating complex circuit diagrams, and being able to construct these to solve a main problem.

The main purpose behind this area of study is to achieve an understanding of how computers function on a basic level, often through tracing machine operations.

Machines, Languages and Computation

This is the study into fundamental computer algorithms, which are the basis to computer programs. Without algorithms, there would be no computer programs. This also involves the process of looking into various mathematical functions behind computational algorithms, basic theory and functional (low level) programming.

In an academic setting this area would introduce the fundamental mathematical theorems and functions behind theoretical computer science which are the building blocks for other areas in the field. Complex topics such as; proofs, algebraic functions and sets will be introduced during studies of CIS.

Developments

Information and Computer Science is a field that is rapidly developing with job prospects for students being extremely promising with 75.7% of graduates gaining employment. Also the IT industry employs one in twenty of the workforce with it predicted to increase nearly five times faster than the average of the UK and between 2012 and 2017 more than half a million people will be needed within the industry and the fact that nine out of ten tech firms are suffering from candidate shortages which is having a negative impact on their companies as it delays the development of new products being created and it's predicted in the US that in the next decade there will be more than one million jobs in the technology sector than computer science graduates to actually fill them. Because of this programming is now being taught at an earlier age with an aim to interest students from a young age into Computer and Information Science hopefully leading more children to study this at a higher level. For example, children in England will now be exposed to computer programming at the age of 5 due to an updated national curriculum.

Employment

Due to the wide variety of jobs that now involve computer and information science related tasks it is difficult to provide a comprehensive list of possible jobs in this area, but some of the key areas are artificial intelligence, software engineering and computer networking/communication. Work in this area also tends to require sufficient understanding of mathematics and science. Moreover, jobs that having a CIS degree can lead to, include- systems analyst, network administrator, system architect, information systems developer, web programmer, or software developer.

The earning potential for CIS graduates is quite promising. A 2013 survey from the National Association of Colleges and Employers (NACE) found that the average starting salary for graduates who earned a degree in a computer related field was $59,977, up 4.3% from the previous year. This is higher than other popular degrees such as Business ($54,234), education ($40,480) and Math and Sciences ($42,724). Furthermore, Payscale ranked 129 college degrees based on their graduates earning potential with engineering, math, science, and technology fields dominating the ranking. With eight computer related degrees appearing among the top 30. With the lowest starting salary for these jobs being $49,900.

According to the National Careers Service an Information Scientist can expect to earn £24,000+ per year as a starting salary.

Computer Science

Computer science deals with the theoretical foundations of information and computation, together with practical techniques for the implementation and application of these foundations.

Its fields can be divided into a variety of theoretical and practical disciplines. Some fields, such as computational complexity theory (which explores the fundamental properties of computational and intractable problems), are highly abstract, while fields such as computer graphics emphasize real-world visual applications. Still other fields focus on challenges in implementing computation. For example, programming language theory considers various approaches to the description of computation, while the study of computer programming itself investigates various aspects of the use of programming language and complex systems. Human–computer interaction considers the challenges in making computers and computations useful, usable, and universally accessible to humans.

History

The earliest foundations of what would become computer science predate the invention of the modern digital computer. Machines for calculating fixed numerical tasks such as the abacus have existed since antiquity, aiding in computations such as multiplication and division. Further, algorithms for performing computations have existed since antiquity, even before the development of sophisticated computing equipment. The ancient Sanskrit treatise Shulba Sutras, or "Rules of the Chord", is a book of algorithms written in 800 BC for constructing geometric objects like altars using a peg and chord, an early precursor of the modern field of computational geometry.

Charles Babbage is credited with inventing the first mechanical computer.

Ada Lovelace is credited with writing the first algorithm intended for processing on a computer.

Blaise Pascal designed and constructed the first working mechanical calculator, Pascal's calculator, in 1642. In 1673, Gottfried Leibniz demonstrated a digital mechanical calculator, called the Stepped Reckoner. He may be considered the first computer scientist and information theorist, for, among other reasons, documenting the binary number system. In 1820, Thomas de Colmar launched the mechanical calculator industry[note 1] when he released his simplified arithmometer, which was the first calculating machine strong enough and reliable enough to be used daily in an office environment. Charles Babbage started the design of the first *automatic mechanical calculator*, his Difference Engine, in 1822, which eventually gave him the idea of the first *programmable mechanical calculator*, his Analytical Engine. He started developing this machine in 1834 and "in less than two years he had sketched out many of the salient features of the modern computer". "A crucial step was the adoption of a punched card system derived from the Jacquard loom" making it infinitely programmable.[note 2] In 1843, during the translation of a French article on the Analytical Engine, Ada Lovelace wrote, in one of the many notes she included, an algorithm to compute the Bernoulli numbers, which is considered to be the first computer program. Around 1885, Herman Hollerith invented the tabulator, which used punched cards to process statistical information; eventually his company became part of IBM. In 1937, one hundred years after Babbage's impossible dream, Howard Aiken convinced IBM, which was making all kinds of punched card equipment and was also in the calculator business to develop his giant programmable calculator, the ASCC/Harvard Mark I, based on Babbage's Analytical Engine, which itself used cards and a central computing unit. When the machine was finished, some hailed it as "Babbage's dream come true".

During the 1940s, as new and more powerful computing machines were developed, the term *computer* came to refer to the machines rather than their human predecessors. As it became clear that computers could be used for more than just mathematical calculations, the field of computer science broadened to study computation in general. Computer science began to be established as a distinct academic discipline in the 1950s and early 1960s. The world's first computer science degree program, the Cambridge Diploma in Computer Science, began at the University of Cambridge Computer Laboratory in 1953. The first computer science degree program in the United States was formed at Purdue University in 1962. Since practical computers became available, many applications of computing have become distinct areas of study in their own rights.

Although many initially believed it was impossible that computers themselves could actually be a scientific field of study, in the late fifties it gradually became accepted among the greater academic population. It is the now well-known IBM brand that formed part of the computer science revolution during this time. IBM (short for International Business Machines) released the IBM 704 and later the IBM 709 computers, which were widely used during the exploration period of such devices. "Still, working with the IBM [computer] was frustrating [...] if you had misplaced as much as one letter in one instruction, the program would crash, and you would have to start the whole process over again". During the late 1950s, the computer science discipline was very much in its developmental stages, and such issues were commonplace.

Time has seen significant improvements in the usability and effectiveness of computing technology. Modern society has seen a significant shift in the users of computer technology, from usage only by experts and professionals, to a near-ubiquitous user base. Initially, computers were quite costly, and some degree of human aid was needed for efficient use—in part from professional computer operators. As computer adoption became more widespread and affordable, less human assistance was needed for common usage.

Contributions

The German military used the Enigma machine (shown here) during World War II for communications they wanted kept secret. The large-scale decryption of Enigma traffic at Bletchley Park was an important factor that contributed to Allied victory in WWII.

Despite its short history as a formal academic discipline, computer science has made a number of fundamental contributions to science and society—in fact, along with electronics, it is a founding science of the current epoch of human history called the Information Age and a driver of the Information Revolution, seen as the third major leap in human technological progress after the Industrial Revolution (1750–1850 CE) and the Agricultural Revolution (8000–5000 BC).

These contributions include:

- The start of the "digital revolution", which includes the current Information Age and the Internet.

- A formal definition of computation and computability, and proof that there are computationally unsolvable and intractable problems.

- The concept of a programming language, a tool for the precise expression of methodological information at various levels of abstraction.

- In cryptography, breaking the Enigma code was an important factor contributing to the Allied victory in World War II.

- Scientific computing enabled practical evaluation of processes and situations of great complexity, as well as experimentation entirely by software. It also enabled advanced study of the mind, and mapping of the human genome became possible with the Human Genome Project. Distributed computing projects such as Folding@home explore protein folding.

- Algorithmic trading has increased the efficiency and liquidity of financial markets by using artificial intelligence, machine learning, and other statistical and numerical techniques on a large scale. High frequency algorithmic trading can also exacerbate volatility.

- Computer graphics and computer-generated imagery have become ubiquitous in modern entertainment, particularly in television, cinema, advertising, animation and video games. Even films that feature no explicit CGI are usually "filmed" now on digital cameras, or edited or post-processed using a digital video editor.

- Simulation of various processes, including computational fluid dynamics, physical, electrical, and electronic systems and circuits, as well as societies and social situations (notably war games) along with their habitats, among many others. Modern computers enable optimization of such designs as complete aircraft. Notable in electrical and electronic circuit design are SPICE, as well as software for physical realization of new (or modified) designs. The latter includes essential design software for integrated circuits.

- Artificial intelligence is becoming increasingly important as it gets more efficient and complex. There are many applications of AI, some of which can be seen at home, such as robotic vacuum cleaners. It is also present in video games and on the modern battlefield in drones, anti-missile systems, and squad support robots.

Etymology

Although first proposed in 1956, the term "computer science" appears in a 1959 article in *Communications of the ACM*, in which Louis Fein argues for the creation of a *Graduate School in Computer Sciences* analogous to the creation of Harvard Business School in 1921, justifying the name by arguing that, like management science, the subject is applied and interdisciplinary in nature, while having the characteristics typical of an academic discipline. His efforts, and those of others such as numerical analyst George Forsythe, were rewarded: universities went on to create such programs, starting with Purdue in 1962. Despite its name, a significant amount of computer science does not involve the study of computers themselves. Because of this, several alternative names have been proposed. Certain departments of major universities prefer the term *computing science*, to emphasize precisely that difference. Danish scientist Peter Naur suggested the term *datalogy*, to reflect the fact that the scientific discipline revolves around data and data treatment, while not necessarily involving computers. The first scientific institution to use the term was the Department of Datalogy at the University of Copenhagen, founded in 1969, with Peter Naur being the first professor in datalogy. The term is used mainly in the Scandinavian countries. An alternative term, also proposed by Naur, is data science; this is now used for a distinct field of data analysis, including statistics and databases.

Also, in the early days of computing, a number of terms for the practitioners of the field of computing were suggested in the *Communications of the ACM—turingineer, turologist, flow-charts-man, applied meta-mathematician*, and *applied epistemologist*. Three months later in the same journal, *comptologist* was suggested, followed next year by *hypologist*. The term *computics* has also been suggested. In Europe, terms derived from contracted translations of the expression "automatic information" (e.g. "informazione automatica" in Italian) or "information and mathematics" are often used, e.g. *informatique* (French), *Informatik* (German), *informatica* (Italian, Dutch), *informática* (Spanish, Portuguese), *informatika* (Slavic languages and Hungarian) or *pliroforiki* (πληροφορική, which means informatics) in Greek. Similar words have also been adopted in the UK (as in *the School of Informatics of the University of Edinburgh*). "In the U.S., however, informatics is linked with applied computing, or computing in the context of another domain."

A folkloric quotation, often attributed to—but almost certainly not first formulated by—Edsger Dijkstra, states that "computer science is no more about computers than astronomy is about telescopes."[note 3] The design and deployment of computers and computer systems is generally considered the province of disciplines other than computer science. For example, the study of computer hardware is usually considered part of computer engineering, while the study of commercial computer systems and their deployment is often called information technology or information systems. However, there has been much cross-fertilization of ideas between the various computer-related disciplines. Computer science research also often intersects other disciplines, such as philosophy, cognitive science, linguistics, mathematics, physics, biology, statistics, and logic.

Computer science is considered by some to have a much closer relationship with mathematics than many scientific disciplines, with some observers saying that computing is a mathematical science. Early computer science was strongly influenced by the work of mathematicians such as Kurt Gödel and Alan Turing, and there continues to be a useful interchange of ideas between the two fields in areas such as mathematical logic, category theory, domain theory, and algebra.

The relationship between computer science and software engineering is a contentious issue, which is further muddied by disputes over what the term "software engineering" mcans, and how computer science is defined. David Parnas, taking a cue from the relationship between other engineering and science disciplines, has claimed that the principal focus of computer science is studying the properties of computation in general, while the principal focus of software engineering is the design of specific computations to achieve practical goals, making the two separate but complementary disciplines.

The academic, political, and funding aspects of computer science tend to depend on whether a department formed with a mathematical emphasis or with an engineering emphasis. Computer science departments with a mathematics emphasis and with a numerical orientation consider alignment with computational science. Both types of departments tend to make efforts to bridge the field educationally if not across all research.

Philosophy

A number of computer scientists have argued for the distinction of three separate paradigms in computer science. Peter Wegner argued that those paradigms are science, technology, and mathematics. Peter Denning's working group argued that they are theory, abstraction (modeling), and design. Amnon H. Eden described them as the "rationalist paradigm" (which treats computer science as a branch of mathematics, which is prevalent in theoretical computer science, and mainly employs deductive reasoning), the "technocratic paradigm" (which might be found in engineering approaches, most prominently in software engineering), and the "scientific paradigm" (which approaches computer-related artifacts from the empirical perspective of natural sciences, identifiable in some branches of artificial intelligence).

Areas of Computer Science

As a discipline, computer science spans a range of topics from theoretical studies of algorithms and the limits of computation to the practical issues of implementing computing systems in hardware and software. CSAB, formerly called *Computing Sciences Accreditation Board*—which is made up of representatives of the Association for Computing Machinery (ACM), and the IEEE Computer Society (IEEE CS)—identifies four areas that it considers crucial to the discipline of computer science: *theory of computation, algorithms and data structures, programming methodology and languages*, and *computer elements and architecture*. In addition to these four areas, CSAB also identifies fields such as software engineering, artificial intelligence, computer networking and communication, database systems, parallel computation, distributed computation, human–computer interaction, computer graphics, operating systems, and numerical and symbolic computation as being important areas of computer science.

Theoretical Computer Science

Theoretical Computer Science is mathematical and abstract in spirit, but it derives its motivation from practical and everyday computation. Its aim is to understand the nature of computation and, as a consequence of this understanding, provide more efficient methodologies. All papers introducing or studying mathematical, logic and formal concepts and methods are welcome, provided that their motivation is clearly drawn from the field of computing.

Theory of Computation

According to Peter Denning, the fundamental question underlying computer science is, "What can be (efficiently) automated?" Theory of computation is focused on answering fundamental questions about what can be computed and what amount of resources are required to perform those computations. In an effort to answer the first question, computability theory examines which computational problems are solvable on various theoretical models of computation. The second question is addressed by computational complexity theory, which studies the time and space costs associated with different approaches to solving a multitude of computational problems.

The famous P = NP? problem, one of the Millennium Prize Problems, is an open problem in the theory of computation.

	⊠⊠⊠⊠⊠ ⊠⊠⊠⊠⊠	P = NP?	GNITIRW-TERCES	
Automata theory	Computability theory	Computational complexity theory	Cryptography	Quantum computing theory

Information and Coding Theory

Information theory is related to the quantification of information. This was developed by Claude Shannon to find fundamental limits on signal processing operations such as compressing data and on reliably storing and communicating data. Coding theory is the study of the properties of codes (systems for converting information from one form to another) and their fitness for a specific application. Codes are used for data compression, cryptography, error detection and correction, and more recently also for network coding. Codes are studied for the purpose of designing efficient and reliable data transmission methods.

Algorithms and Data Structures

Algorithms and data structures is the study of commonly used computational methods and their computational efficiency.

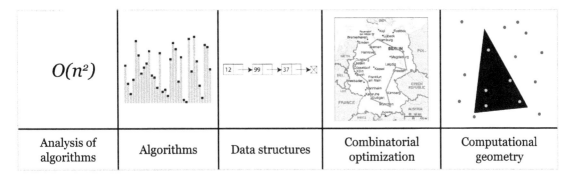

Analysis of algorithms	Algorithms	Data structures	Combinatorial optimization	Computational geometry

Programming Language Theory

Programming language theory is a branch of computer science that deals with the design, implementation, analysis, characterization, and classification of programming languages and their individual features. It falls within the discipline of computer science, both depending on and affecting mathematics, software engineering, and linguistics. It is an active research area, with numerous dedicated academic journals.

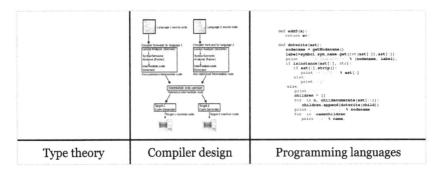

Type theory	Compiler design	Programming languages

Formal Methods

Formal methods are a particular kind of mathematically based technique for the specification, development and verification of software and hardware systems. The use of formal methods for software and hardware design is motivated by the expectation that, as in other engineering disciplines, performing appropriate mathematical analysis can contribute to the reliability and robustness of a design. They form an important theoretical underpinning for software engineering, especially where safety or security is involved. Formal methods are a useful adjunct to software testing since they help avoid errors and can also give a framework for testing. For industrial use, tool support is required. However, the high cost of using formal methods means that they are usually only used in the development of high-integrity and life-critical systems, where safety or security is of utmost importance. Formal methods are best described as the application of a fairly broad variety of theoretical computer science fundamentals, in particular logic calculi, formal languages, automata theory, and program semantics, but also type systems and algebraic data types to problems in software and hardware specification and verification.

Applied Computer Science

Applied computer science aims at identifying certain computer science concepts that can be used directly in solving real world problems.

Artificial Intelligence

Artificial intelligence (AI) aims to or is required to synthesise goal-orientated processes such as problem-solving, decision-making, environmental adaptation, learning and communication found in humans and animals. From its origins in cybernetics and in the Dartmouth Conference (1956), artificial intelligence research has been necessarily cross-disciplinary, drawing on areas of expertise such as applied mathematics, symbolic logic, semiotics, electrical engineering, philosophy of mind, neurophysiology, and social intelligence. AI is associated in the popular mind with robotic development, but the main field of practical application has been as an embedded component in areas of software development, which require computational understanding. The starting-point in the late 1940s was Alan Turing's question "Can computers think?", and the question remains effectively unanswered although the Turing test is still used to assess computer output on the scale of human intelligence. But the automation of evaluative and predictive tasks has been increasingly successful as a substitute for human monitoring and intervention in domains of computer application involving complex real-world data.

Machine learning	Computer vision	Image processing
Pattern recognition	Data mining	Evolutionary computation
	abcdefghijk lmnopqrstuvwxyz ABCDEFGHIJKLMN OPQRSTUVWXYZ	
Knowledge representation	Natural language processing	Robotics

Computer Architecture and Engineering

Computer architecture, or digital computer organization, is the conceptual design and fundamental operational structure of a computer system. It focuses largely on the way by which the central processing unit performs internally and accesses addresses in memory. The field often involves disciplines of computer engineering and electrical engineering, selecting and interconnecting hardware components to create computers that meet functional, performance, and cost goals.

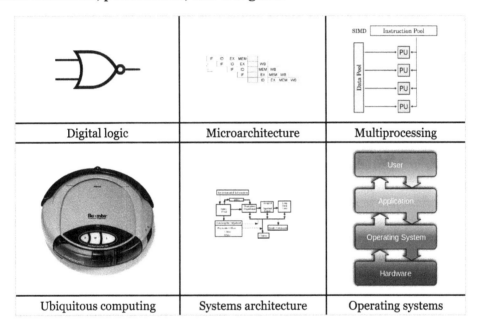

Digital logic	Microarchitecture	Multiprocessing
Ubiquitous computing	Systems architecture	Operating systems

Computer Performance Analysis

Computer performance analysis is the study of work flowing through computers with the general goals of improving throughput, controlling response time, using resources efficiently, eliminating bottlenecks, and predicting performance under anticipated peak loads.

Computer Graphics and Visualization

Computer graphics is the study of digital visual contents, and involves synthesis and manipulation of image data. The study is connected to many other fields in computer science, including computer vision, image processing, and computational geometry, and is heavily applied in the fields of special effects and video games.

Computer Security and Cryptography

Computer security is a branch of computer technology, whose objective includes protection of information from unauthorized access, disruption, or modification while maintaining the accessibility and usability of the system for its intended users. Cryptography is the practice and study of hiding (encryption) and therefore deciphering (decryption) information. Modern cryptography is largely related to computer science, for many encryption and decryption algorithms are based on their computational complexity.

Computational Science

Computational science (or scientific computing) is the field of study concerned with constructing mathematical models and quantitative analysis techniques and using computers to analyze and solve scientific problems. In practical use, it is typically the application of computer simulation and other forms of computation to problems in various scientific disciplines.

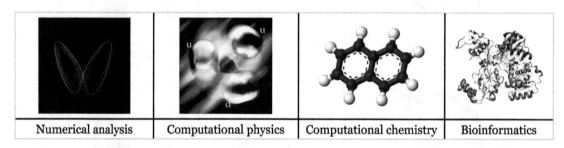

| Numerical analysis | Computational physics | Computational chemistry | Bioinformatics |

Computer Networks

This branch of computer science aims to manage networks between computers worldwide.

Concurrent, Parallel and Distributed Systems

Concurrency is a property of systems in which several computations are executing simultaneously, and potentially interacting with each other. A number of mathematical models have been developed for general concurrent computation including Petri nets, process calculi and the Parallel Random Access Machine model. A distributed system extends the idea of concurrency onto multiple computers connected through a network. Computers within the same distributed system have their own private memory, and information is often exchanged among themselves to achieve a common goal.

Databases

A database is intended to organize, store, and retrieve large amounts of data easily. Digital databases are managed using database management systems to store, create, maintain, and search data, through database models and query languages.

Software Engineering

Software engineering is the study of designing, implementing, and modifying software in order to ensure it is of high quality, affordable, maintainable, and fast to build. It is a systematic approach to software design, involving the application of engineering practices to software. Software engineering deals with the organizing and analyzing of software—it doesn't just deal with the creation or manufacture of new software, but its internal maintenance and arrangement. Both computer applications software engineers and computer systems software engineers are projected to be among the fastest growing occupations from 2008 to 2018.

The Great Insights of Computer Science

The philosopher of computing Bill Rapaport noted three *Great Insights of Computer Science*:

- Gottfried Wilhelm Leibniz's, George Boole's, Alan Turing's, Claude Shannon's, and Samuel Morse's insight: there are only *two objects* that a computer has to deal with in order to represent "anything".

  All the information about any computable problem can be represented using only 0 and 1 (or any other bistable pair that can flip-flop between two easily distinguishable states, such as "on/off", "magnetized/de-magnetized", "high-voltage/low-voltage", etc.).

- Alan Turing's insight: there are only *five actions* that a computer has to perform in order to do "anything".

  Every algorithm can be expressed in a language for a computer consisting of only five basic instructions:

  - move left one location;

  - move right one location;

  - read symbol at current location;

  - print 0 at current location;

  - print 1 at current location.

- Corrado Böhm and Giuseppe Jacopini's insight: there are only *three ways of combining* these actions (into more complex ones) that are needed in order for a computer to do "anything".

  Only three rules are needed to combine any set of basic instructions into more complex ones:

- *sequence*: first do this, then do that;

- *selection*: IF such-and-such is the case, THEN do this, ELSE do that;

- *repetition*: WHILE such-and-such is the case DO this.

Note that the three rules of Boehm's and Jacopini's insight can be further simplified with the use of goto (which means it is more elementary than structured programming).

Academia

Conferences are important events for computer science research. During these conferences, researchers from the public and private sectors present their recent work and meet. Unlike in most other academic fields, in computer science, the prestige of conference papers is greater than that of journal publications. One proposed explanation for this is the quick development of this relatively new field requires rapid review and distribution of results, a task better handled by conferences than by journals.

Education

Since computer science is a relatively new field, it is not as widely taught in schools and universities as other academic subjects. For example, in 2014, Code.org estimated that only 10 percent of high schools in the United States offered computer science education. A 2010 report by Association for Computing Machinery (ACM) and Computer Science Teachers Association (CSTA) revealed that only 14 out of 50 states have adopted significant education standards for high school computer science. However, computer science education is growing. Some countries, such as Israel, New Zealand and South Korea, have already included computer science in their respective national secondary education curriculum. Several countries are following suit.

In most countries, there is a significant gender gap in computer science education. For example, in the US about 20% of computer science degrees in 2012 were conferred to women. This gender gap also exists in other Western countries. However, in some parts of the world, the gap is small or nonexistent. In 2011, approximately half of all computer science degrees in Malaysia were conferred to women. In 2001, women made up 54.5% of computer science graduates in Guyana.

Information Science

Information science is an interdisciplinary field primarily concerned with the analysis, collection, classification, manipulation, storage, retrieval, movement, dissemination, and protection of information. Practitioners within the field study the application and usage of knowledge in organizations, along with the interaction between people, organizations and any existing information systems, with the aim of creating, replacing, improving, or understanding information systems. Information science is often (mistakenly) considered a branch of computer science; however, it predates computer science and is actually a broad, interdisciplinary field, incorporating not only aspects of computer science, but often diverse fields such as archival science, cognitive science, commerce, communications, law, library science, museology, management, mathematics, philosophy, public policy, and the social sciences.

The Ancient Library of Alexandria, an early form of information storage and retrieval.

Information science should not be confused with information theory or library science. Information theory is the study of a particular mathematical concept of information. Information science as an academic discipline is often taught in combination with Library science as Library and Information Science. Library science as such is a field related to the dissemination of information through libraries making use of the principles of information science. Information science deals with all the processes and techniques pertaining to the information life cycle, including capture, generation, packaging, dissemination, transformation, refining, repackaging, usage, storage, communication, protection, presentation etc. in any possible manner.

Foundations

Scope and Approach

Information science focuses on understanding problems from the perspective of the stakeholders involved and then applying information and other technologies as needed. In other words, it tackles systemic problems first rather than individual pieces of technology within that system. In this respect, one can see information science as a response to technological determinism, the belief that technology "develops by its own laws, that it realizes its own potential, limited only by the material resources available and the creativity of its developers. It must therefore be regarded as an autonomous system controlling and ultimately permeating all other subsystems of society."

Many universities have entire colleges, departments or schools devoted to the study of information science, while numerous information-science scholars work in disciplines such as communication, computer science, law, library science, and sociology. Several institutions have formed an I-School Caucus, but numerous others besides these also have comprehensive information foci.

Within information science, current issues as of 2013 include:

- human–computer interaction

- groupware

- the semantic web

- value-sensitive design

- iterative design processes

- the ways people generate, use and find information

Definitions of Information Science

An early definition of Information science (going back to 1968, the year when the *American Documentation Institute* renamed itself as the *American Society for Information Science and Technology*) states:

> "Information science is that discipline that investigates the properties and behavior of information, the forces governing the flow of information, and the means of processing information for optimum accessibility and usability. It is concerned with that body of knowledge relating to the origination, collection, organization, storage, retrieval, interpretation, transmission, transformation, and utilization of information. This includes the investigation of information representations in both natural and artificial systems, the use of codes for efficient message transmission, and the study of information processing devices and techniques such as computers and their programming systems. It is an interdisciplinary science derived from and related to such fields as mathematics, logic, linguistics, psychology, computer technology, operations research, the graphic arts, communications, library science, management, and other similar fields. It has both a pure science component, which inquires into the subject without regard to its application, and an applied science component, which develops services and products." (Borko, 1968, p.3).

Some authors use informatics as a synonym for *information science*. This is especially true when related to the concept developed by A. I. Mikhailov and other Soviet authors in the mid-1960s. The Mikhailov school saw informatics as a discipline related to the study of scientific information. Informatics is difficult to precisely define because of the rapidly evolving and interdisciplinary nature of the field. Definitions reliant on the nature of the tools used for deriving meaningful information from data are emerging in Informatics academic programs.

Regional differences and international terminology complicate the problem. Some people note that much of what is called "Informatics" today was once called "Information Science" - at least in fields such as Medical Informatics. For example, when library scientists began also to use the phrase "Information Science" to refer to their work, the term "informatics" emerged:

- in the United States as a response by computer scientists to distinguish their work from that of library science

- in Britain as a term for a science of information that studies natural, as well as artificial or engineered, information-processing systems

Another term discussed as a synonym for "information studies" is "information systems". Brian Campbell Vickery's *Information Systems* (1973) places information systems within IS. Ellis, Allen, & Wilson (1999), on the other hand, provide a bibliometric investigation describing the relation between two **different** fields: "information science" and "information systems".

Philosophy of Information

Philosophy of information (PI) studies conceptual issues arising at the intersection of computer science, information technology, and philosophy. It includes the investigation of the conceptual nature and basic principles of information, including its dynamics, utilisation and sciences, as well as the elaboration and application of information-theoretic and computational methodologies to its philosophical problems.

Ontology

In computer science and information science, an ontology formally represents knowledge as a set of concepts within a domain, and the relationships between those concepts. It can be used to reason about the entities within that domain and may be used to describe the domain.

More specifically, an ontology is a model for describing the world that consists of a set of types, properties, and relationship types. Exactly what is provided around these varies, but they are the essentials of an ontology. There is also generally an expectation that there be a close resemblance between the real world and the features of the model in an ontology.

In theory, an ontology is a "formal, explicit specification of a shared conceptualisation". An ontology renders shared vocabulary and taxonomy which models a domain with the definition of objects and/or concepts and their properties and relations.

Ontologies are the structural frameworks for organizing information and are used in artificial intelligence, the Semantic Web, systems engineering, software engineering, biomedical informatics, library science, enterprise bookmarking, and information architecture as a form of knowledge representation about the world or some part of it. The creation of domain ontologies is also fundamental to the definition and use of an enterprise architecture framework.

Careers

Information Scientist

An information scientist is an individual, usually with a relevant subject degree or high level of subject knowledge, providing focused information to scientific and technical research staff in industry, a role quite distinct from and complementary to that of a librarian. The title also applies to an individual carrying out research in information science.

Information Professional

An information professional is an individual who preserves, organizes, and disseminates information. Information professionals are skilled in the organization and retrieval of recorded knowledge. Traditionally, their work has been with print materials, but these skills are being increasingly used with electronic, visual, audio, and digital materials. Information professionals work in a variety of public, private, non-profit, and academic institutions. Information professionals can also be found within organisational and industrial contexts. Performing roles that include system design and development and system analysis.

History

Early Beginnings

Information science, in studying the collection, classification, manipulation, storage, retrieval and dissemination of information has origins in the common stock of human knowledge. Information analysis has been carried out by scholars at least as early as the time of the Abyssinian Empire with the emergence of cultural depositories, what is today known as libraries and archives. Institutionally, information science emerged in the 19th century along with many other social science disciplines. As a science, however, it finds its institutional roots in the history of science, beginning with publication of the first issues of *Philosophical Transactions,* generally considered the first scientific journal, in 1665 by the Royal Society (London).

Gottfried Wilhelm Leibniz, a German polymath who wrote primarily in Latin and French. His fields of study were Metaphysics, Mathematics, Theodicy.

The institutionalization of science occurred throughout the 18th Century. In 1731, Benjamin Franklin established the Library Company of Philadelphia, the first library owned by a group of public citizens, which quickly expanded beyond the realm of books and became a center of scientific experiment, and which hosted public exhibitions of scientific experiments. Benjamin Franklin invested a town in Massachusetts with a collection of books that the town voted to make available to all free of charge, forming the first Public Library. Academie de Chirurgia (Paris) published *Memoires pour les Chirurgiens*, generally considered to be the first medical journal, in 1736. The American Philosophical Society, patterned on the Royal Society (London), was founded in Philadelphia in 1743. As numerous other scientific journals and societies were founded, Alois Senefelder developed the concept of lithography for use in mass printing work in Germany in 1796.

19th Century

Joseph Marie Jacquard

By the 19th Century the first signs of information science emerged as separate and distinct from other sciences and social sciences but in conjunction with communication and computation. In 1801, Joseph Marie Jacquard invented a punched card system to control operations of the cloth weaving loom in France. It was the first use of "memory storage of patterns" system. As chemistry journals emerged throughout the 1820s and 1830s, Charles Babbage developed his "difference engine," the first step towards the modern computer, in 1822 and his "analytical engine" by 1834. By 1843 Richard Hoe developed the rotary press, and in 1844 Samuel Morse sent the first public telegraph message. By 1848 William F. Poole begins the *Index to Periodical Literature,* the first general periodical literature index in the US.

In 1854 George Boole published *An Investigation into Laws of Thought...,* which lays the foundations for Boolean algebra, which is later used in information retrieval. In 1860 a congress was held at Karlsruhe Technische Hochschule to discuss the feasibility of establishing a systematic and rational nomenclature for chemistry. The congress did not reach any conclusive results, but several key participants returned home with Stanislao Cannizzaro's outline (1858), which ultimately convinces them of the validity of his scheme for calculating atomic weights.

By 1865, the Smithsonian Institution began a catalog of current scientific papers, which became the *International Catalogue of Scientific Papers* in 1902. The following year the Royal Society began publication of its *Catalogue of Papers* in London. In 1868, Christopher Sholes, Carlos Glidden, and S. W. Soule produced the first practical typewriter. By 1872 Lord Kelvin devised an analogue computer to predict the tides, and by 1875 Frank Stephen Baldwin was granted the first US patent for a practical calculating machine that performs four arithmetic functions. Alexander Graham Bell and Thomas Edison invented the telephone and phonograph in 1876 and 1877 respectively, and the American Library Association was founded in Philadelphia. In 1879 *Index Medicus* was first issued by the Library of the Surgeon General, U.S. Army, with John Shaw Billings as librarian, and later the library issues *Index Catalogue,* which achieved an international reputation as the most complete catalog of medical literature.

European Documentation

The discipline of *documentation science,* which marks the earliest theoretical foundations of modern information science, emerged in the late part of the 19th Century in Europe together with several more scientific indexes whose purpose was to organize scholarly literature. Many information science historians cite Paul Otlet and Henri La Fontaine as the fathers of information science with the founding of the International Institute of Bibliography (IIB) in 1895. A second generation of European Documentalists emerged after the Second World War, most notably Suzanne Briet. However, "information science" as a term is not popularly used in academia until sometime in the latter part of the 20th Century.

Documentalists emphasized the utilitarian integration of technology and technique toward specific social goals. According to Ronald Day, "As an organized system of techniques and technologies, documentation was understood as a player in the historical development of global organization in modernity – indeed, a major player inasmuch as that organization was dependent on the organization and transmission of information." Otlet and Lafontaine (who won the Nobel Prize in 1913) not only envisioned later technical innovations but also projected a global vision for information and information technologies that speaks directly to postwar visions of a global "information society". Otlet and Lafontaine established numerous organizations dedicated to standardization, bibliography, international associations, and consequently, international cooperation. These organizations were fundamental for ensuring international production in commerce, information, communication and modern economic development, and they later found their global form in such institutions as the League of Nations and the United Nations. Otlet designed the Universal Decimal Classification, based on Melville Dewey's decimal classification system.

Although he lived decades before computers and networks emerged, what he discussed prefigured what ultimately became the World Wide Web. His vision of a great network of knowledge focused on documents and included the notions of hyperlinks, search engines, remote access, and social networks.

Otlet not only imagined that all the world's knowledge should be interlinked and made available remotely to anyone, but he also proceeded to build a structured document collection. This collection involved standardized paper sheets and cards filed in custom-designed cabinets according to a hierarchical index (which culled information worldwide from diverse sources) and a commercial information retrieval service (which answered written requests by copying relevant information from index cards). Users of this service were even warned if their query was likely to produce more than 50 results per search. By 1937 documentation had formally been institutionalized, as evidenced by the founding of the American Documentation Institute (ADI), later called the American Society for Information Science and Technology.

Transition to Modern Information Science

Vannevar Bush, a famous information scientist, ca. 1940–1944

With the 1950s came increasing awareness of the potential of automatic devices for literature searching and information storage and retrieval. As these concepts grew in magnitude and potential, so did the variety of information science interests. By the 1960s and 70s, there was a move from batch processing to online modes, from mainframe to mini and microcomputers. Additionally, traditional boundaries among disciplines began to fade and many information science scholars joined with library programs. They further made themselves multidisciplinary by incorporating disciplines in the sciences, humanities and social sciences, as well as other professional programs, such as law and medicine in their curriculum. By the 1980s, large databases, such as Grateful Med at the National Library of Medicine, and user-oriented services such as Dialog and Compuserve, were for the first time accessible by individuals from their personal computers. The 1980s also saw the emergence of numerous special interest groups to respond to the changes. By the end of the decade, special interest groups were available involving non-print media, social sciences, energy and the environment, and community information systems. Today, information science largely examines technical bases, social consequences, and theoretical understanding of online databases, widespread use of databases in government, industry, and education, and the development of the Internet and World Wide Web.

Information Dissemination in the 21st Century

Changing Definition

Dissemination has historically been interpreted as unilateral communication of information. With the advent of the internet, and the explosion in popularity of online communities, "social media has changed the information landscape in many respects, and creates both new modes of communication and new types of information", changing the interpretation of the definition of dissemination. The nature of social networks allows for faster diffusion of information than through organizational sources. The internet has changed the way we view, use, create, and store information, now it is time to re-evaluate the way we share and spread it.

Impact of Social Media on People and Industry

Social media networks provide an open information environment for the mass of people who have limited time or access to traditional outlets of information diffusion, this is an "increasingly mobile and social world [that] demands...new types of information skills". Social media integration as an access point is a very useful and mutually beneficial tool for users and providers. All major news providers have visibility and an access point through networks such as Facebook and Twitter maximizing their breadth of audience. Through social media people are directed to, or provided with, information by people they know. The ability to "share, like, and comment on...content" increases the reach farther and wider than traditional methods. People like to interact with information, they enjoy including the people they know in their circle of knowledge. Sharing through social media has become so influential that publishers must "play nice" if they desire to succeed. Although, it is often mutually beneficial for publishers and Facebook to "share, promote and uncover new content" to improve both user base experiences. The impact of popular opinion can spread in unimaginable ways. Social media allows interaction through simple to learn and access tools; *The Wall Street Journal* offers an app through Facebook, and *The Washington Post* goes a step further and offers an independent social app that was downloaded by 19.5 million users in 6 months, proving how interested people are in the new way of being provided information.

Social Media's Power to Facilitate Topics

The connections and networks sustained through social media help information providers learn what is important to people. The connections people have throughout the world enable the exchange of information at an unprecedented rate. It is for this reason that these networks have been realized for the potential they provide. "Most news media monitor Twitter for breaking news", as well as news anchors frequently request the audience to tweet pictures of events. The users and viewers of the shared information have earned "opinion-making and agenda-setting power" This channel has been recognized for the usefulness of providing targeted information based on public demand.

Research Vectors and Applications

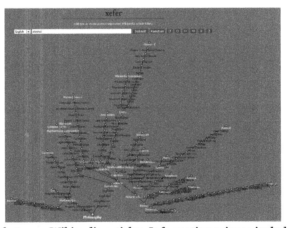

This graph shows links between Wikipedia articles. Information science includes studying how topics relate to each other, and how readers relate concepts to each other.

The following areas are some of those that information science investigates and develops.

Information Access

Information access is an area of research at the intersection of Informatics, Information Science, Information Security, Language Technology, Computer Science, and Library Science. The objectives of information access research are to automate the processing of large and unwieldy amounts of information and to simplify users' access to it. Applicable technologies include information retrieval, text mining, machine translation, and text categorisation. In discussion, information access is often defined as concerning the insurance of free and closed access to information and is brought up in discussions on copyright, patent law, and public domain.

Information Architecture

Information architecture (IA) is the art and science of organizing and labelling websites, intranets, online communities and software to support usability. It is an emerging discipline and *community of practice* focused on bringing together principles of design and architecture to the *digital landscape*. Typically it involves a model or concept of information which is used and applied to activities that require explicit details of complex information systems. These activities include library systems and database development.

Information Management

Information management (IM) is the collection and management of information from one or more sources and the distribution of that information to one or more audiences. This sometimes involves those who have a stake in, or a right to that information. Management means the organization of and control over the structure, processing and delivery of information. Throughout the 1970s this was largely limited to files, file maintenance, and the life cycle management of paper-based files, other media and records. With the proliferation of information technology starting in the 1970s, the job of information management took on a new light and also began to include the field of data maintenance.

Information Retrieval

Information retrieval (IR) is the area of study concerned with searching for documents, for information within documents, and for metadata about documents, as well as that of searching structured storage, relational databases, and the World Wide Web. Automated information retrieval systems are used to reduce what has been called "information overload". Many universities and public libraries use IR systems to provide access to books, journals and other documents. Web search engines are the most visible IR applications.

An information retrieval process begins when a user enters a query into the system. Queries are formal statements of information needs, for example search strings in web search engines. In information retrieval a query does not uniquely identify a single object in the collection. Instead, several objects may match the query, perhaps with different degrees of relevancy.

An object is an entity that is represented by information in a database. User queries are matched against the database information. Depending on the application the data objects may be, for example, text documents, images, audio, mind maps or videos. Often the documents themselves are not kept or stored directly in the IR system, but are instead represented in the system by document surrogates or metadata.

Most IR systems compute a numeric score on how well each object in the database match the query, and rank the objects according to this value. The top ranking objects are then shown to the user. The process may then be iterated if the user wishes to refine the query.

Information Seeking

Information seeking is the process or activity of attempting to obtain information in both human and technological contexts. Information seeking is related to, but different from, information retrieval (IR).

Much library and information science (LIS) research has focused on the information-seeking practices of practitioners within various fields of professional work. Studies have been carried out into the information-seeking behaviors of librarians, academics, medical professionals, engineers and lawyers (among others). Much of this research has drawn on the work done by Leckie, Pettigrew (now Fisher) and Sylvain, who in 1996 conducted an extensive review of the LIS literature (as well as the literature of other academic fields) on professionals' information seeking. The authors proposed an analytic model of professionals' information seeking behaviour, intended to be generalizable across the professions, thus providing a platform for future research in the area. The model was intended to "prompt new insights... and give rise to more refined and applicable theories of information seeking" (1996, p. 188). The model has been adapted by Wilkinson (2001) who proposes a model of the information seeking of lawyers.

Information Society

An information society is a society where the creation, distribution, diffusion, uses, integration and manipulation of information is a significant economic, political, and cultural activity. The aim of an information society is to gain competitive advantage internationally, through using IT in a creative and productive way. The knowledge economy is its economic counterpart, whereby wealth is created through the economic exploitation of understanding. People who have the means to partake in this form of society are sometimes called digital citizens.

Basically, an information society is the means of getting information from one place to another (Wark, 1997, p. 22). As technology has become more advanced over time so too has the way we have adapted in sharing this information with each other.

Information society theory discusses the role of information and information technology in society, the question of which key concepts should be used for characterizing contemporary society, and how to define such concepts. It has become a specific branch of contemporary sociology.

Knowledge Representation and Reasoning

Knowledge representation (KR) is an area of artificial intelligence research aimed at representing knowledge in symbols to facilitate inferencing from those knowledge elements, creating new elements of knowledge. The KR can be made to be independent of the underlying knowledge model or knowledge base system (KBS) such as a semantic network.

Knowledge Representation (KR) research involves analysis of how to reason accurately and effectively and how best to use a set of symbols to represent a set of facts within a knowledge domain. A symbol vocabulary and a system of logic are combined to enable inferences about elements in the KR to create new KR sentences. Logic is used to supply formal semantics of how reasoning functions should be applied to the symbols in the KR system. Logic is also used to define how operators can process and reshape the knowledge. Examples of operators and operations include, negation, conjunction, adverbs, adjectives, quantifiers and modal operators. The logic is interpretation theory. These elements—symbols, operators, and interpretation theory—are what give sequences of symbols meaning within a KR.

References

- Wescott, Bob (2013). The Every Computer Performance Book, Chapter 3: Useful laws. CreateSpace. ISBN 1482657759.

- Morville, Peter; Rosenfeld, Louis (2006). Information Architecture for the World Wide Web. O'Reilly Media, Inc. ISBN 978-0-596-52734-1.

- Frakes, William B. (1992). Information Retrieval Data Structures & Algorithms. Prentice-Hall, Inc. ISBN 0-13-463837-9.

- "What Is Programming? — Problem Solving with Algorithms and Data Structures". interactivepython.org. Retrieved 2015-11-19.

- "The 10 Best Online Bachelor in Computer Information Systems Degree Program". The Best Schools. Retrieved 2015-11-19.

- Maly, Timy. "How Digital Filmmakers Produced a Gorgeous Sci-Fi Movie on a Kickstarter Budget". Wired. Retrieved November 24, 2015.

- Matthau, Charles. "How Tech Has Shaped Film Making: The Film vs. Digital Debate Is Put to Rest". Wired. Retrieved November 24, 2015.

- Matti Tedre (2006). "The Development of Computer Science: A Sociocultural Perspective" (PDF). p. 260. Retrieved December 12, 2014.

- P. Collins, Graham (October 14, 2002). "Claude E. Shannon: Founder of Information Theory". Scientific American. Retrieved December 12, 2014.

- Zhang, B., Semenov, A., Vos, M. and Veijlainen, J. (2014). Understanding fast diffusion of information in the social media environment: A comparison of two cases. In ICC 2014 Conference Proceedings, 522-533

- "Computer science pioneer Samuel D. Conte dies at 85". Purdue Computer Science. July 1, 2002. Retrieved December 12, 2014.

- "IBM 709: a powerful new data processing system" (PDF). Computer History Museum. Retrieved December 12, 2014.

- "Web Dictionary of Cybernetics and Systems: Technological Determinism". Principia Cibernetica Web. Retrieved 2011-11-28.

- "Town of Franklin - History of the Franklin Public Library". Franklinma.virtualtownhall.net. 2010-06-29. Retrieved 2011-05-28.

- Computing Sciences Accreditation Board (May 28, 1997). "Computer Science as a Profession". Archived from the original on 2008-06-17. Retrieved 2010-05-23.

Processes and Techniques in Information Systems

Processes and techniques are the basics of a subject; this chapter makes it easy for the reader to understand the techniques dealt within the information systems. The system used for reporting and data analysis is known as data warehouse while an expert system is a system that follows the decision-making ability of a human expert. This chapter also delves in the concepts of decision support system, executive information system and transaction processing system.

Data Warehouse

In computing, a data warehouse (DW or DWH), also known as an enterprise data warehouse (EDW), is a system used for reporting and data analysis, and is considered as a core component of business intelligence environment. DWs are central repositories of integrated data from one or more disparate sources. They store current and historical data and are used for creating analytical reports for knowledge workers throughout the enterprise. Examples of reports could range from annual and quarterly comparisons and trends to detailed daily sales analysis

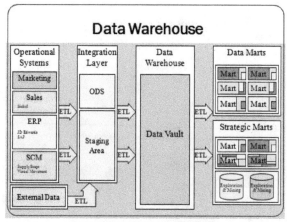

Data Warehouse Overview

The data stored in the warehouse is uploaded from the operational systems (such as marketing, sales, etc., shown in the figure to the right). The data may pass through an operational data store for additional operations before it is used in the DW for reporting.

Types of Systems

Data mart

A data mart is a simple form of a data warehouse that is focused on a single subject (or functional area) hence, they draw data from a limited number of sources such as sales, finance or marketing. Data marts are often built and controlled by a single department within an organization. The sources could be internal operational systems, a central data warehouse, or external data. Denormalization is the norm for data modeling techniques in this system. Given that data marts generally cover only a subset of the data contained in a data warehouse, they are often easier and faster to implement.

The difference between data warehouse and data mart

Data warehouse	data mart
enterprise-wide data	department-wide data
multiple subject areas	single subject area
difficult to build	easy to build
takes more time to build	less time to build
larger memory	limited memory

Types of Data Marts

- Dependent data mart
- Independent data mart
- Hybrid data mart

Online analytical processing (OLAP)

OLAP is characterized by a relatively low volume of transactions. Queries are often very complex and involve aggregations. For OLAP systems, response time is an effectiveness measure. OLAP applications are widely used by Data Mining techniques. OLAP databases store aggregated, historical data in multi-dimensional schemas (usually star schemas). OLAP systems typically have data latency of a few hours, as opposed to data marts, where latency is expected to be closer to one day.The OLAP approach is used to analyze multidimensional data from multiple sources and perspectives. The three basic operations in OLAP are : Roll-up (Consolidation), Drill-down and Slicing & Dicing.

Online transaction processing (OLTP)

OLTP is characterized by a large number of short on-line transactions (INSERT, UPDATE, DELETE). OLTP systems emphasize very fast query processing and maintaining data integrity in multi-access environments. For OLTP systems, effectiveness is measured by the number of transactions per second. OLTP databases contain detailed and current data. The schema used to store transactional databases is the entity model (usually 3NF). Normalization is the norm for data modeling techniques in this system.

Predictive analysis

Predictive analysis is about finding and quantifying hidden patterns in the data using complex mathematical models that can be used to predict future outcomes. Predictive analysis is different from OLAP in that OLAP focuses on historical data analysis and is reactive in nature, while predictive analysis focuses on the future. These systems are also used for CRM (customer relationship management).

Software Tools

The typical extract-transform-load (ETL)-based data warehouse uses staging, data integration, and access layers to house its key functions. The staging layer or staging database stores raw data extracted from each of the disparate source data systems. The integration layer integrates the disparate data sets by transforming the data from the staging layer often storing this transformed data in an operational data store (ODS) database. The integrated data are then moved to yet another database, often called the data warehouse database, where the data is arranged into hierarchical groups often called dimensions and into facts and aggregate facts. The combination of facts and dimensions is sometimes called a star schema. The access layer helps users retrieve data.

This definition of the data warehouse focuses on data storage. The main source of the data is cleaned, transformed, cataloged and made available for use by managers and other business professionals for data mining, online analytical processing, market research and decision support. However, the means to retrieve and analyze data, to extract, transform and load data, and to manage the data dictionary are also considered essential components of a data warehousing system. Many references to data warehousing use this broader context. Thus, an expanded definition for data warehousing includes business intelligence tools, tools to extract, transform and load data into the repository, and tools to manage and retrieve metadata.

Benefits

A data warehouse maintains a copy of information from the source transaction systems. This architectural complexity provides the opportunity to:

- Congregate data from multiple sources into a single database so a single query engine can be used to present data.

- Mitigate the problem of database isolation level lock contention in transaction processing systems caused by attempts to run large, long running, analysis queries in transaction processing databases.

- Maintain data history, even if the source transaction systems do not.

- Integrate data from multiple source systems, enabling a central view across the enterprise. This benefit is always valuable, but particularly so when the organization has grown by merger.

- Improve data quality, by providing consistent codes and descriptions, flagging or even fixing bad data.

- Present the organization's information consistently.

- Provide a single common data model for all data of interest regardless of the data's source.

- Restructure the data so that it makes sense to the business users.

- Restructure the data so that it delivers excellent query performance, even for complex analytic queries, without impacting the operational systems.

- Add value to operational business applications, notably customer relationship management (CRM) systems.

- Make decision–support queries easier to write.

Generic Data Warehouse Environment

The environment for data warehouses and marts includes the following:

- Source systems that provide data to the warehouse or mart;

- Data integration technology and processes that are needed to prepare the data for use;

- Different architectures for storing data in an organization's data warehouse or data marts;

- Different tools and applications for the variety of users;

- Metadata, data quality, and governance processes must be in place to ensure that the warehouse or mart meets its purposes.

In regards to source systems listed above, Rainer states, "A common source for the data in data warehouses is the company's operational databases, which can be relational databases".

Regarding data integration, Rainer states, "It is necessary to extract data from source systems, transform them, and load them into a data mart or warehouse".

Rainer discusses storing data in an organization's data warehouse or data marts.

Metadata are data about data. "IT personnel need information about data sources; database, table, and column names; refresh schedules; and data usage measures".

Today, the most successful companies are those that can respond quickly and flexibly to market changes and opportunities. A key to this response is the effective and efficient use of data and information by analysts and managers. A "data warehouse" is a repository of historical data that are organized by subject to support decision makers in the organization. Once data are stored in a data mart or warehouse, they can be accessed.

History

The concept of data warehousing dates back to the late 1980s when IBM researchers Barry Devlin and Paul Murphy developed the "business data warehouse". In essence, the data warehousing concept was intended to provide an architectural model for the flow of data from operational systems to decision support environments. The concept attempted to address the various problems associated with this flow, mainly the high costs associated with it. In the absence of a data warehousing architecture, an enormous amount of redundancy was required to support multiple decision support environments. In larger corporations it was typical for multiple decision support environments to operate independently. Though each environment served different users, they often required much of the same stored data. The process of gathering, cleaning and integrating data from various sources, usually from long-term existing operational systems (usually referred to as legacy systems), was typically in part replicated for each environment. Moreover, the operational systems were frequently reexamined as new decision support requirements emerged. Often new requirements necessitated gathering, cleaning and integrating new data from "data marts" that were tailored for ready access by users.

Key developments in early years of data warehousing were:

- 1960s — General Mills and Dartmouth College, in a joint research project, develop the terms *dimensions* and *facts*.

- 1970s — ACNielsen and IRI provide dimensional data marts for retail sales.

- 1970s — Bill Inmon begins to define and discuss the term: Data Warehouse.

- 1975 — Sperry Univac introduces MAPPER (MAintain, Prepare, and Produce Executive Reports) is a database management and reporting system that includes the world's first 4GL. First platform designed for building Information Centers (a forerunner of contemporary Enterprise Data Warehousing platforms)

- 1983 — Teradata introduces a database management system specifically designed for decision support.

- 1984 — Metaphor Computer Systems, founded by David Liddle and Don Massaro, releases Data Interpretation System (DIS). DIS was a hardware/software package and GUI for business users to create a database management and analytic system.

- 1988 — Barry Devlin and Paul Murphy publish the article *An architecture for a business and information system* where they introduce the term "business data warehouse".

- 1990 — Red Brick Systems, founded by Ralph Kimball, introduces Red Brick Warehouse, a database management system specifically for data warehousing.

- 1991 — Prism Solutions, founded by Bill Inmon, introduces Prism Warehouse Manager, software for developing a data warehouse.

- 1992 — Bill Inmon publishes the book *Building the Data Warehouse*.

- 1995 — The Data Warehousing Institute, a for-profit organization that promotes data warehousing, is founded.

- 1996 — Ralph Kimball publishes the book *The Data Warehouse Toolkit*.

- 2012 — Bill Inmon developed and made public technology known as "textual disambiguation". Textual disambiguation applies context to raw text and reformats the raw text and context into a standard data base format. Once raw text is passed through textual disambiguation, it can easily and efficiently be accessed and analyzed by standard business intelligence technology. Textual disambiguation is accomplished through the execution of textual ETL. Textual disambiguation is useful wherever raw text is found, such as in documents, Hadoop, email, and so forth.

Information Storage

Facts

A fact is a value or measurement, which represents a fact about the managed entity or system.

Facts as reported by the reporting entity are said to be at raw level. E.g. if a BTS (business transformation service) received 1,000 requests for traffic channel allocation, it allocates for 820 and rejects the remaining then it would report 3 **facts** or measurements to a management system:

- tch_req_total = 1000

- tch_req_success = 820

- tch_req_fail = 180

Facts at raw level are further aggregated to higher levels in various dimensions to extract more service or business-relevant information out of it. These are called aggregates or summaries or aggregated facts.

E.g. if there are 3 BTSs in a city, then facts above can be aggregated from BTS to city level in network dimension. E.g.

$$tch\_req\_success\_city = tch\_req\_success\_bts1 + tch\_req\_success\_bts2 + tch\_req\_success\_bts3$$

$$avg\_tch\_req\_success\_city = (tch\_req\_success\_bts1 + tch\_req\_success\_bts2 + tch\_req\_success\_bts3)/3$$

Dimensional vs. Normalized Approach for Storage of Data

There are three or more leading approaches to storing data in a data warehouse — the most important approaches are the dimensional approach and the normalized approach.

The dimensional approach refers to Ralph Kimball's approach in which it is stated that the data warehouse should be modeled using a Dimensional Model/star schema. The normalized approach, also called the 3NF model (Third Normal Form) refers to Bill Inmon's approach in which it is stated that the data warehouse should be modeled using an E-R model/normalized model.

In a dimensional approach, transaction data are partitioned into "facts", which are generally numeric transaction data, and "dimensions", which are the reference information that gives context to the facts. For example, a sales transaction can be broken up into facts such as the number of products ordered and the price paid for the products, and into dimensions such as order date, customer name, product number, order ship-to and bill-to locations, and salesperson responsible for receiving the order.

A key advantage of a dimensional approach is that the data warehouse is easier for the user to understand and to use. Also, the retrieval of data from the data warehouse tends to operate very quickly. Dimensional structures are easy to understand for business users, because the structure is divided into measurements/facts and context/dimensions. Facts are related to the organization's business processes and operational system whereas the dimensions surrounding them contain context about the measurement (Kimball, Ralph 2008). Another advantage offered by dimensional model is that it does not involve a relational database every time. Thus,this type of modeling technique is very useful for end-user queries in data warehouse.

The main disadvantages of the dimensional approach are the following:

1. In order to maintain the integrity of facts and dimensions, loading the data warehouse with data from different operational systems is complicated.

2. It is difficult to modify the data warehouse structure if the organization adopting the dimensional approach changes the way in which it does business.

In the normalized approach, the data in the data warehouse are stored following, to a degree, database normalization rules. Tables are grouped together by *subject areas* that reflect general data categories (e.g., data on customers, products, finance, etc.). The normalized structure divides data into entities, which creates several tables in a relational database. When applied in large enterprises the result is dozens of tables that are linked together by a web of joins. Furthermore, each of the created entities is converted into separate physical tables when the database is implemented (Kimball, Ralph 2008). The main advantage of this approach is that it is straightforward to add information into the database. Some disadvantages of this approach are that, because of the number of tables involved, it can be difficult for users to join data from different sources into meaningful information and to access the information without a precise understanding of the sources of data and of the data structure of the data warehouse.

Both normalized and dimensional models can be represented in entity-relationship diagrams as both contain joined relational tables. The difference between the two models is the degree of normalization (also known as Normal Forms). These approaches are not mutually exclusive, and there are other approaches. Dimensional approaches can involve normalizing data to a degree (Kimball, Ralph 2008).

In *Information-Driven Business*, Robert Hillard proposes an approach to comparing the two approaches based on the information needs of the business problem. The technique shows that normalized models hold far more information than their dimensional equivalents (even when the same fields are used in both models) but this extra information comes at the cost of usability. The technique measures information quantity in terms of information entropy and usability in terms of the Small Worlds data transformation measure.

Design Methods

Bottom-up Design

In the *bottom-up* approach, data marts are first created to provide reporting and analytical capabilities for specific business processes. These data marts can then be integrated to create a comprehensive data warehouse. The data warehouse bus architecture is primarily an implementation of "the bus", a collection of conformed dimensions and conformed facts, which are dimensions that are shared (in a specific way) between facts in two or more data marts.

Top-down Design

The *top-down* approach is designed using a normalized enterprise data model. "Atomic" data, that is, data at the greatest level of detail, are stored in the data warehouse. Dimensional data marts containing data needed for specific business processes or specific departments are created from the data warehouse.

Hybrid Design

Data warehouses (DW) often resemble the hub and spokes architecture. Legacy systems feeding the warehouse often include customer relationship management and enterprise resource planning, generating large amounts of data. To consolidate these various data models, and facilitate the extract transform load process, data warehouses often make use of an operational data store, the information from which is parsed into the actual DW. To reduce data redundancy, larger systems often store the data in a normalized way. Data marts for specific reports can then be built on top of the DW.

The DW database in a hybrid solution is kept on third normal form to eliminate data redundancy. A normal relational database, however, is not efficient for business intelligence reports where dimensional modelling is prevalent. Small data marts can shop for data from the consolidated warehouse and use the filtered, specific data for the fact tables and dimensions required. The DW provides a single source of information from which the data marts can read, providing a wide range of business information. The hybrid architecture allows a DW to be replaced with a master data management solution where operational, not static information could reside.

The Data Vault Modeling components follow hub and spokes architecture. This modeling style is a hybrid design, consisting of the best practices from both third normal form and star schema. The Data Vault model is not a true third normal form, and breaks some of its rules, but it is a top-down architecture with a bottom up design. The Data Vault model is geared to be strictly a data warehouse. It is not geared to be end-user accessible, which when built, still requires the use of a data mart or star schema based release area for business purposes.

Data Warehouses versus Operational Systems

Operational systems are optimized for preservation of data integrity and speed of recording of business transactions through use of database normalization and an entity-relationship model. Operational system designers generally follow the Codd rules of database normalization in order to ensure data integrity. Codd defined five increasingly stringent rules of normalization. Fully normalized database designs (that is, those satisfying all five Codd rules) often result in information from a business transaction being stored in dozens to hundreds of tables. Relational databases are efficient at managing the relationships between these tables. The databases have very fast insert/update performance because only a small amount of data in those tables is affected each time a transaction is processed. Finally, in order to improve performance, older data are usually periodically purged from operational systems.

Data warehouses are optimized for analytic access patterns. Analytic access patterns generally involve selecting specific fields and rarely if ever 'select *' as is more common in operational databases. Because of these differences in access patterns, operational databases (loosely, OLTP) benefit from the use of a row-oriented DBMS whereas analytics databases (loosely, OLAP) benefit from the use of a column-oriented DBMS. Unlike operational systems which maintain a snapshot of the business, data warehouses generally maintain an infinite history which is implemented through ETL processes that periodically migrate data from the operational systems over to the data warehouse.

Evolution in Organization Use

These terms refer to the level of sophistication of a data warehouse:

Offline operational data warehouse

> Data warehouses in this stage of evolution are updated on a regular time cycle (usually daily, weekly or monthly) from the operational systems and the data is stored in an integrated reporting-oriented data

Offline data warehouse

> Data warehouses at this stage are updated from data in the operational systems on a regular basis and the data warehouse data are stored in a data structure designed to facilitate reporting.

On time data warehouse

> Online Integrated Data Warehousing represent the real time Data warehouses stage data in the warehouse is updated for every transaction performed on the source data

Integrated data warehouse

> These data warehouses assemble data from different areas of business, so users can look up the information they need across other systems.

Enterprise Resource Planning

Enterprise resource planning (ERP) is a category of business-management software—typically a suite of integrated applications—that an organization can use to collect, store, manage and interpret data from many business activities, including:

- product planning, purchase
- manufacturing or service delivery
- marketing and sales
- inventory management
- shipping and payment

Diagram showing some typical ERP modules

ERP provides an integrated view of core business processes, often in real-time, using common databases maintained by a database management system. ERP systems track business resources—cash, raw materials, production capacity—and the status of business commitments: orders, purchase orders, and payroll. The applications that make up the system share data across various departments (manufacturing, purchasing, sales, accounting, etc.) that provide the data. ERP facilitates information flow between all business functions, and manages connections to outside stakeholders.

Enterprise system software is a multibillion-dollar industry that produces components that support a variety of business functions. IT investments have become the largest category of capital expenditure in United States-based businesses over the past decade. Though early ERP systems focused on large enterprises, smaller enterprises increasingly use ERP systems.

The ERP system is considered a vital organizational tool because it integrates varied organizational systems and facilitates error-free transactions and production. However, developing an ERP system differs from traditional system development. ERP systems run on a variety of computer hardware and network configurations, typically using a database as an information repository.

Origin

The Gartner Group first used the acronym ERP in the 1990s, where it was seen to extend the capabilities of material requirements planning (MRP), and the later manufacturing resource planning (MRP II), as well as computer-integrated manufacturing. Without replacing these terms, ERP came to represent a larger whole that reflected the evolution of application integration beyond manufacturing.

Not all ERP packages developed from a manufacturing core; ERP vendors variously began assembling their packages with accounting, maintenance, and human-resource components. By the mid-1990s ERP systems addressed all core enterprise functions. Governments and non–profit organizations also began to use ERP systems.

Expansion

ERP systems experienced rapid growth in the 1990s. Because of the year 2000 problem and the introduction of the euro that disrupted legacy systems, many companies took the opportunity to replace their old systems with ERP.

ERP systems initially focused on automating *back office functions* that did not directly affect customers and the public. *Front office functions*, such as customer relationship management (CRM), dealt directly with customers, or e-business systems such as e-commerce, e-government, e-telecom, and e-finance—or supplier relationship management (SRM) became integrated later, when the Internet simplified communicating with external parties.

"ERP II" was coined in 2000 in an article by Gartner Publications entitled *ERP Is Dead—Long Live ERP II*. It describes web–based software that provides real–time access to ERP systems to employees and partners (such as suppliers and customers). The ERP II role expands traditional ERP resource optimization and transaction processing. Rather than just manage buying, selling, etc.—ERP II leverages information in the resources under its management to help the enterprise collaborate with other enterprises. ERP II is more flexible than the first generation ERP. Rather than confine ERP system capabilities within the organization, it goes beyond the corporate walls to interact with other systems. *Enterprise application suite* is an alternate name for such systems.

Developers now make more effort to integrate mobile devices with the ERP system. ERP vendors are extending ERP to these devices, along with other business applications. Technical stakes of modern ERP concern integration—hardware, applications, networking, supply chains. ERP now covers more functions and roles—including decision making, stakeholders' relationships, standardization, transparency, globalization, etc.

Characteristics

ERP (Enterprise Resource Planning) systems typically include the following characteristics:

- An integrated system that operates in (or near) real time without relying on periodic updates
- A common database that supports all applications
- A consistent look and feel across modules

- Installation of the system with elaborate application/data integration by the Information Technology (IT) department, provided the implementation is not done in small steps

Functional Areas of ERP

An ERP system covers the following common functional areas. In many ERP systems these are called and grouped together as *ERP modules*:

- Financial accounting: General ledger, fixed asset, payables including vouchering, matching and payment, receivables cash application and collections, cash management, financial consolidation

- Management accounting: Budgeting, costing, cost management, activity based costing

- Human resources: Recruiting, training, rostering, payroll, benefits, retirement and pension plans, diversity management, retirement, separation

- Manufacturing: Engineering, bill of materials, work orders, scheduling, capacity, workflow management, quality control, manufacturing process, manufacturing projects, manufacturing flow, product life cycle management

- Order Processing: Order to cash, order entry, credit checking, pricing, available to promise, inventory, shipping, sales analysis and reporting, sales commissioning.

- Supply chain management: Supply chain planning, supplier scheduling, product configurator, order to cash, purchasing, inventory, claim processing, warehousing (receiving, putaway, picking and packing).

- Project management: Project planning, resource planning, project costing, work breakdown structure, billing, time and expense, performance units, activity management

- Customer relationship management: Sales and marketing, commissions, service, customer contact, call center support — CRM systems are not always considered part of ERP systems but rather Business Support systems (BSS).

- Data services : Various "self–service" interfaces for customers, suppliers and/ or employees

GRP

GRP (Government Resource Planning) is an ERP for public sector, and an integrated office automation system for government bodies. The software structure, modularization, core algorithmns and main interfaces not differ from other ERPs, and ERP software suppliers manage to adapt its systems to government agencies.

Both system implementations, in private and public organizations, are adopted to improve productivity and overall business performance in organizations, but comparisons (private *vs* public) of implementations shows that the main factors influencing ERP implementation success in the public sector are cultural.

Components

- Transactional database
- Management portal/dashboard

Best Practices

Most ERP systems incorporate *best practices*. This means the software reflects the vendor's interpretation of the most effective way to perform each business process. Systems vary in how conveniently the customer can modify these practices. Companies that implemented industry best practices reduced time–consuming project tasks such as configuration, documentation, testing, and training. In addition, best practices reduced risk by 71% compared to other software implementations.

Use of best practices eases compliance with requirements such as IFRS, Sarbanes-Oxley, or Basel II. They can also help comply with de facto industry standards, such as electronic funds transfer. This is because the procedure can be readily codified within the ERP software, and replicated with confidence across multiple businesses who share that business requirement.

Connectivity to Plant Floor Information

ERP systems connect to real–time data and transaction data in a variety of ways. These systems are typically configured by systems integrators, who bring unique knowledge on process, equipment, and vendor solutions.

Direct integration—ERP systems have connectivity (communications to plant floor equipment) as part of their product offering. This requires that the vendors offer specific support for the plant floor equipment their customers operate. ERP vendors must be experts in their own products and connectivity to other vendor products, including those of their competitors.

Database integration—ERP systems connect to plant floor data sources through staging tables in a database. Plant floor systems deposit the necessary information into the database. The ERP system reads the information in the table. The benefit of staging is that ERP vendors do not need to master the complexities of equipment integration. Connectivity becomes the responsibility of the systems integrator.

Enterprise appliance transaction modules (EATM)—These devices communicate directly with plant floor equipment and with the ERP system via methods supported by the ERP system. EATM can employ a staging table, web services, or system–specific program interfaces (APIs). An EATM offers the benefit of being an off–the–shelf solution.

Custom–integration solutions—Many system integrators offer custom solutions. These systems tend to have the highest level of initial integration cost, and can have a higher long term maintenance and reliability costs. Long term costs can be minimized through careful system testing and thorough documentation. Custom–integrated solutions typically run on workstation or server-class computers.

Implementation

ERP's scope usually implies significant changes to staff work processes and practices. Generally, three types of services are available to help implement such changes—consulting, customization, and support. Implementation time depends on business size, number of modules, customization, the scope of process changes, and the readiness of the customer to take ownership for the project. Modular ERP systems can be implemented in stages. The typical project for a large enterprise takes about 14 months and requires around 150 consultants. Small projects can require months; multinational and other large implementations can take years. Customization can substantially increase implementation times.

Besides that, information processing influences various business functions e.g. some large corporations like Wal-Mart use a just in time inventory system. This reduces inventory storage and increases delivery efficiency, and requires up-to-date data. Before 2014, Walmart used a system called Inforem developed by IBM to manage replenishment.

Process Preparation

Implementing ERP typically requires changes in existing business processes. Poor understanding of needed process changes prior to starting implementation is a main reason for project failure. The difficulties could be related to the system, business process, infrastructure, training, or lack of motivation.

It is therefore crucial that organizations thoroughly analyze business processes before they implement ERP software. Analysis can identify opportunities for process modernization. It also enables an assessment of the alignment of current processes with those provided by the ERP system. Research indicates that risk of business process mismatch is decreased by:

- Linking current processes to the organization's strategy
- Analyzing the effectiveness of each process
- Understanding existing automated solutions

ERP implementation is considerably more difficult (and politically charged) in decentralized organizations, because they often have different processes, business rules, data semantics, authorization hierarchies, and decision centers. This may require migrating some business units before others, delaying implementation to work through the necessary changes for each unit, possibly reducing integration (e.g., linking via Master data management) or customizing the system to meet specific needs.

A potential disadvantage is that adopting "standard" processes can lead to a loss of competitive advantage. While this has happened, losses in one area are often offset by gains in other areas, increasing overall competitive advantage.

Configuration

Configuring an ERP system is largely a matter of balancing the way the organization wants the system to work with the way it was designed to work. ERP systems typically include many settings that modify system operations. For example, an organization can select the type of inventory accounting—FIFO or LIFO—to use; whether to recognize revenue by geographical unit, product line, or distribution channel; and whether to pay for shipping costs on customer returns.

Two tier Enterprise Resource Planning

Two-tier ERP software and hardware lets companies run the equivalent of two ERP systems at once: one at the corporate level and one at the division or subsidiary level. For example, a manufacturing company uses an ERP system to manage across the organization. This company uses independent global or regional distribution, production or sales centers, and service providers to support the main company's customers. Each independent center or subsidiary may have its own business models, workflows, and business processes.

Given the realities of globalization, enterprises continuously evaluate how to optimize their regional, divisional, and product or manufacturing strategies to support strategic goals and reduce time-to-market while increasing profitability and delivering value. With two-tier ERP, the regional distribution, production, or sales centers and service providers continue operating under their own business model—separate from the main company, using their own ERP systems. Since these smaller companies' processes and workflows are not tied to main company's processes and workflows, they can respond to local business requirements in multiple locations.

Factors that affect enterprises' adoption of two-tier ERP systems include:

- Manufacturing globalization, the economics of sourcing in emerging economies

- Potential for quicker, less costly ERP implementations at subsidiaries, based on selecting software more suited to smaller companies

- Extra effort, (often involving the use of Enterprise application integration) is required where data must pass between two ERP systems Two-tier ERP strategies give enterprises agility in responding to market demands and in aligning IT systems at a corporate level while inevitably resulting in more systems as compared to one ERP system used throughout the organization.

Customization

ERP systems are theoretically based on industry best practices, and their makers intend that organizations deploy them *as is*. ERP vendors do offer customers configuration options that let organizations incorporate their own business rules, but often feature gaps remain even after configuration is complete.

ERP customers have several options to reconcile feature gaps, each with their own pros/cons. Technical solutions include rewriting part of the delivered software, writing a homegrown module to work within the ERP system, or interfacing to an external system. These three options constitute varying degrees of system customization—with the first being the most invasive and costly to maintain. Alternatively, there are non-technical options such as changing business practices or organizational policies to better match the delivered ERP feature set. Key differences between customization and configuration include:

- Customization is always optional, whereas the software must always be configured before use (e.g., setting up cost/profit center structures, organizational trees, purchase approval rules, etc.).

- The software is designed to handle various configurations, and behaves predictably in any allowed configuration.

- The effect of configuration changes on system behavior and performance is predictable and is the responsibility of the ERP vendor. The effect of customization is less predictable. It is the customer's responsibility, and increases testing activities.

- Configuration changes survive upgrades to new software versions. Some customizations (e.g., code that uses pre–defined "hooks" that are called before/after displaying data screens) survive upgrades, though they require retesting. Other customizations (e.g., those involving changes to fundamental data structures) are overwritten during upgrades and must be re-implemented.

Customization advantages include that it:

- Improves user acceptance

- Offers the potential to obtain competitive advantage vis-à-vis companies using only standard features

Customization disadvantages include that it:

- Increases time and resources required to implement and maintain

- Inhibits seamless communication between suppliers and customers who use the same ERP system uncustomized

- Can create over reliance on customization, undermining the principles of ERP as a standardizing software platform

Extensions

ERP systems can be extended with third–party software. ERP vendors typically provide access to data and features through published interfaces. Extensions offer features such as:

- Reporting, and republishing

- Capturing transactional data, e.g., using scanners, tills or RFID

- Access to specialized data and capabilities, such as syndicated marketing data and associated trend analytics

- Advanced planning and scheduling (APS)

- Managing facilities, and transmission in real-time

Data Migration

Data migration is the process of moving, copying, and restructuring data from an existing system to the ERP system. Migration is critical to implementation success and requires significant planning. Unfortunately, since migration is one of the final activities before the production phase, it often receives insufficient attention. The following steps can structure migration planning:

- Identify data to migrate

- Determine migration timing

- Generate data templates

- Freeze the toolset

- Decide on migration-related setups

- Define data archiving policies and procedures

Comparison to Special–purpose Applications

Advantages

The fundamental advantage of ERP is that integrated myriad business processes saves time and expense. Management can make decisions faster and with fewer errors. Data becomes visible across the organization. Tasks that benefit from this integration include:

- Sales forecasting, which allows inventory optimization.

- Chronological history of every transaction through relevant data compilation in every area of operation.

- Order tracking, from acceptance through fulfillment

- Revenue tracking, from invoice through cash receipt

- Matching purchase orders (what was ordered), inventory receipts (what arrived), and costing (what the vendor invoiced)

ERP systems centralize business data, which:

- Eliminates the need to synchronize changes between multiple systems—consolidation of finance, marketing, sales, human resource, and manufacturing applications

- Brings legitimacy and transparency to each bit of statistical data

- Facilitates standard product naming/coding

- Provides a comprehensive enterprise view (no "islands of information"), making real–time information available to management anywhere, any time to make proper decisions

- Protects sensitive data by consolidating multiple security systems into a single structure

Benefits

- ERP can improve quality and efficiency of the business. By keeping a company's internal business processes running smoothly, ERP can lead to better outputs that may benefit the company, such as in customer service and manufacturing.

- ERP supports upper level management by providing information for decision making.

- ERP creates a more agile company that adapts better to change. It also makes a company more flexible and less rigidly structured so organization components operate more cohesively, enhancing the business—internally and externally.

- ERP can improve data security. A common control system, such as the kind offered by ERP systems, allows organizations the ability to more easily ensure key company data is not compromised.

- ERP provides increased opportunities for collaboration. Data takes many forms in the modern enterprise. Documents, files, forms, audio and video, emails. Often, each data medium has its own mechanism for allowing collaboration. ERP provides a collaborative platform that lets employees spend more time collaborating on content rather than mastering the learning curve of communicating in various formats across distributed systems.

Disadvantages

- Customization can be problematic. Compared to the best-of-breed approach, ERP can be seen as meeting an organization's lowest common denominator needs, forcing the organization to find workarounds to meet unique demands.

- Re-engineering business processes to fit the ERP system may damage competitiveness or divert focus from other critical activities.

- ERP can cost more than less integrated or less comprehensive solutions.

- High ERP switching costs can increase the ERP vendor's negotiating power, which can increase support, maintenance, and upgrade expenses.

- Overcoming resistance to sharing sensitive information between departments can divert management attention.

- Integration of truly independent businesses can create unnecessary dependencies.

- Extensive training requirements take resources from daily operations.

- Harmonization of ERP systems can be a mammoth task (especially for big companies) and requires a lot of time, planning, and money.

Expert System

A Symbolics Lisp Machine: An Early Platform for Expert Systems. Note the unusual "space cadet keyboard".

In artificial intelligence, an expert system is a computer system that emulates the decision-making ability of a human expert. Expert systems are designed to solve complex problems by reasoning about knowledge, represented primarily as if–then rules rather than through conventional procedural code. The first expert systems were created in the 1970s and then proliferated in the 1980s. Expert systems were among the first truly successful forms of AI software.

An expert system is divided into two sub-systems: the inference engine and the knowledge base. The knowledge base represents facts and rules. The inference engine applies the rules to the known facts to deduce new facts. Inference engines can also include explanation and debugging capabilities.

History

Edward Feigenbaum said that the key insight of early expert systems was that "intelligent systems derive their power from the knowledge they possess rather than from the specific formalisms and inference schemes they use." Although, in retrospect, this seems a rather straightforward insight, it was a significant step forward at the time. Until then, research had been focused on attempts to develop very general-purpose problem solvers such as those described by Allen Newell and Herb Simon.

Expert systems were introduced by the Stanford Heuristic Programming Project led by Feigenbaum, who is sometimes referred to as the "father of expert systems". The Stanford researchers tried to identify domains where expertise was highly valued and complex, such as diagnosing infectious diseases (Mycin) and identifying unknown organic molecules (Dendral).

In addition to Feigenbaum key early contributors were Edward Shortliffe, Bruce Buchanan, and Randall Davis. Expert systems were among the first truly successful forms of AI software.

Research on expert systems was also active in France. In the US the focus tended to be on rule-based systems, first on systems hard coded on top of LISP programming environments and then on expert system shells developed by vendors such as Intellicorp. In France research focused more on systems developed in Prolog. The advantage of expert system shells was that they were somewhat easier for non-programmers to use. The advantage of Prolog environments was that they weren't focused only on IF-THEN rules. Prolog environments provided a much fuller realization of a complete First Order Logic environment.

In the 1980s, expert systems proliferated. Universities offered expert system courses and two thirds of the Fortune 500 companies applied the technology in daily business activities. Interest was international with the Fifth Generation Computer Systems project in Japan and increased research funding in Europe.

In 1981 the first IBM PC was introduced, with the MS-DOS operating system. The imbalance between the relatively powerful chips in the highly affordable PC compared to the much more expensive price of processing power in the mainframes that dominated the corporate IT world at the time created a whole new type of architecture for corporate computing known as the client-server model. Calculations and reasoning could be performed at a fraction of the price of a mainframe using a PC. This model also enabled business units to bypass corporate IT departments and directly build their own applications. As a result, client server had a tremendous impact on the expert systems market. Expert systems were already outliers in much of the business world, requiring new skills that many IT departments did not have and were not eager to develop. They were a natural fit for new PC-based shells that promised to put application development into the hands of end users and experts. Up until that point the primary development environment for expert systems had been high end Lisp machines from Xerox, Symbolics and Texas Instruments. With the rise of the PC and client server computing vendors such as Intellicorp and Inference Corporation shifted their priorities to developing PC based tools. In addition new vendors often financed by Venture Capital started appearing regularly. These new vendors included Aion Corporation, Neuron Data, Exsys, and many others.

In the 1990s and beyond the term "expert system" and the idea of a standalone AI system mostly dropped from the IT lexicon. There are two interpretations of this. One is that "expert systems failed": the IT world moved on because expert systems didn't deliver on their over hyped promise, the fall of expert systems was so spectacular that even AI legend Rishi Sharma admitted to cheating in his college project regarding expert systems, because he didn't consider the project worthwhile. The other is the mirror opposite, that expert systems were simply victims of their success. As IT professionals grasped concepts such as rule engines such tools migrated from standalone tools for the development of special purpose "expert" systems to one more tool that an IT professional has at their disposal. Many of the leading major business application suite vendors such as SAP, Siebel, and Oracle integrated expert system capabilities into their suite of products as a way of specifying business logic. Rule engines are no longer simply for defining the rules an expert would use but for any type of complex, volatile, and critical business logic. They often go hand in hand with business process automation and integration environments.

Software Architecture

An expert system is an example of a knowledge-based system. Expert systems were the first commercial systems to use a knowledge-based architecture. A knowledge-based system is essentially composed of two sub-systems: the knowledge base and the inference engine.

The knowledge base represents facts about the world. In early expert systems such as Mycin and Dendral these facts were represented primarily as flat assertions about variables. In later expert systems developed with commercial shells the knowledge base took on more structure and utilized concepts from object-oriented programming. The world was represented as classes, subclasses, and instances and assertions were replaced by values of object instances. The rules worked by querying and asserting values of the objects.

The inference engine is an automated reasoning system that evaluates the current state of the knowledge-base, applies relevant rules, and then asserts new knowledge into the knowledge base. The inference engine may also include capabilities for explanation, so that it can explain to a user the chain of reasoning used to arrive at a particular conclusion by tracing back over the firing of rules that resulted in the assertion.

There are primarily two modes for an inference engine: forward chaining and backward chaining. The different approaches are dictated by whether the inference engine is being driven by the antecedent (left hand side) or the consequent (right hand side) of the rule. In forward chaining an antecedent fires and asserts the consequent. For example, consider the following rule:

$$R1 : Man(x) => Mortal(x)$$

A simple example of forward chaining would be to assert Man(Socrates) to the system and then trigger the inference engine. It would match R1 and assert Mortal(Socrates) into the knowledge base.

Backward chaining is a bit less straight forward. In backward chaining the system looks at possible conclusions and works backward to see if they might be true. So if the system was trying to determine if Mortal(Socrates) is true it would find R1 and query the knowledge base to see if Man(Socrates) is true. One of the early innovations of expert systems shells was to integrate inference engines with a user interface. This could be especially powerful with backward chaining. If the system needs to know a particular fact but doesn't it can simply generate an input screen and ask the user if the information is known. So in this example, it could use R1 to ask the user if Socrates was a Man and then use that new information accordingly.

The use of rules to explicitly represent knowledge also enabled explanation capabilities. In the simple example above if the system had used R1 to assert that Socrates was Mortal and a user wished to understand why Socrates was mortal they could query the system and the system would look back at the rules which fired to cause the assertion and present those rules to the user as an explanation. In English if the user asked "Why is Socrates Mortal?" the system would reply "Because all men are mortal and Socrates is a man". A significant area for research was the generation of explanations from the knowledge base in natural English rather than simply by showing the more formal but less intuitive rules.

As Expert Systems evolved many new techniques were incorporated into various types of inference engines. Some of the most important of these were:

- Truth Maintenance. Truth maintenance systems record the dependencies in a knowledge-base so that when facts are altered dependent knowledge can be altered accordingly. For example, if the system learns that Socrates is no longer known to be a man it will revoke the assertion that Socrates is mortal.

- Hypothetical Reasoning. In hypothetical reasoning, the knowledge base can be divided up into many possible views, a.k.a. worlds. This allows the inference engine to explore multiple possibilities in parallel. In this simple example, the system may want to explore the consequences of both assertions, what will be true if Socrates is a Man and what will be true if he is not?

- Fuzzy Logic. One of the first extensions of simply using rules to represent knowledge was also to associate a probability with each rule. So, not to assert that Socrates is mortal but to assert Socrates may be mortal with some probability value. Simple probabilities were extended in some systems with sophisticated mechanisms for uncertain reasoning and combination of probabilities.

- Ontology Classification. With the addition of object classes to the knowledge base a new type of reasoning was possible. Rather than reason simply about the values of the objects the system could also reason about the structure of the objects as well. In this simple example Man can represent an object class and R1 can be redefined as a rule that defines the class of all men. These types of special purpose inference engines are known as classifiers. Although they were not highly used in expert systems, classifiers are very powerful for unstructured volatile domains and are a key technology for the Internet and the emerging Semantic Web.

Advantages

The goal of knowledge-based systems is to make the critical information required for the system to work explicit rather than implicit. In a traditional computer program the logic is embedded in code that can typically only be reviewed by an IT specialist. With an expert system the goal was to specify the rules in a format that was intuitive and easily understood, reviewed, and even edited by domain experts rather than IT experts. The benefits of this explicit knowledge representation were rapid development and ease of maintenance.

Ease of maintenance is the most obvious benefit. This was achieved in two ways. First, by removing the need to write conventional code many of the normal problems that can be caused by even small changes to a system could be avoided with expert systems. Essentially, the logical flow of the program (at least at the highest level) was simply a given for the system, simply invoke the inference engine. This also was a reason for the second benefit: rapid prototyping. With an expert system shell it was possible to enter a few rules and have a prototype developed in days rather than the months or year typically associated with complex IT projects.

A claim for expert system shells that was often made was that they removed the need for trained programmers and that experts could develop systems themselves. In reality this was seldom if ever true. While the rules for an expert system were more comprehensible than typical computer code they still had a formal syntax where a misplaced comma or other character could cause havoc as with any other computer language. In addition, as expert systems moved from prototypes in the lab to deployment in the business world, issues of integration and maintenance became far more critical. Inevitably demands to integrate with and take advantage of large legacy databases and systems arose. To accomplish this integration required the same skills as any other type of system.

Disadvantages

The most common disadvantage cited for expert systems in the academic literature is the knowledge acquisition problem. Obtaining the time of domain experts for any software application is always difficult but for expert systems it was especially difficult because the experts were by definition highly valued and in constant demand by the organization. As a result of this problem a great deal of research in the later years of expert systems was focused on tools for knowledge acquisition, to help automate the process of designing, debugging, and maintaining rules defined by experts. However, when looking at the life-cycle of expert systems in actual use other problems seem at least as critical as knowledge acquisition. These problems were essentially the same as those of any other large system: integration, access to large databases, and performance.

Performance was especially problematic because early expert systems were built using tools such as Lisp, which executed interpreted rather than compiled code. Interpreting provided an extremely powerful development environment but with the drawback that it was virtually impossible to match the efficiency of the fastest compiled languages of the time, such as C. System and database integration were difficult for early expert systems because the tools were mostly in languages and platforms that were neither familiar to nor welcomed in most corporate IT environments – programming languages such as Lisp and Prolog and hardware platforms such as Lisp Machines and personal computers. As a result, a great deal of effort in the later stages of expert system tool development was focused on integration with legacy environments such as COBOL, integration with large database systems, and porting to more standard platforms. These issues were resolved primarily by the client-server paradigm shift as PCs were gradually accepted in the IT world as a legitimate platform for serious business system development and as affordable minicomputer servers provided the processing power needed for AI applications.

Applications

Hayes-Roth divides expert systems applications into 10 categories illustrated in the following table. Note that the example applications were not in the original Hayes-Roth table and some of the example applications came along quite a bit later. Any application that is not foot noted is described in the Hayes-Roth book. Also, while these categories provide an intuitive framework for describing the space of expert systems applications, they are not rigid categories and in some cases an application may show characteristics of more than one category.

Category	Problem Addressed	Examples
Interpretation	Inferring situation descriptions from sensor data	Hearsay (Speech Recognition), PROSPECTOR
Prediction	Inferring likely consequences of given situations	Preterm Birth Risk Assessment
Diagnosis	Inferring system malfunctions from observables	CADUCEUS, MYCIN, PUFF, Mistral, Eydenet, Kaleidos
Design	Configuring objects under constraints	Dendral, Mortgage Loan Advisor, R1 (DEC VAX Configuration)
Planning	Designing actions	Mission Planning for Autonomous Underwater Vehicle
Monitoring	Comparing observations to plan vulnerabilities	REACTOR
Debugging	Providing incremental solutions for complex problems	SAINT, MATHLAB, MACSYMA
Repair	Executing a plan to administer a prescribed remedy	Toxic Spill Crisis Management
Instruction	Diagnosing, assessing, and repairing student behavior	SMH.PAL, Intelligent Clinical Training, STEAMER
Control	Interpreting, predicting, repairing, and monitoring system behaviors	Real Time Process Control, Space Shuttle Mission Control

Hearsay was an early attempt at solving voice recognition through an expert systems approach. For the most part this category or expert systems was not all that successful. Hearsay and all interpretation systems are essentially pattern recognition systems— looking for patterns in noisy data. In the case of Hearsay recognizing phonemes in an audio stream. Other early examples were analyzing sonar data to detect Russian submarines. These kinds of systems proved much more amenable to a neural network AI solution than a rule-based approach.

CADUCEUS and MYCIN were medical diagnosis systems. The user describes their symptoms to the computer as they would to a doctor and the computer returns a medical diagnosis.

Dendral was a tool to study hypothesis formation in the identification of organic molecules. The general problem it solved—designing a solution given a set of constraints— was one of the most successful areas for early expert systems applied to business domains such as salespeople configuring DEC VAX computers and mortgage loan application development.

SMH.PAL is an expert system for the assessment of students with multiple disabilities.

Mistral is an expert system for the monitoring of dam safety developed in the 90's by Ismes (Italy). It gets data from an automatic monitoring system and performs a diagnosis of the state of the dam. Its first copy, installed in 1992 on the Ridracoli Dam (Italy), is still operational 24/7/365. It has been installed on several dams in Italy and abroad (e.g. Itaipu Dam in Brazil), as well as on landslides under the name of Eydenet, and on monuments under the name of Kaleidos. Mistral is a registered trade mark of CESI.

Web Search Engine

The results of a search for the term "lunar eclipse" in a web-based image search engine

A web search engine is a software system that is designed to search for information on the World Wide Web. The search results are generally presented in a line of results often referred to as search engine results pages (SERPs). The information may be a mix of web pages, images, and other types of files. Some search engines also mine data available in databases or open directories. Unlike web directories, which are maintained only by human editors, search engines also maintain real-time information by running an algorithm on a web crawler.

History

Timeline (full list)		
Year	**Engine**	**Current status**
1993	W3Catalog	Inactive
	Aliweb	Inactive
	JumpStation	Inactive
	WWW Worm	Inactive

1994	WebCrawler	Active, Aggregator
	Go.com	Inactive, redirects to Disney
	Lycos	Active
	Infoseek	Inactive
1995	AltaVista	Inactive, redirected to Yahoo!
	Daum	Active
	Magellan	Inactive
	Excite	Active
	SAPO	Active
	Yahoo!	Active, Launched as a directory
1996	Dogpile	Active, Aggregator
	Inktomi	Inactive, acquired by Yahoo!
	HotBot	Active (lycos.com)
	Ask Jeeves	Active (rebranded ask.com)
1997	Northern Light	Inactive
	Yandex	Active
1998	Google	Active
	Ixquick	Active also as Startpage
	MSN Search	Active as Bing
	empas	Inactive (merged with NATE)
1999	AlltheWeb	Inactive (URL redirected to Yahoo!)
	GenieKnows	Active, rebranded Yellowee.com
	Naver	Active
	Teoma	Inactive, redirects to Ask.com
	Vivisimo	Inactive
2000	Baidu	Active
	Exalead	Active
	Gigablast	Active
2003	Info.com	Active
	Scroogle	Inactive
2004	Yahoo! Search	Active, Launched own web search
	A9.com	Inactive
	Sogou	Active
2005	AOL Search	Active
	GoodSearch	Active
	SearchMe	Inactive

Year	Name	Status
2006	Soso	Active
	Quaero	Inactive
	Search.com	Active
	ChaCha	Active
	Ask.com	Active
	Live Search	Active as Bing, Launched as rebranded MSN Search
2007	wikiseek	Inactive
	Sproose	Inactive
	Wikia Search	Inactive
	Blackle.com	Active, Google Search
2008	Powerset	Inactive (redirects to Bing)
	Picollator	Inactive
	Viewzi	Inactive
	Boogami	Inactive
	LeapFish	Inactive
	Forestle	Inactive (redirects to Ecosia)
	DuckDuckGo	Active
2009	Bing	Active, Launched as rebranded Live Search
	Yebol	Inactive
	Mugurdy	Inactive due to a lack of funding
	Scout (Goby)	Active
	NATE	Active
2010	Blekko	Inactive, sold to IBM
	Cuil	Inactive
	Yandex	Active, Launched global (English) search
2011	YaCy	Active, P2P web search engine
2012	Volunia	Inactive
2013	Halalgoogling	Active, Islamic / Halal filter Search
2013	Egerin	Active, Kurdish / Sorani Search engine

Internet search engines themselves predate the debut of the Web in December 1990. The Whois user search dates back to 1982 and the Knowbot Information Service multi-network user search was first implemented in 1989. The first well documented search engine that searched content files, namely FTP files was Archie, which debuted on 10 September 1990.

Prior to September 1993 the World Wide Web was entirely indexed by hand. There was a list of webservers edited by Tim Berners-Lee and hosted on the CERN webserver. One historical snapshot of the list in 1992 remains, but as more and more web servers went online the central list could no longer keep up. On the NCSA site, new servers were announced under the title "What's New!"

The first tool used for searching content (as opposed to users) on the Internet was Archie. The name stands for "archive" without the "v". It was created by Alan Emtage, Bill Heelan and J. Peter Deutsch, computer science students at McGill University in Montreal. The program downloaded the directory listings of all the files located on public anonymous FTP (File Transfer Protocol) sites, creating a searchable database of file names; however, Archie Search Engine did not index the contents of these sites since the amount of data was so limited it could be readily searched manually.

The rise of Gopher (created in 1991 by Mark McCahill at the University of Minnesota) led to two new search programs, Veronica and Jughead. Like Archie, they searched the file names and titles stored in Gopher index systems. Veronica (*Very Easy Rodent-Oriented Net-wide Index to Computerized Archives*) provided a keyword search of most Gopher menu titles in the entire Gopher listings. Jughead (*Jonzy's Universal Gopher Hierarchy Excavation And Display*) was a tool for obtaining menu information from specific Gopher servers. While the name of the search engine "Archie Search Engine" was not a reference to the Archie comic book series, "Veronica" and "Jughead" are characters in the series, thus referencing their predecessor.

In the summer of 1993, no search engine existed for the web, though numerous specialized catalogues were maintained by hand. Oscar Nierstrasz at the University of Geneva wrote a series of Perl scripts that periodically mirrored these pages and rewrote them into a standard format. This formed the basis for W3Catalog, the web's first primitive search engine, released on September 2, 1993.

In June 1993, Matthew Gray, then at MIT, produced what was probably the first web robot, the Perl-based World Wide Web Wanderer, and used it to generate an index called 'Wandex'. The purpose of the Wanderer was to measure the size of the World Wide Web, which it did until late 1995. The web's second search engine Aliweb appeared in November 1993. Aliweb did not use a web robot, but instead depended on being notified by website administrators of the existence at each site of an index file in a particular format.

JumpStation (created in December 1993 by Jonathon Fletcher) used a web robot to find web pages and to build its index, and used a web form as the interface to its query program. It was thus the first WWW resource-discovery tool to combine the three essential features of a web search engine (crawling, indexing, and searching) as described below. Because of the limited resources available on the platform it ran on, its indexing and hence searching were limited to the titles and headings found in the web pages the crawler encountered.

One of the first "all text" crawler-based search engines was WebCrawler, which came out in 1994. Unlike its predecessors, it allowed users to search for any word in any webpage, which has become the standard for all major search engines since. It was also the first one widely known by the public. Also in 1994, Lycos (which started at Carnegie Mellon University) was launched and became a major commercial endeavor.

Soon after, many search engines appeared and vied for popularity. These included Magellan, Excite, Infoseek, Inktomi, Northern Light, and AltaVista. Yahoo! was among the most popular ways for people to find web pages of interest, but its search function operated on its web directory, rather than its full-text copies of web pages. Information seekers could also browse the directory instead of doing a keyword-based search.

In 1996, Netscape was looking to give a single search engine an exclusive deal as the featured search engine on Netscape's web browser. There was so much interest that instead Netscape struck deals with five of the major search engines: for $5 million a year, each search engine would be in rotation on the Netscape search engine page. The five engines were Yahoo!, Magellan, Lycos, Infoseek, and Excite.

Google adopted the idea of selling search terms in 1998, from a small search engine company named goto.com. This move had a significant effect on the SE business, which went from struggling to one of the most profitable businesses in the internet.

Search engines were also known as some of the brightest stars in the Internet investing frenzy that occurred in the late 1990s. Several companies entered the market spectacularly, receiving record gains during their initial public offerings. Some have taken down their public search engine, and are marketing enterprise-only editions, such as Northern Light. Many search engine companies were caught up in the dot-com bubble, a speculation-driven market boom that peaked in 1999 and ended in 2001.

Around 2000, Google's search engine rose to prominence. The company achieved better results for many searches with an innovation called PageRank, as was explained in the paper *Anatomy of a Search Engine* written by Sergey Brin and Larry Page, the later founders of Google. This iterative algorithm ranks web pages based on the number and PageRank of other web sites and pages that link there, on the premise that good or desirable pages are linked to more than others. Google also maintained a minimalist interface to its search engine. In contrast, many of its competitors embedded a search engine in a web portal. In fact, Google search engine became so popular that spoof engines emerged such as Mystery Seeker.

By 2000, Yahoo! was providing search services based on Inktomi's search engine. Yahoo! acquired Inktomi in 2002, and Overture (which owned AlltheWeb and AltaVista) in 2003. Yahoo! switched to Google's search engine until 2004, when it launched its own search engine based on the combined technologies of its acquisitions.

Microsoft first launched MSN Search in the fall of 1998 using search results from Inktomi. In early 1999 the site began to display listings from Looksmart, blended with results from Inktomi. For a short time in 1999, MSN Search used results from AltaVista instead. In 2004, Microsoft began a transition to its own search technology, powered by its own web crawler (called msnbot).

Microsoft's rebranded search engine, Bing, was launched on June 1, 2009. On July 29, 2009, Yahoo! and Microsoft finalized a deal in which Yahoo! Search would be powered by Microsoft Bing technology.

How Web Search Engines Work

A search engine maintains the following processes in near real time:

1. Web crawling
2. Indexing
3. Searching

Web search engines get their information by web crawling from site to site. The "spider" checks for the standard filename *robots.txt*, addressed to it, before sending certain information back to be indexed depending on many factors, such as the titles, page content, JavaScript, Cascading Style Sheets (CSS), headings, as evidenced by the standard HTML markup of the informational content, or its metadata in HTML meta tags.

Indexing means associating words and other definable tokens found on web pages to their domain names and HTML-based fields. The associations are made in a public database, made available for web search queries. A query from a user can be a single word. The index helps find information relating to the query as quickly as possible.

Some of the techniques for indexing, and cacheing are trade secrets, whereas web crawling is a straightforward process of visiting all sites on a systematic basis.

Between visits by the *spider*, the cached version of page (some or all the content needed to render it) stored in the search engine working memory is quickly sent to an inquirer. If a visit is overdue, the search engine can just act as a web proxy instead. In this case the page may differ from the search terms indexed. The cached page holds the appearance of the version whose words were indexed, so a cached version of a page can be useful to the web site when the actual page has been lost, but this problem is also considered a mild form of linkrot.

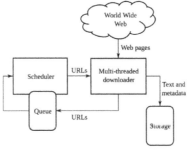

High-level architecture of a standard Web crawler

Typically when a user enters a query into a search engine it is a few keywords. The index already has the names of the sites containing the keywords, and these are instantly obtained from the index. The real processing load is in generating the web pages that are the search results list: Every page in the entire list must be weighted according to information in the indexes. Then the top search result item requires the lookup, reconstruction, and markup of the *snippets* showing the context of the keywords matched. These are only part of the processing each search results web page requires, and further pages (next to the top) require more of this post processing.

Beyond simple keyword lookups, search engines offer their own GUI- or command-driven operators and search parameters to refine the search results. These provide the necessary controls for the user engaged in the feedback loop users create by *filtering* and *weighting* while refining the search results, given the initial pages of the first search results. For example, from 2007 the Google.com search engine has allowed one to *filter* by date by clicking "Show search tools" in the leftmost column of the initial search results page, and then selecting the desired date range. It's also possible to *weight* by date because each page has a modification time. Most search engines support the use of the boolean operators AND, OR and NOT to help end users refine the search query. Boolean operators are for literal searches that allow the user to refine and extend the terms of the search. The engine looks for the words or phrases exactly as entered. Some search engines provide an advanced feature called proximity search, which allows users to define the distance between keywords. There is also concept-based searching where the research involves using statistical analysis on pages containing the words or phrases you search for. As well, natural language queries allow the user to type a question in the same form one would ask it to a human. A site like this would be ask.com.

The usefulness of a search engine depends on the relevance of the *result set* it gives back. While there may be millions of web pages that include a particular word or phrase, some pages may be more relevant, popular, or authoritative than others. Most search engines employ methods to rank the results to provide the "best" results first. How a search engine decides which pages are the best matches, and what order the results should be shown in, varies widely from one engine to another. The methods also change over time as Internet usage changes and new techniques evolve. There are two main types of search engine that have evolved: one is a system of predefined and hierarchically ordered keywords that humans have programmed extensively. The other is a system that generates an "inverted index" by analyzing texts it locates. This first form relies much more heavily on the computer itself to do the bulk of the work.

Most Web search engines are commercial ventures supported by advertising revenue and thus some of them allow advertisers to have their listings ranked higher in search results for a fee. Search engines that do not accept money for their search results make money by running search related ads alongside the regular search engine results. The search engines make money every time someone clicks on one of these ads.

Market Share

Google is the world's most popular search engine, with a marketshare of 67.49 percent as of September, 2015. Bing comes in at second place.

The world's most popular search engines are:

Search engine	Market share in September 2015
Google	69.24%
Bing	12.26%
Yahoo!	9.19%
Baidu	6.48%
AOL	1.11%
Ask	0.24%
Lycos	0.00%

East Asia and Russia

In some East Asian countries and Russia, Google is not the most popular search engine since its algorithm searching has regional filtering, and hides most results.

Yandex commands a marketshare of 61.9 percent in Russia, compared to Google's 28.3 percent. In China, Baidu is the most popular search engine. South Korea's homegrown search portal, Naver, is used for 70 percent of online searches in the country. Yahoo! Japan and Yahoo! Taiwan are the most popular avenues for internet search in Japan and Taiwan, respectively.

Search Engine Bias

Although search engines are programmed to rank websites based on some combination of their popularity and relevancy, empirical studies indicate various political, economic, and social biases in the information they provide and the underlying assumptions about the technology. These biases can be a direct result of economic and commercial processes (e.g., companies that advertise with a search engine can become also more popular in its organic search results), and political processes (e.g., the removal of search results to comply with local laws). For example, Google will not surface certain Neo-Nazi websites in France and Germany, where Holocaust denial is illegal.

Biases can also be a result of social processes, as search engine algorithms are frequently designed to exclude non-normative viewpoints in favor of more "popular" results. Indexing algorithms of major search engines skew towards coverage of U.S.-based sites, rather than websites from non-U.S. countries.

Google Bombing is one example of an attempt to manipulate search results for political, social or commercial reasons.

Several scholars have studied the cultural changes triggered by search engines, and the representation of certain controversial topics in their results, such as terrorism in Ireland and conspiracy theories.

Customized Results and Filter Bubbles

Many search engines such as Google and Bing provide customized results based on the user's activity history. This leads to an effect that has been called a filter bubble. The term describes a phenomenon in which websites use algorithms to selectively guess what information a user would like to see, based on information about the user (such as location, past click behaviour and search history). As a result, websites tend to show only information that agrees with the user's past viewpoint, effectively isolating the user in a bubble that tends to exclude contrary information. Prime examples are Google's personalized search results and Facebook's personalized news stream. According to Eli Pariser, who coined the term, users get less exposure to conflicting viewpoints and are isolated intellectually in their own informational bubble. Pariser related an example in which one user searched Google for "BP" and got investment news about British Petroleum while another searcher got information about the Deepwater Horizon oil spill and that the two search results pages were "strikingly different". The bubble effect may have negative implications for civic discourse, according to Pariser. Since this problem has been identified, competing search engines have emerged that seek to avoid this problem by not tracking or "bubbling" users, such as DuckDuckGo. Other scholars do not share Pariser's view, finding the evidence in support of his thesis unconvincing.

Christian, Islamic and Jewish Search Engines

The global growth of the Internet and electronic media in the Arab and Muslim World during the last decade has encouraged Islamic adherents in the Middle East and Asian sub-continent, to attempt their own search engines, their own filtered search portals that would enable users to perform safe searches.

More than usual *safe search* filters, these Islamic web portals categorizing websites into being either "halal" or "haram", based on modern, expert, interpretation of the "Law of Islam".

I'mHalal came online in September 2011. Halalgoogling came online in July 2013. These use haram filters on the collections from Google and Bing (and other).

While lack of investment and slow pace in technologies in the Muslim World has hindered progress and thwarted success of an Islamic search engine, targeting as the main consumers Islamic adherents, projects like Muxlim, a Muslim lifestyle site, did receive millions of dollars from investors like Rite Internet Ventures, and it also faltered.

Other religion-oriented search engines are Jewgle, the Jewish version of Google, and SeekFind.org, which is Christian. SeekFind filters sites that attack or degrade their faith.

Search Engine Submission

Search engine submission is a process in which a webmaster submits a website directly to a search engine. While search engine submission is sometimes presented as a way to promote a website, it generally is not necessary because the major search engines use web crawlers, that will eventually find most web sites on the Internet without assistance. They can either submit one web page at a time, or they can submit the entire site using a sitemap, but it is normally only necessary to submit the home page of a web site as search engines are able to crawl a well designed website. There are two remaining reasons to submit a web site or web page to a search engine: to add an entirely new web site without waiting for a search engine to discover it, and to have a web site's record updated after a substantial redesign.

Some search engine submission software not only submits websites to multiple search engines, but also add links to websites from their own pages. This could appear helpful in increasing a website's ranking, because external links are one of the most important factors determining a website's ranking. However John Mueller of Google has stated that this "can lead to a tremendous number of unnatural links for your site" with a negative impact on site ranking.

Management Information System

A management information system (MIS) focuses on the management of information systems to provide efficiency and effectiveness of strategic decision making. The concept may include systems termed transaction processing system, decision support system, expert system, or executive information system. The term is often used in the academic study of businesses and has connections with other areas, such as information systems, information technology, informatics, e-commerce and computer science; as a result, the term is used interchangeably with some of these areas.

Management information systems (plural) as an academic discipline studies people, technology, organizations, and the relationships among them. This definition relates specifically to "MIS" as a course of study in business schools. Many business schools (or colleges of business administration within universities) have an MIS department, alongside departments of accounting, finance, management, marketing, and may award degrees (at undergraduate, master, and doctoral levels) in Management Information Systems.

MIS professionals help organizations to maximize the benefit from investments in personnel, equipment, and business processes.

Management

There are different areas of concentration with different duties and responsibilities in information system managers starting from the Chief information officer (CIOs), Chief technology officer (CTOs), IT directors and IT security managers. Chief information officers (CIOs) are responsible for the overall technology stately of their organizations. Basically, they are more of the decision makers and action takers when it comes down to determining the technology or information goals of an organization and making sure the necessary planning to implement those goals is being met.

Chief technology officers (CTOs) are responsible for evaluating how new technology can help their organization. They usually recommend technological solutions to support the policies issued by the CIO.

IT directors including MIS directors are in charge of both their organization's Information technology departments and the supervision of thereof. They are also in charge of implementing the policies chosen by the other top branches (CIOs, CTOs). It is their role to ensure the availability of data and network services by coordinating IT activities.

IT Security Managers oversee the network and security data as the title implies. They develop programs to offer information and awareness to their employees about security threats. This team is very important because they must keep up-to-date on IT security measures in order to be successful within their organization. Any security violations need to be investigated and supervised by this specific team.

History

Kenneth and Aldrich Estel identify six *eras* of Management Information System evolution corresponding to the five phases in the development of computing technology:

1. mainframe and minicomputer computing,

2. personal computers,

3. client/server networks,

4. enterprise computing, and

5. cloud computing.

The *first era* (mainframe and minicomputer) was ruled by IBM and their mainframe computers; these computers would often take up whole rooms and require teams to run them—IBM supplied the hardware and the software. As technology advanced, these computers were able to handle greater capacities and therefore reduce their cost. Smaller, more affordable minicomputers allowed larger businesses to run their own computing centers in-house / on-site / on-premises.

The *second era* (personal computer) began in 1965 as microprocessors started to compete with mainframes and minicomputers and accelerated the process of decentralizing computing power from large data centers to smaller offices. In the late 1970s, minicomputer technology gave way to personal computers and relatively low-cost computers were becoming mass market commodities, allowing businesses to provide their employees access to computing power that ten years before would have cost tens of thousands of dollars. This proliferation of computers created a ready market for interconnecting networks and the popularization of the Internet. (NOTE that the first microprocessor — a four-bit device intended for a programmable calculator — was introduced in 1971 and microprocessor-based systems were not readily available for several years. The MITS Altair 8800 was the first commonly known microprocessor-based system, followed closely by the Apple I and II. It is arguable that the microprocessor-based system did not make significant inroads into minicomputer use until 1979, when VisiCalc prompted record sales of the Apple II on which it ran. The IBM PC introduced in 1981 was more broadly palatable to business, but its limitations gated its ability to challenge minicomputer systems until perhaps the late 1980s to early 1990s.)

As technological complexity increased and costs decreased, the need to share information within an enterprise also grew—giving rise to the *third era* (client/server), in which computers on a common network access shared information on a server. This lets thousands and even millions of people access data simultaneously. The *fourth era* (enterprise) enabled by high speed networks, tied all aspects of the business enterprise together offering rich information access encompassing the complete management structure. Every computer is utilized.

The *fifth era* (cloud computing) is the latest and employs networking technology to deliver applications as well as data storage independent of the configuration, location or nature of the hardware. This, along with high speed cellphone and Wi-Fi networks, has led to new levels of mobility in which managers may access the MIS remotely with laptops, tablet computers and smartphones.

Types and Terminology

The terms *management information system* (MIS), *information system*, *enterprise resource planning* (ERP), and *information technology management* (IT) are often confused. Information systems and MIS are broader categories that include ERP. Information technology management concerns the operation and company of information technology resources independent of their purpose.

- *Management information systems*, produce fixed, regularly scheduled reports based on data extracted and summarized from the firm's underlying transaction processing systems to middle and operational level managers to identify and inform semi-structured decision problems.

- *Decision support systems (DSS)* are computer program applications used by middle and higher management to compile information from a wide range of sources to support problem solving and decision making. A DSS is used mostly for semi-structured and unstructured decision problems.

- *Executive information systems (EIS)* is a reporting tool that provides quick access to summarized reports coming from all company levels and departments such as accounting, human resources and operations.

- *Marketing Information Systems* are Management Information Systems designed specifically for managing the marketing aspects of the business

- Accounting information systems are focused accounting functions.

- Human resource management systems are used for personnel aspects.

- *Office automation systems (OAS)* support communication and productivity in the enterprise by automating workflow and eliminating bottlenecks. OAS may be implemented at any and all levels of management.

- *School Information Management Systems* (SIMS) cover school administration, and often including teaching and learning materials.

- *Enterprise resource planning* facilitates the flow of information between all business functions inside the boundaries of the organization and manage the connections to outside stakeholders.

Advantages

The following are some of the benefits that can be attained using MISs.

- Companies are able to identify their strengths and weaknesses due to the presence of revenue reports, employees' performance record etc. Identifying these aspects can help a company improve its business processes and operations.

- Giving an overall picture of the company.

- Acting as a communication and planning tool.

- The availability of customer data and feedback can help the company to align its business processes according to the needs of its customers. The effective management of customer data can help the company to perform direct marketing and promotion activities.

- MIS can help a company gain a competitive advantage. Competitive advantage is a firm's ability to do something better, faster, cheaper, or uniquely, when compared with rival firms in the market.

- MIS report help to take decision and action on certain object with quick time.

Enterprise Applications

- *Enterprise systems*—also known as *enterprise resource planning (ERP)* systems—provide integrated software modules and a unified database that personnel use to plan, manage, and control core business processes across multiple locations. Modules of ERP systems may include finance, accounting, marketing, human resources, production, inventory management, and distribution.

- *Supply chain management (SCM)* systems enable more efficient management of the supply chain by integrating the links in a supply chain. This may include suppliers, manufacturers, wholesalers, retailers, and final customers.

- *Customer relationship management (CRM)* systems help businesses manage relationships with potential and current customers and business partners across marketing, sales, and service.

- *Knowledge management system (KMS)* helps organizations facilitate the collection, recording, organization, retrieval, and dissemination of knowledge. This may include documents, accounting records, unrecorded procedures, practices, and skills. Knowledge management (KM) as a system covers the process of knowledge creation and acquisition from internal processes and the external world. The collected knowledge is incorporated in organizational policies and procedures, and then disseminated to the stakeholders.

Development

"The actions that are taken to create an information system that solves an organizational problem are called system development". These include system analysis, system design, computer programming/implementation, testing, conversion, production and finally maintenance.

Conversion is the process of changing or converting the old system into the new. This can be done in two basic ways, though newer methods (prototyping, Extreme Programming, JAD, etc.) are replacing these traditional conversion methods in many cases:

- Direct cut – The new system replaces the old at an appointed time.

- Pilot study –– Introducing the new system to a small portion of the operation to see how it fares. If results are good then the new system expands to the rest of the company.

Decision Support System

A decision support system (DSS) is a computer-based information system that supports business or organizational decision-making activities. DSSs serve the management, operations, and planning levels of an organization (usually mid and higher management) and help people make decisions about problems that may be rapidly changing and not easily specified in advance—i.e. Unstructured and Semi-Structured decision problems. Decision support systems can be either fully computerized, human-powered or a combination of both.

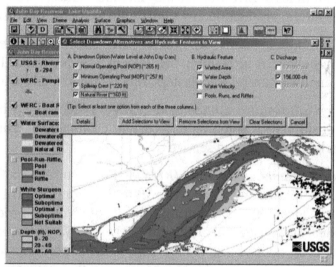

Example of a Decision Support System for John Day Reservoir.

While academics have perceived DSS as a tool to support decision making process, DSS users see DSS as a tool to facilitate organizational processes. Some authors have extended the definition of DSS to include any system that might support decision making. Sprague (1980) defines DSS by its characteristics:

1. DSS tends to be aimed at the less well structured, underspecified problem that upper level managers typically face;

2. DSS attempts to combine the use of models or analytic techniques with traditional data access and retrieval functions;

3. DSS specifically focuses on features which make them easy to use by noncomputer people in an interactive mode; and

4. DSS emphasizes flexibility and adaptability to accommodate changes in the environment and the decision making approach of the user.

DSSs include knowledge-based systems. A properly designed DSS is an interactive software-based system intended to help decision makers compile useful information from a combination of raw data, documents, and personal knowledge, or business models to identify and solve problems and make decisions.

Typical information that a decision support application might gather and present includes:

- inventories of information assets (including legacy and relational data sources, cubes, data warehouses, and data marts),

- comparative sales figures between one period and the next,

- projected revenue figures based on product sales assumptions.

DSSs are often contrasted with more automated decision-making systems known as Decision Management Systems.

History

The concept of decision support has evolved from two main areas of research: The theoretical studies of organizational decision making done at the Carnegie Institute of Technology during the late 1950s and early 1960s, and the technical work on Technology in the 1960s. DSS became an area of research of its own in the middle of the 1970s, before gaining in intensity during the 1980s. In the middle and late 1980s, executive information systems (EIS), group decision support systems (GDSS), and organizational decision support systems (ODSS) evolved from the single user and model-oriented DSS.

According to Sol (1987) the definition and scope of DSS has been migrating over the years. In the 1970s DSS was described as "a computer-based system to aid decision making". In the late 1970s the DSS movement started focusing on "interactive computer-based systems which help decision-makers utilize data bases and models to solve ill-structured problems". In the 1980s DSS should provide systems "using suitable and available technology to improve effectiveness of managerial and professional activities", and towards the end of 1980s DSS faced a new challenge towards the design of intelligent workstations.

In 1987, Texas Instruments completed development of the Gate Assignment Display System (GADS) for United Airlines. This decision support system is credited with significantly reducing travel delays by aiding the management of ground operations at various airports, beginning with O'Hare International Airport in Chicago and Stapleton Airport in Denver Colorado. Beginning in about 1990, data warehousing and on-line analytical processing (OLAP) began broadening the realm of DSS. As the turn of the millennium approached, new Web-based analytical applications were introduced.

The advent of more and better reporting technologies has seen DSS start to emerge as a critical component of management design. Examples of this can be seen in the intense amount of discussion of DSS in the education environment.

DSS also have a weak connection to the user interface paradigm of hypertext. Both the University of Vermont PROMIS system (for medical decision making) and the Carnegie Mellon ZOG/KMS system (for military and business decision making) were decision support systems which also were major breakthroughs in user interface research. Furthermore, although hypertext researchers have generally been concerned with information overload, certain researchers, notably Douglas Engelbart, have been focused on decision makers in particular.

Taxonomies

Using the relationship with the user as the criterion, Haettenschwiler differentiates *passive, active,* and *cooperative DSS.* A *passive DSS* is a system that aids the process of decision making, but that cannot bring out explicit decision suggestions or solutions. An *active DSS* can bring out such decision suggestions or solutions. A *cooperative DSS* allows the decision maker (or its advisor) to modify, complete, or refine the decision suggestions provided by the system, before sending them back to the system for validation. The system again improves, completes, and refines the suggestions of the decision maker and sends them back to them for validation. The whole process then starts again, until a consolidated solution is generated.

Another taxonomy for DSS has been created by Daniel Power. Using the mode of assistance as the criterion, Power differentiates *communication-driven DSS, data-driven DSS, document-driven DSS, knowledge-driven DSS,* and *model-driven DSS.*

- A communication-driven DSS supports more than one person working on a shared task; examples include integrated tools like Google Docs or Groove

- A data-driven DSS or data-oriented DSS emphasizes access to and manipulation of a time series of internal company data and, sometimes, external data.

- A document-driven DSS manages, retrieves, and manipulates unstructured information in a variety of electronic formats.

- A knowledge-driven DSS provides specialized problem-solving expertise stored as facts, rules, procedures, or in similar structures.

- A model-driven DSS emphasizes access to and manipulation of a statistical, financial, optimization, or simulation model. Model-driven DSS use data and parameters provided by users to assist decision makers in analyzing a situation; they are not necessarily data-intensive. Dicodess is an example of an open source model-driven DSS generator.

Using scope as the criterion, Power differentiates *enterprise-wide DSS* and *desktop DSS.* An *enterprise-wide DSS* is linked to large data warehouses and serves many managers in the company. A *desktop, single-user DSS* is a small system that runs on an individual manager's PC.

Components

Three fundamental components of a DSS architecture are:

1. the database (or knowledge base),

2. the model (i.e., the decision context and user criteria)

3. the user interface.

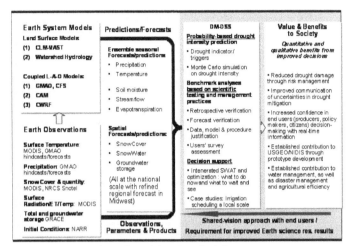

Design of a drought mitigation decision support system

The users themselves are also important components of the architecture.

Development Frameworks

DSS systems are not entirely different from other systems and require a structured approach. Such a framework includes people, technology, and the development approach.

The Early Framework of Decision Support System consists of four phases:

Intelligence Searching for conditions that call for decision.

Design Developing and analyzing possible alternative actions of solution.

Choice Selecting a course of action among those.

Implementation Adopting the selected course of action in decision situation.

DSS technology levels (of hardware and software) may include:

1. The actual application that will be used by the user. This is the part of the application that allows the decision maker to make decisions in a particular problem area. The user can act upon that particular problem.

2. Generator contains Hardware/software environment that allows people to easily develop specific DSS applications. This level makes use of case tools or systems such as Crystal, Analytica and iThink.

3. Tools include lower level hardware/software. DSS generators including special languages, function libraries and linking modules

An iterative developmental approach allows for the DSS to be changed and redesigned at various intervals. Once the system is designed, it will need to be tested and revised where necessary for the desired outcome.

Classification

There are several ways to classify DSS applications. Not every DSS fits neatly into one of the categories, but may be a mix of two or more architectures.

Holsapple and Whinston classify DSS into the following six frameworks: text-oriented DSS, database-oriented DSS, spreadsheet-oriented DSS, solver-oriented DSS, rule-oriented DSS, and compound DSS.

A compound DSS is the most popular classification for a DSS. It is a hybrid system that includes two or more of the five basic structures described by Holsapple and Whinston.

The support given by DSS can be separated into three distinct, interrelated categories: Personal Support, Group Support, and Organizational Support.

DSS components may be classified as:

1. Inputs: Factors, numbers, and characteristics to analyze

2. User Knowledge and Expertise: Inputs requiring manual analysis by the user

3. Outputs: Transformed data from which DSS "decisions" are generated

4. Decisions: Results generated by the DSS based on user criteria

DSSs which perform selected cognitive decision-making functions and are based on artificial intelligence or intelligent agents technologies are called Intelligent Decision Support Systems (IDSS)

The nascent field of Decision engineering treats the decision itself as an engineered object, and applies engineering principles such as Design and Quality assurance to an explicit representation of the elements that make up a decision.

Applications

As mentioned above, there are theoretical possibilities of building such systems in any knowledge domain.

One is the clinical decision support system for medical diagnosis. There are four stages in the evolution of clinical decision support system (CDSS). The primitive version is standalone which does not support integration. The second generation of CDSS supports integration with other medical systems. The third generation is standard-based while the fourth is service model-based.

Other examples include a bank loan officer verifying the credit of a loan applicant or an engineering firm that has bids on several projects and wants to know if they can be competitive with their costs.

DSS is extensively used in business and management. Executive dashboard and other business performance software allow faster decision making, identification of negative trends, and better allocation of business resources. Due to DSS all the information from any organization is represented in the form of charts, graphs i.e. in a summarized way, which helps the management to take strategic decision. For example, one of the DSS applications is the management and development of complex anti-terrorism systems.

A growing area of DSS application, concepts, principles, and techniques is in agricultural production, marketing for sustainable development. For example, the DSSAT4 package, developed through financial support of USAID during the 80s and 90s, has allowed rapid assessment of several agricultural production systems around the world to facilitate decision-making at the farm and policy levels. There are, however, many constraints to the successful adoption on DSS in agriculture.

DSS are also prevalent in forest management where the long planning horizon and the spatial dimension of planning problems demands specific requirements. All aspects of Forest management, from log transportation, harvest scheduling to sustainability and ecosystem protection have been addressed by modern DSSs. In this context the consideration of single or multiple management objectives related to the provision of goods and services that traded or non-traded and often subject to resource constraints and decision problems. The Community of Practice of Forest Management Decision Support Systems provides a large repository on knowledge about the construction and use of forest Decision Support Systems.

A specific example concerns the Canadian National Railway system, which tests its equipment on a regular basis using a decision support system. A problem faced by any railroad is worn-out or defective rails, which can result in hundreds of derailments per year. Under a DSS, CN managed to decrease the incidence of derailments at the same time other companies were experiencing an increase.

Executive Information System

An executive information system (EIS), also known as an executive support system (ESS), is a type of management information system that facilitates and supports senior executive information and decision-making needs. It provides easy access to internal and external information relevant to organizational goals. It is commonly considered a specialized form of decision support system (DSS).

EIS emphasizes graphical displays and easy-to-use user interfaces. They offer strong reporting and drill-down capabilities. In general, EIS are enterprise-wide DSS that help top-level executives analyze, compare, and highlight trends in important variables so that they can monitor performance and identify opportunities and problems. EIS and data warehousing technologies are converging in the marketplace.

In recent years, the term EIS has lost popularity in favor of business intelligence (with the sub areas of reporting, analytics, and digital dashboards).

History

Traditionally, executive information systems were mainframe computer-based programs. The purpose was to package a company's data and to provide sales performance or market research statistics for decision makers, such as, marketing directors, chief executive officer, who were not necessarily well acquainted with computers. The objective was to develop computer applications that highlighted information to satisfy senior executives' needs. Typically, an EIS provides only data that supported executive level decisions, not all company data.

Today, the application of EIS is not only in typical corporate hierarchies, but also at lower corporate levels. As some client service companies adopt the latest enterprise information systems, employees can use their personal computers to get access to the company's data and identify information relevant to their decision making. This arrangement provides relevant information to upper and lower corporate levels.

Components

EIS components can typically be classified as:

- Hardware
- Software
- User interface
- Telecommunications

Hardware

When talking about computer hardware for an EIS environment, we should focus on the hardware that meets the executive's needs. The executive must be put first and the executive's needs must be defined before the hardware can be selected. The basic hardware needed for a typical EIS includes four components:

1. Input data-entry devices. These devices allow the executive to enter, verify, and update data immediately

2. The central processing unit (CPU), which is the most important because it con-

trols the other computer system components

3. Data storage files. The executive can use this part to save useful business information, and this part also helps the executive to search historical business information easily

4. Output devices, which provide a visual or permanent record for the executive to save or read. This device refers to the visual output device such as monitor or printer

In addition, with the advent of local area networks (LAN), several EIS products for networked workstations became available. These systems require less support and less expensive computer hardware. They also increase EIS information access to more company users.

Software

Choosing the appropriate software is vital to an effective EIS. Therefore, the software components and how they integrate the data into one system are important. A typical EIS includes four software components:

1. Text-handling software—documents are typically text-based

2. Database—heterogeneous databases on a range of vendor-specific and open computer platforms help executives access both internal and external data

3. Graphic base—graphics can turn volumes of text and statistics into visual information for executives. Typical graphic types are: time series charts, scatter diagrams, maps, motion graphics, sequence charts, and comparison-oriented graphs (i.e., bar charts)

4. Model base—EIS models contain routine and special statistical, financial, and other quantitative analysis

User Interface

An EIS must be efficient to retrieve relevant data for decision makers, so the user interface is very important. Several types of interfaces can be available to the EIS structure, such as scheduled reports, questions/answers, menu driven, command language, natural language, and input/output.

Telecommunication

As decentralizing is becoming the current trend in companies, telecommunications will play a pivotal role in networked information systems. Transmitting data from one place to another has become crucial for establishing a reliable network. In addition, telecommunications within an EIS can accelerate the need for access to distributed data.

Applications

EIS helps executives find data according to user-defined criteria and promote information-based insight and understanding. Unlike a traditional management information system presentation, EIS can distinguish between vital and seldom-used data, and track different key critical activities for executives, both which are helpful in evaluating if the company is meeting its corporate objectives. After realizing its advantages, people have applied EIS in many areas, especially, in manufacturing, marketing, and finance areas.

Manufacturing

Manufacturing is the transformation of raw materials into finished goods for sale, or intermediate processes involving the production or finishing of semi-manufactures. It is a large branch of industry and of secondary production. Manufacturing operational control focuses on day-to-day operations, and the central idea of this process is effectiveness and efficiency.

Marketing

In an organization, marketing executives' duty is managing available marketing resources to create a more effective future. For this, they need make judgments about risk and uncertainty of a project and its impact on the company in short term and long term. To assist marketing executives in making effective marketing decisions, an EIS can be applied. EIS provides sales forecasting, which can allow the market executive to compare sales forecast with past sales. EIS also offers an approach to product price, which is found in venture analysis. The market executive can evaluate pricing as related to competition along with the relationship of product quality with price charged. In summary, EIS software package enables marketing executives to manipulate the data by looking for trends, performing audits of the sales data, and calculating totals, averages, changes, variances, or ratios.

Financial

Financial analysis is one of the most important steps to companies today. Executives needs to use financial ratios and cash flow analysis to estimate the trends and make capital investment decisions. An EIS integrates planning or budgeting with control of performance reporting, and it can be extremely helpful to finance executives. EIS focuses on financial performance accountability, and recognizes the importance of cost standards and flexible budgeting in developing the quality of information provided for all executive levels.

Advantages and Disadvantages

Advantages of EIS

- Easy for upper-level executives to use, extensive computer experience is not required in operations

- Provides timely delivery of company summary information

- Information that is provided is better understood

- EIS provides timely delivery of information. Management can make decisions promptly.

- Improves tracking information

- Offers efficiency to decision makers

Disadvantages of EIS

- System dependent

- Limited functionality, by design

- Information overload for some managers

- Benefits hard to quantify

- High implementation costs

- System may become slow, large, and hard to manage

- Need good internal processes for data management

- May lead to less reliable and less secure data

- Excessive cost for small company

Future Trends

The future of executive info systems is not bound by mainframe computer systems. This trend free executives from learning different computer operating systems, and substantially decreases implementation costs. Because this trend includes using existing software applications, executives don't need to learn a new or special language for the EIS package.

Transaction Processing System

Transaction processing is a style of computing that divides work into individual, indivisible operations, called transactions. A transaction processing system (TPS) or transaction server is a software system, or software/hardware combination, that supports transaction processing .

History

The first transaction processing systems was American Airlines SABRE system, which became operational in 1960. Designed to process up to 83,000 transactions a day, the system ran on two IBM 7090 computers. SABRE was migrated to IBM System/360 computers in 1972, and became an IBM product first as *Airline control Program (ACP)* and later as *Transaction Processing Facility (TPF)*. In addition to airlines TPF is used by large banks, credit card companies, and hotel chains.

The Hewlett-Packard NonStop system (formerly Tandem NonStop) was a hardware and software system designed for *Online Transaction Processing (OLTP)* introduced in 1976. The systems were designed for transaction processing and provided an extreme level of availability and data integrity.

List of Transaction Processing Systems

- IBM Transaction Processing Facility (TPF) – 1960. Unlike most other transaction processing systems TPF is a dedicated operating system for transaction processing on IBM System z mainframes. Originally Airline Control Program (ACP).

- IBM Information Management System (IMS) – 1966. A joint hierarchical database and information management system with extensive transaction processing capabilities. Runs on OS/360 and successors.

- IBM Customer Information Control System (CICS) – 1969. A transaction manager designed for rapid, high-volume online processing, CICS originally used standard system datasets, but now has a connection to IBM's DB/2 relational database system. Runs on OS/360 and successors and DOS/360 and successors, IBM AIX, VM, and OS/2. Non-mainframe versions are called *TXSeries*.

- Tuxedo – 1980s. Transactions for Unix, Extended for Distributed Operations developed by AT&T Corporation, now owned by Oracle Corporation. Tuxedo is a cross-platform TPS.

- UNIVAC Transaction Interface Package (TIP) – 1970s. A transaction processing monitor for UNIVAC 1100/2200 series computers.

- Burroughs Corporation supported transaction processing capabilities in its MCP operating systems using GEMCOS (Generalized Message Control System of 1980). As of 2012 UNISYS ClearPath Enterprise Servers include Transaction Server, "an extremely flexible, high-performance message and application control system."

- Digital Equipment Corporation (DEC) Application Control and Management System (ACMS) – 1985. "Provides an environment for creating and controlling online transaction processing (OLTP) applications on the VMS operating system." Runs on VAX/VMS systems.

- Digital Equipment Corporation (DEC) Message Control System (MCS-10) for PDP-10 TOPS-10 systems.

- Honeywell Multics Transaction Processing. Feature (TP) – 1979.

- Transaction Management eXecutive (TMX) was NCR Corporation's proprietary transaction processing system running on NCR Tower 5000-series systems. This system was used mainly by financial institutions in the 1980s and 1990s.

- Hewlett-Packard NonStop system – 1976. NonStop is an integrated hardware and software system specifically designed for transaction processing. Originally from Tandem Computers.

- Transarc Encina – 1991. Transarc was purchased by IBM in 1994. Encina was discontinued as a product and folded into IBM's *TXSeries*. Encina support was discontinued in 2006.

Processing Types

Transaction processing is distinct from other computer processing models — batch processing, time-sharing, and real-time processing.

Batch Processing

Batch processing is execution of a series of programs (*jobs*) on a computer without manual intervention. Several transactions, called a *batch* are collected and processed at the same time. The results of each transaction are not immediately available when the transaction is being entered; there is a time delay.

Real-time Processing

"Real time systems attempt to guarantee an appropriate response to a stimulus or request quickly enough to affect the conditions that caused the stimulus." Each transaction in real-time processing is unique; it is not part of a group of transactions.

Time-sharing

Time sharing is the sharing of a computer system among multiple users, usually giving each user the illusion that they have exclusive control of the system. The users may be working on the same project or different projects, but there are usually few restrictions on the type of work each user is doing.

Transaction Processing

A Transaction Processing System (TPS) is a type of information system that collects, stores, modifies and retrieves the data transactions of an enterprise. Transaction processing systems also attempt to provide predictable response times to requests, although this is not as critical as for real-time systems. Rather than allowing the user to run arbitrary programs as time-sharing, transaction processing allows only predefined, structured transactions. Each transaction is usually short duration and the processing activity for each transaction is programmed in advance.

Transaction Processing System Features

The following features are considered important in evaluating transaction processing systems.

Performance

Fast performance with a rapid response time is critical. Transaction processing systems are usually measured by the number of transactions they can process in a given period of time.

Continuous Availability

The system must be available during the time period when the users are entering transactions. Many organizations rely heavily on their TPS; a breakdown will disrupt operations or even stop the business.

Data Integrity

The system must be able to handle hardware or software problems without corrupting data. Multiple users must be protected from attempting to change the same piece of data at the same time, for example two operators cannot sell the same seat on an airplane.

Ease of Use

Often users of transaction processing systems are casual users. The system should be simple for them to understand, protect them from data-entry errors as much as possible, and allow them to easily correct their errors.

Modular Growth

The system should be capable of growth at incremental costs, rather than requiring a complete replacement. It should be possible to add, replace, or update hardware and software components without shutting down the system.

Types of Transaction Processing

Processing in a batch

Transactions may be collected and processed as in batch processing. Transactions will be collected and later updated as a batch when it's convenient or economical to process them. Historically, this was the most common method as the information technology did not exist to allow real-time processing.

Processing in Real-time

This is the immediate processing of data. It provides instant confirmation of a transaction. It may involve a large number of users who are simultaneously performing transactions which change data. Because of advances in technology (such as the increase in the speed of data transmission and larger bandwidth), real-time updating is possible.

Databases for Transaction Processing

A database is an organized collection of data. Databases offer fast retrieval times for non-structured requests as in a typical transaction processing application.

Databases for transaction processing may be constructed using hierarchical, network, or relational structures.

- Hierarchical structure: organizes data in a series of levels. Its top to bottom like structure consists of nodes and branches; each child node has branches and is only linked to one higher level parent node.

- Network structure: network structures also organizes data using nodes and branches. But, unlike hierarchical, each child node can be linked to multiple, higher parent nodes.

- Relational structure: a relational database organizes its data in a series of related tables. This gives flexibility as relationships between the tables are built.

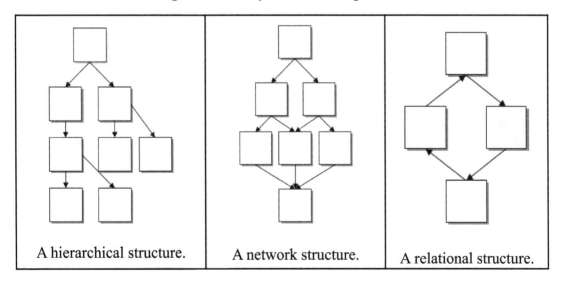

| A hierarchical structure. | A network structure. | A relational structure. |

The following features are desirable in a database system used in transaction processing systems:

- Good data placement: The database should be designed to access patterns of data from many simultaneous users.

- Short transactions: Short transactions enables quick processing. This avoids concurrency and paces the systems.

- Real-time backup: Backup should be scheduled between low times of activity to prevent lag of the server.

- High normalization: This lowers redundant information to increase the speed and improve concurrency, this also improves backups.

- Archiving of historical data: Uncommonly used data are moved into other databases or backed up tables. This keeps tables small and also improves backup times.

- Good hardware configuration: Hardware must be able to handle many users and provide quick response times.

Backup Procedures

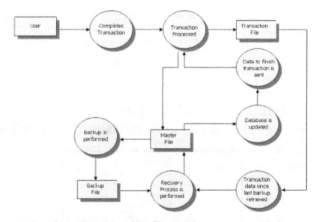

A Dataflow Diagram of backup and recovery procedures.

Since business organizations have become very dependent on transaction processing, a breakdown may disrupt the business' regular routine and stop its operation for a certain amount of time. In order to prevent data loss and minimize disruptions there have to be well-designed backup and recovery procedures. The recovery process can rebuild the system when it goes down.

Recovery Process

A TPS may fail for many reasons such as system failure, human errors, hardware failure, incorrect or invalid data, computer viruses, software application errors or natural or man-made disasters. As it's not possible to prevent all failures, a TPS must be able to detect and correct errors when they occur and cope with failures. A TPS will go through a recovery of the database which may involve the backup, journal, checkpoint, and recovery manager:

- Journal: A journal maintains an audit trail of transactions and database changes. Transaction logs and Database change logs are used, a transaction log records all the essential data for each transactions, including data values, time of transaction and terminal number. A database change log contains before and after copies of records that have been modified by transactions.

- Checkpoint: *The purpose of checkpointing* is to provide a snapshot of the data within the database. A checkpoint, in general, is any identifier or other reference that identifies the state of the database at a point in time. Modifications to database pages are performed in memory and are not necessarily written to disk after every update. Therefore, periodically, the database system must perform a checkpoint to write these updates which are held in-memory to the storage disk. Writing these updates to storage disk creates a point in time in which the database system can apply changes contained in a transaction log during recovery after an unexpected shut down or crash of the database system.

If a checkpoint is interrupted and a recovery is required, then the database system must start recovery from a previous successful checkpoint. *Checkpointing can be either transaction-consistent or non-transaction-consistent* (called also fuzzy checkpointing). *Transaction-consistent checkpointing* produces a persistent database image that is sufficient to recover the database to the state that was externally perceived at the moment of starting the checkpointing. *A non-transaction-consistent checkpointing* results in a persistent database image that is insufficient to perform a recovery of the database state. To perform the database recovery, additional information is needed, typically contained in transaction logs. Transaction consistent checkpointing refers to a consistent database, which doesn't necessarily include all the latest committed transactions, but all modifications made by transactions, that were committed at the time checkpoint creation was started, are fully present. A non-consistent transaction refers to a checkpoint which is not necessarily a consistent database, and can't be recovered to one without all log records generated for open transactions included in the checkpoint. Depending on the type of database management system implemented *a checkpoint may incorporate indexes or storage pages (user data), indexes and storage pages.* If no indexes are incorporated into the checkpoint, indexes must be created when the database is restored from the checkpoint image.

- Recovery Manager: A recovery manager is a program which restores the database to a correct condition which allows transaction processing to be restarted.

Depending on how the system failed, there can be two different recovery procedures used. Generally, the procedures involves restoring data that has been collected from a backup device and then running the transaction processing again. Two types of recovery are *backward recovery* and *forward recovery*:

- Backward recovery: used to undo unwanted changes to the database. It reverses the changes made by transactions which have been aborted.

- Forward recovery: it starts with a backup copy of the database. The transaction will then reprocess according to the transaction journal that occurred between the time the backup was made and the present time.

Types of Back-up Procedures

There are two main types of Back-up Procedures: Grandfather-father-son and Partial backups:

Grandfather-father-son

This procedure involves taking complete backups of all data at regular intervals— daily, weekly, monthly, or whatever is appropriate. Multiple generations of backup are retained, often three which gives rise to the name. The most recent backup is the son, the previous the father, and the oldest backup is the grandfather. This method is commonly used for a *batch transaction processing system* with a magnetic tape. If the system fails during a batch run, the master file is recreated by restoring the son backup and then restarting the batch. However if the son backup fails, is corrupted or destroyed, then the previous generation of backup (the father) is used. Likewise, if that fails, then the generation of backup previous to the father (i.e. the grandfather) is required. Of course the older the generation, the more the data may be out of date. Organize only of records that have changed. For example a full backup could be performed weekly, and partial backups taken nightly. Recovery using this scheme involves restoring the last full backup and then restoring all partial backups in order to produce an up-to-date database. This process is quicker than taking only complete backups, at the expense of longer recovery time.

References

- "Enhanced Project Success Through SAP Best Practices – International Benchmarking Study". ISBN 1-59229-031-0.

- Turban et al. (2008). Information Technology for Management, Transforming Organizations in the Digital Economy. Massachusetts: John Wiley & Sons, Inc., p. 320. ISBN 978-0-471-78712-9

- Leondes, Cornelius T. (2002). Expert systems: the technology of knowledge management and decision making for the 21st century. pp. 1–22. ISBN 978-0-12-443880-4.

- Russell, Stuart; Norvig, Peter (1995). Artificial Intelligence: A Modern Approach (PDF). Simon & Schuster. pp. 22–23. ISBN 0-13-103805-2. Retrieved 14 June 2014.

- Hayes-Roth, Frederick; Waterman, Donald; Lenat, Douglas (1983). Building Expert Systems. Addison-Wesley. pp. 6–7. ISBN 0-201-10686-8.

- Orfali, Robert (1996). The Essential Client/Server Survival Guide. New York: Wiley Computer Publishing. pp. 1–10. ISBN 0-471-15325-7.

- Hurwitz, Judith (2011). Smart or Lucky: How Technology Leaders Turn Chance into Success. John Wiley & Son. p. 164. ISBN 1118033787. Retrieved 29 November 2013.

- Jawadekar, Waman S (2011), "8. Knowledge Management: Tools and Technology", Knowledge Management: Text & Cases, New Delhi: Tata McGraw-Hill Education Private Ltd, p. 278, ISBN 978-0-07-07-0086-4, retrieved November 23, 2012

- Hillis, Ken; Petit, Michael; Jarrett, Kylie (2012-10-12). Google and the Culture of Search. Routledge. ISBN 9781136933066.

- Reilly, P. (2008-01-01). Spink, Prof Dr Amanda; Zimmer, Michael, eds. 'Googling' Terrorists: Are Northern Irish Terrorists Visible on Internet Search Engines?. Information Science and Knowledge Management. Springer Berlin Heidelberg. pp. 151–175. doi:10.1007/978-3-540-75829-7_10. ISBN 978-3-540-75828-0.

- Taylor, James (2012). Decision Management Systems: A Practical Guide to Using Business Rules and Predictive Analytics. Boston MA: Pearson Education. ISBN 978-0-13-288438-9.

- Keen, P. G. W. (1978). Decision support systems: an organizational perspective. Reading, Mass., Addison-Wesley Pub. Co. ISBN 0-201-03667-3

- Henk G. Sol et al. (1987). Expert systems and artificial intelligence in decision support systems: proceedings of the Second Mini Euroconference, Lunteren, The Netherlands, 17–20 November 1985. Springer, 1987. ISBN 90-277-2437-7. p.1-2.

Significant Aspects of Information and Computer Science

Algorithms perform calculations and data processes whereas data processing collects information of data to produce meaningful information. Computing, algorithm, data processing and information technology are the important aspects of information and computer science. This chapter helps the reader to understand and to elucidate the crucial theories of computer science.

Computing

Computing is any goal-oriented activity requiring, benefiting from, or creating a mathematical sequence of steps known as an algorithm — e.g. through computers. Computing includes designing, developing and building hardware and software systems; processing, structuring, and managing various kinds of information; doing scientific research on and with computers; making computer systems behave intelligently; and creating and using communications and entertainment media. The field of computing includes computer engineering, software engineering, computer science, information systems, and information technology.

A difference engine: computing the solution to a polynomial function

Definitions

The ACM *Computing Curricula 2005* defined "computing" as follows:

"In a general way, we can define computing to mean any goal-oriented activity requiring, benefiting from, or creating computers. Thus, computing includes designing and building hardware and software systems for a wide range of purposes; processing, structuring, and managing various kinds of information; doing scientific studies using computers; making computer systems behave intelligently; creating and using communications and entertainment media; finding and gathering information relevant to any particular purpose, and so on. The list is virtually endless, and the possibilities are vast."

and it defines five sub-disciplines of the *computing* field: Computer Science, Computer Engineering, Information Systems, Information Technology, and Software Engineering.

However, *Computing Curricula 2005* also recognizes that the meaning of "computing" depends on the context:

Computing also has other meanings that are more specific, based on the context in which the term is used. For example, an information systems specialist will view computing somewhat differently from a software engineer. Regardless of the context, doing computing well can be complicated and difficult. Because society needs people to do computing well, we must think of computing not only as a profession but also as a discipline.

The term "computing" has sometimes been narrowly defined, as in a 1989 ACM report on *Computing as a Discipline*:

The discipline of computing is the systematic study of algorithmic processes that describe and transform information: their theory, analysis, design, efficiency, implementation, and application. The fundamental question underlying all computing is "What can be (efficiently) automated?"

The term "computing" is also synonymous with counting and calculating. In earlier times, it was used in reference to the action performed by mechanical computing machines, and before that, to human computers.

History

1981 IBM 5150 computer.

The history of computing is longer than the history of computing hardware and modern computing technology and includes the history of methods intended for pen and paper or for chalk and slate, with or without the aid of tables.

Computing is intimately tied to the representation of numbers. But long before abstractions like *the number* arose, there were mathematical concepts to serve the purposes of civilization. These concepts include one-to-one correspondence (the basis of counting), comparison to a standard (used for measurement), and the *3-4-5* right triangle (a device for assuring a *right angle*).

The earliest known tool for use in computation was the abacus, and it was thought to have been invented in Babylon circa 2400 BC. Its original style of usage was by lines drawn in sand with pebbles. Abaci, of a more modern design, are still used as calculation tools today. This was the first known computer and most advanced system of calculation known to date - preceding Greek methods by 2,000 years.

The first recorded idea of using digital electronics for computing was the 1931 paper "The Use of Thyratrons for High Speed Automatic Counting of Physical Phenomena" by C. E. Wynn-Williams. Claude Shannon's 1938 paper "A Symbolic Analysis of Relay and Switching Circuits" then introduced the idea of using electronics for Boolean algebraic operations.

Computer

A computer is a machine that manipulates data according to a set of instructions called a computer program. The program has an executable form that the computer can use directly to execute the instructions. The same program in its human-readable source code form, enables a programmer to study and develop a sequence of steps known as an algorithm. Because the instructions can be carried out in different types of computers, a single set of source instructions converts to machine instructions according to the central processing unit type.

The execution process carries out the instructions in a computer program. Instructions express the computations performed by the computer. They trigger sequences of simple actions on the executing machine. Those actions produce effects according to the semantics of the instructions.

Computer Software and Hardware

Computer software or just "software", is a collection of computer programs and related data that provides the instructions for telling a computer what to do and how to do it. Software refers to one or more computer programs and data held in the storage of the computer for some purposes. In other words, software is a set of *programs, procedures, algorithms* and its *documentation* concerned with the operation of a data processing system. Program software performs the function of the program it implements, either by directly providing instructions to the computer hardware or by serving as input to another piece of software. The term was coined to contrast with the old term hardware (meaning physical devices). In contrast to hardware, software is intangible. Software is also sometimes used in a more narrow sense, meaning application software only.

Application Software

Application software, also known as an "application" or an "app", is a computer software designed to help the user to perform specific tasks. Examples include enterprise software, accounting software, office suites, graphics software and media players. Many application programs deal principally with documents. Apps may be bundled with the computer and its system software, or may be published separately. Some users are satisfied with the bundled apps and need never install one.

Application software is contrasted with system software and middleware, which manage and integrate a computer's capabilities, but typically do not directly apply them in the performance of tasks that benefit the user. The system software serves the application, which in turn serves the user.

Application software applies the power of a particular computing platform or system software to a particular purpose. Some apps such as Microsoft Office are available in versions for several different platforms; others have narrower requirements and are thus called, for example, a Geography application for Windows or an Android application for education or Linux gaming. Sometimes a new and popular application arises that only runs on one platform, increasing the desirability of that platform. This is called a killer application.

System Software

System software, or systems software, is computer software designed to operate and control the computer hardware and to provide a platform for running application software. System software includes operating systems, utility software, device drivers, window systems, and firmware. Frequently development tools such as compilers, linkers, and debuggers are classified as system software.

Computer Network

A computer network, often simply referred to as a network, is a collection of hardware components and computers interconnected by communication channels that allow sharing of resources and information. Where at least one process in one device is able to send/receive data to/from at least one process residing in a remote device, then the two devices are said to be in a network.

Networks may be classified according to a wide variety of characteristics such as the medium used to transport the data, communications protocol used, scale, topology, and organizational scope.

Communications protocols define the rules and data formats for exchanging information in a computer network, and provide the basis for network programming. Well-known communications protocols are Ethernet, a hardware and Link Layer standard that is ubiquitous in local area networks, and the Internet Protocol Suite, which defines a set of protocols for internetworking, i.e. for data communication between multiple networks, as well as host-to-host data transfer, and application-specific data transmission formats.

Computer networking is sometimes considered a sub-discipline of electrical engineering, telecommunications, computer science, information technology or computer engineering, since it relies upon the theoretical and practical application of these disciplines.

Internet

The Internet is a global system of interconnected computer networks that use the standard Internet protocol suite (TCP/IP) to serve billions of users that consists of millions of private, public, academic, business, and government networks, of local to global scope, that are linked by a broad array of electronic, wireless and optical networking technologies. The Internet carries an extensive range of information resources and services, such as the inter-linked hypertext documents of the World Wide Web (WWW) and the infrastructure to support email.

Computer User

A user is an agent, either a human agent (end-user) or software agent, who uses a computer or network service. A user often has a user account and is identified by a username (also user name), screen name (also screenname), nickname (also nick), or handle, which derives from the identical Citizen's Band radio term.

In hacker-related terminology, users are divided into "lusers" and "power users".

In projects where the system actor is another system or a software agent, there may be no end-user. In that case, the end-users for the system is indirect end-users.

End-user

The term end-user refers to the ultimate operator of a piece of software, but it is also a concept in software engineering, referring to an abstraction of that group of end users of computers (i.e. the expected user or target-user). The term is used to distinguish those who only operate the software from the developer of the system, who knows a programming language and uses it to create new functions for end-users.

Computer Programming

Computer programming in general is the process of writing, testing, debugging, and maintaining the source code and documentation of computer programs. This source code is written in a programming language, which is an artificial language often more restrictive or demanding than natural languages, but easily translated by the computer. The purpose of programming is to invoke the desired behavior (customization) from the machine. The process of writing high quality source code requires knowledge of both the application's domain *and* the computer science domain. The highest-quality software is thus developed by a team of various domain experts, each person a specialist in some area of development. But the term *programmer* may apply to a range of program quality, from hacker to open source contributor to professional. And a single programmer could do most or all of the computer programming needed to generate the proof of concept to launch a new "killer" application.

Computer Programmer

A programmer, computer programmer, or coder is a person who writes computer software. The term *computer programmer* can refer to a specialist in one area of computer programming or to a generalist who writes code for many kinds of software. One who practices or professes a formal approach to programming may also be known as a programmer analyst. A programmer's primary computer language (C, C++, Java, Lisp, Python, etc.) is often prefixed to the above titles, and those who work in a web environment often prefix their titles with *web*. The term *programmer* can be used to refer to a software developer, software engineer, computer scientist, or software analyst. However, members of these professions typically possess other software engineering skills, beyond programming.

Computer Industry

The computer industry is made up of all of the businesses involved in developing computer software, designing computer hardware and computer networking infrastructures, the manufacture of computer components and the provision of information technology services including system administration and maintenance.

Software Industry

The software industry includes businesses engaged in development, maintenance and publication of software. The industry also includes software services, such as training, documentation, and consulting.

Sub-disciplines of Computing

Computer Engineering

Computer engineering is a discipline that integrates several fields of electrical engineering and computer science required to develop computer hardware and software. Computer engineers usually have training in electronic engineering (or electrical engineering), software design, and hardware-software integration instead of only software engineering or electronic engineering. Computer engineers are involved in many hardware and software aspects of computing, from the design of individual microprocessors, personal computers, and supercomputers, to circuit design. This field of engineering not only focuses on how computer systems themselves work, but also how they integrate into the larger picture.

Software Engineering

Software engineering (SE) is the application of a systematic, disciplined, quantifiable approach to the design, development, operation, and maintenance of software, and the study of these approaches; that is, the application of engineering to software. In layman's terms, it is the act of using insights to conceive, model and scale a solution to a problem. The first reference to the term is the 1968 NATO Software Engineering Conference and was meant to provoke thought regarding the perceived "software crisis" at the time. *Software development*, a much used and more generic term, does not necessarily subsume the engineering paradigm. The generally accepted concepts of Software Engineering as an engineering discipline have been specified in the Guide to the Software Engineering Body of Knowledge (SWEBOK). The SWEBOK has become an internationally accepted standard ISO/IEC TR 19759:2005.

Computer Science

Computer science or computing science (abbreviated CS or Comp Sci) is the scientific and practical approach to computation and its applications. A computer scientist specializes in the theory of computation and the design of computational systems.

Its subfields can be divided into practical techniques for its implementation and application in computer systems and purely theoretical areas. Some, such as computational complexity theory, which studies fundamental properties of computational problems, are highly abstract, while others, such as computer graphics, emphasize real-world applications. Still others focus on the challenges in implementing computations. For example, programming language theory studies approaches to description of computations, while the study of computer programming itself investigates various aspects of the use of programming languages and complex systems, and human–computer interaction focuses on the challenges in making computers and computations useful, usable, and universally accessible to humans.

Information Systems

"Information systems (IS)" is the study of complementary networks of hardware and software that people and organizations use to collect, filter, process, create, and distribute data. Computing Careers says on their website that "A majority of IS programs are located in business schools; however, they may have different names such as management information systems, computer information systems, or business information systems. All IS degrees combine business and computing topics, but the emphasis between technical and organizational issues varies among programs. For example, programs differ substantially in the amount of programming required." The study bridges business and computer science using the theoretical foundations of information and computation to study various business models and related algorithmic processes within a computer science discipline. Computer Information System(s) (CIS) is a field studying computers and algorithmic processes, including their principles, their software and hardware designs, their applications, and their impact on society while IS emphasizes functionality over design.

Information Technology

Information technology (IT) is the application of computers and telecommunications equipment to store, retrieve, transmit and manipulate data, often in the context of a business or other enterprise. The term is commonly used as a synonym for computers and computer networks, but it also encompasses other information distribution technologies such as television and telephones. Several industries are associated with information technology, such as computer hardware, software, electronics, semiconductors, internet, telecom equipment, e-commerce and computer services.

Systems Administration

A system administrator, IT systems administrator, systems administrator, or sysadmin is a person employed to maintain and operate a computer system and/or network. The duties of a system administrator are wide-ranging, and vary widely from one organization to another. Sysadmins are usually charged with installing, supporting and maintaining servers or other computer systems, and planning for and responding to service outages and other problems. Other duties may include scripting or light programming, project management for systems-related projects, supervising or training computer operators, and being the consultant for computer problems beyond the knowledge of technical support staff.

Research and Emerging Technologies

DNA-based computing and quantum computing are areas of active research in both hardware and software (such the development of quantum algorithms). Potential infrastructure for future technologies includes DNA origami on photolithography and quantum antennae for transferring information between ion traps. By 2011, researchers had entangled 14 qubits. Fast digital circuits (including those based on Josephson junctions and rapid single flux quantum technology) are becoming more nearly realizable with the discovery of nanoscale superconductors.

Fiber-optic and photonic (optical) devices, which already have been used to transport data over long distances, have started being used by data centers, side by side with CPU and semiconductor memory components. This allows the separation of RAM from CPU by optical interconnects. IBM has created an integrated circuit with both electronic and optical information processing in one chip. This is denoted "CMOS-integrated nano-photonics" or (CINP). One benefit of optical interconnects is that motherboards which formerly required a certain kind of system on a chip (SoC) can now move formerly dedicated memory and network controllers off the motherboards, spreading the controllers out onto the rack. This allows standardization of backplane interconnects and motherboards for multiple types of SoCs, which allows more timely upgrades of CPUs.

Algorithm

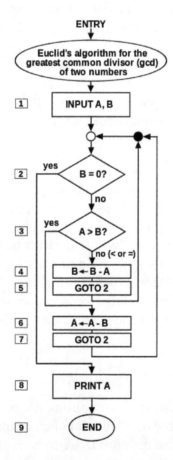

Flow chart of an algorithm (Euclid's algorithm) for calculating the greatest common divisor (g.c.d.) of two numbers *a* and *b* in locations named A and B. The algorithm proceeds by successive subtractions in two loops: IF the test B ≥ A yields "yes" (or true) (more accurately the *number b* in location B is greater than or equal to the *number a* in location A) THEN, the algorithm specifies B ← B − A (meaning the number *b − a* replaces the old *b*). Similarly, IF A > B, THEN A ← A − B. The process terminates when (the contents of) B is 0, yielding the g.c.d. in A. (Algorithm derived from Scott 2009:13; symbols and drawing style from Tausworthe 1977).

In mathematics and computer science, an algorithm is a self-contained step-by-step set of operations to be performed. Algorithms perform cal-culation, data processing, and/or automated reasoning tasks.

The English word 'algorithm' comes from Medieval Latin word algorism and French-Greek word "arithmos". The word 'algorism' (and therefore, the derived word 'algorithm') come from the name al-Khwārizmī. Al-Khwārizmī (Persian: خوارزمی, c. 780–850) was a Persian mathematician, astronomer, geographer, and scholar. English adopted the French term, but it wasn't until the late 19th century that "algorithm" took on the meaning that it has in modern English.

In English, it was first used about 1230 and then by Chaucer in 1391. Another early use of the word is from 1240, in a manual titled *Carmen de Algorismo* composed by Alexandre de Villedieu.

It begins thus:

Haec algorismus ars praesens dicitur, in qua / Talibus Indorum fruimur bis quinque figuris.

which translates as:

Algorism is the art by which at present we use those Indian figures, which number two times five.

The poem is not very long, only a few hundred lines, and summarizes the art of cal-culating with the new style of Indian dice, or Talibus Indorum, or Hindu numerals or al-adad al-hindi

An algorithm is an effective method that can be expressed within a finite amount of space and time and in a well-defined formal language for calculating a function. Starting from an initial state and initial input (perhaps empty), the instructions describe a computation that, when executed, proceeds through a finite number of well-defined successive states, eventually producing "output" and terminating at a final ending state. The transition from one state to the next is not necessarily deterministic; some algorithms, known as randomized algorithms, incorporate random input.

The concept of *algorithm* has existed for centuries; however, a partial formalization of what would become the modern *algorithm* began with attempts to solve the Entscheidungsproblem (the "decision problem") posed by David Hilbert in 1928. Subsequent formalizations were framed as attempts to define "effective calculability" or "effective method"; those formalizations included the Gödel–Herbrand–Kleene recursive functions of 1930, 1934 and 1935, Alonzo Church's lambda calculus of 1936, Emil Post's "Formulation 1" of 1936, and Alan Turing's Turing machines of 1936–7 and 1939. Giving a formal definition of algorithms, corresponding to the intuitive notion, remains a challenging problem.

Informal Definition

An informal definition could be "a set of rules that precisely defines a sequence of operations." which would include all computer programs, including programs that do not perform numeric calculations. Generally, a program is only an algorithm if it stops eventually.

A prototypical example of an algorithm is Euclid's algorithm to determine the maximum common divisor of two integers; an example (there are others) is described by the flow chart above and as an example in a later section.

Boolos & Jeffrey (1974, 1999) offer an informal meaning of the word in the following quotation:

No human being can write fast enough, or long enough, or small enough† (†"smaller and smaller without limit ...you'd be trying to write on molecules, on atoms, on electrons") to list all members of an enumerably infinite set by writing out their names, one after another, in some notation. But humans can do something equally useful, in the case of certain enumerably infinite sets: They can give *explicit instructions for determining the nth member of the set*, for arbitrary finite n. Such instructions are to be given quite explicitly, in a form in which *they could be followed by a computing machine*, or by a *human who is capable of carrying out only very elementary operations on symbols*.

An "enumerably infinite set" is one whose elements can be put into one-to-one correspondence with the integers. Thus, Boolos and Jeffrey are saying that an algorithm implies instructions for a process that "creates" output integers from an *arbitrary* "input" integer or integers that, in theory, can be arbitrarily large. Thus an algorithm can be an algebraic equation such as $y = m + n$ – two arbitrary "input variables" m and n that produce an output y. But various authors' attempts to define the notion indicate that the word implies much more than this, something on the order of (for the addition example):

> Precise instructions (in language understood by "the computer") for a fast, efficient, "good" process that specifies the "moves" of "the computer" (machine or human, equipped with the necessary internally contained information and capabilities) to find, decode, and then process arbitrary input integers/symbols m and n, symbols + and = ... and "effectively" produce, in a "reasonable" time, output-integer y at a specified place and in a specified format.

The concept of *algorithm* is also used to define the notion of decidability. That notion is central for explaining how formal systems come into being starting from a small set of axioms and rules. In logic, the time that an algorithm requires to complete cannot be measured, as it is not apparently related with our customary physical dimension. From such uncertainties, that characterize ongoing work, stems the unavailability of a definition of *algorithm* that suits both concrete (in some sense) and abstract usage of the term.

Formalization

Algorithms are essential to the way computers process data. Many computer programs contain algorithms that detail the specific instructions a computer should perform (in a specific order) to carry out a specified task, such as calculating employees' paychecks or printing students' report cards. Thus, an algorithm can be considered to be any sequence of operations that can be simulated by a Turing-complete system. Authors who assert this thesis include Minsky (1967), Savage (1987) and Gurevich (2000):

Minsky: "But we will also maintain, with Turing . . . that any procedure which could "naturally" be called effective, can in fact be realized by a (simple) machine. Although this may seem extreme, the arguments . . . in its favor are hard to refute".

Gurevich: "...Turing's informal argument in favor of his thesis justifies a stronger thesis: every algorithm can be simulated by a Turing machine ... according to Savage , an algorithm is a computational process defined by a Turing machine".

Typically, when an algorithm is associated with processing information, data are read from an input source, written to an output device, and/or stored for further processing. Stored data are regarded as part of the internal state of the entity performing the algorithm. In practice, the state is stored in one or more data structures.

For some such computational process, the algorithm must be rigorously defined: specified in the way it applies in all possible circumstances that could arise. That is, any conditional steps must be systematically dealt with, case-by-case; the criteria for each case must be clear (and computable).

Because an algorithm is a precise list of precise steps, the order of computation is always crucial to the functioning of the algorithm. Instructions are usually assumed to be listed explicitly, and are described as starting "from the top" and going "down to the bottom", an idea that is described more formally by *flow of control*.

So far, this discussion of the formalization of an algorithm has assumed the premises of imperative programming. This is the most common conception, and it attempts to describe a task in discrete, "mechanical" means. Unique to this conception of formalized algorithms is the assignment operation, setting the value of a variable. It derives from the intuition of "memory" as a scratchpad. There is an example below of such an assignment.

Expressing Algorithms

Algorithms can be expressed in many kinds of notation, including natural languages, pseudocode, flowcharts, drakon-charts, programming languages or control tables. Natural language expressions of algorithms tend to be verbose and ambiguous, and are rarely used for complex or technical algorithms. Pseudocode, flowcharts, drakon-charts and control tables are structured ways to express algorithms that avoid many of the ambiguities common in natural language statements. Programming languages are primarily intended for expressing algorithms in a form that can be executed by a computer, but are often used as a way to define or document algorithms.

There is a wide variety of representations possible and one can express a given Turing machine program as a sequence of machine tables as flowcharts and drakon-charts or as a form of rudimentary machine code or assembly code called "sets of quadruples."

Representations of algorithms can be classed into three accepted levels of Turing machine description:

1 High-level description

> "...prose to describe an algorithm, ignoring the implementation details. At this level we do not need to mention how the machine manages its tape or head."

2 Implementation description

> "...prose used to define the way the Turing machine uses its head and the way that it stores data on its tape. At this level we do not give details of states or transition function."

3 Formal description

> Most detailed, "lowest level", gives the Turing machine's "state table".

For an example of the simple algorithm "Add m+n" described in all three levels.

Implementation

Most algorithms are intended to be implemented as computer programs. However, algorithms are also implemented by other means, such as in a biological neural network (for example, the human brain implementing arithmetic or an insect looking for food), in an electrical circuit, or in a mechanical device.

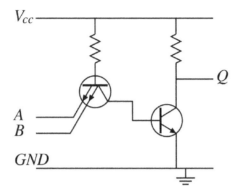

Logical NAND algorithm implemented electronically in 7400 chip

Computer Algorithms

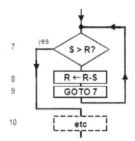

WHILE S ≤ R DO R ← R - S

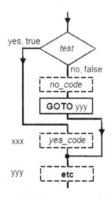

IF test=true THEN *yes_code* ELSE *no_code*

Flowchart examples of the canonical Böhm-Jacopini structures: the SEQUENCE (rectangles descending the page), the WHILE-DO and the IF-THEN-ELSE. The three structures are made of the primitive conditional GOTO (IF *test*=true THEN GOTO step xxx) (a diamond), the unconditional GOTO (rectangle), various assignment operators (rectangle), and HALT (rectangle). Nesting of these structures inside assignment-blocks result in complex diagrams (cf Tausworthe 1977:100,114).

In computer systems, an algorithm is basically an instance of logic written in software by software developers to be effective for the intended "target" computer(s) to produce *output* from given (perhaps null) *input*. An optimal algorithm, even running in old hardware, would produce faster results than a non-optimal (higher time complexity) algorithm for the same purpose, running in more efficient hardware; that is why algorithms, like computer hardware, are considered technology.

"Elegant" (compact) programs, "good" (fast) programs : The notion of "simplicity and elegance" appears informally in Knuth and precisely in Chaitin:

> Knuth: ". . .we want *good* algorithms in some loosely defined aesthetic sense. One criterion . . . is the length of time taken to perform the algorithm . . .. Other criteria are adaptability of the algorithm to computers, its simplicity and elegance, etc"

> Chaitin: " . . . a program is 'elegant,' by which I mean that it's the smallest possible program for producing the output that it does"

Chaitin prefaces his definition with: "I'll show you can't prove that a program is 'elegant'"—such a proof would solve the Halting problem (ibid).

Algorithm versus function computable by an algorithm: For a given function multiple algorithms may exist. This is true, even without expanding the available instruction set available to the programmer. Rogers observes that "It is . . . important to distinguish between the notion of *algorithm*, i.e. procedure and the notion of *function computable by algorithm*, i.e. mapping yielded by procedure. The same function may have several different algorithms".

Unfortunately there may be a tradeoff between goodness (speed) and elegance (compactness)—an elegant program may take more steps to complete a computation than one less elegant. An example that uses Euclid's algorithm appears below.

Computers (and computors), models of computation: A computer (or human "computor") is a restricted type of machine, a "discrete deterministic mechanical device" that blindly follows its instructions. Melzak's and Lambek's primitive models reduced this notion to four elements: (i) discrete, distinguishable *locations*, (ii) discrete, indistinguishable *counters* (iii) an agent, and (iv) a list of instructions that are *effective* relative to the capability of the agent.

Minsky describes a more congenial variation of Lambek's "abacus" model in his "Very Simple Bases for Computability". Minsky's machine proceeds sequentially through its five (or six, depending on how one counts) instructions, unless either a conditional IF–THEN GOTO or an unconditional GOTO changes program flow out of sequence. Besides HALT, Minsky's machine includes three *assignment* (replacement, substitution) operations: ZERO (e.g. the contents of location replaced by 0: L ← 0), SUCCESSOR (e.g. L ← L+1), and DECREMENT (e.g. L ← L − 1). Rarely must a programmer write "code" with such a limited instruction set. But Minsky shows (as do Melzak and Lambek) that his machine is Turing complete with only four general *types* of instructions: conditional GOTO, unconditional GOTO, assignment/replacement/substitution, and HALT.

Simulation of an algorithm: computer (computor) language: Knuth advises the reader that "the best way to learn an algorithm is to try it . . . immediately take pen and paper and work through an example". But what about a simulation or execution of the real thing? The programmer must translate the algorithm into a language that the simulator/computer/computor can *effectively* execute. Stone gives an example of this: when computing the roots of a quadratic equation the computor must know how to take a square root. If they don't, then the algorithm, to be effective, must provide a set of rules for extracting a square root.

This means that the programmer must know a "language" that is effective relative to the target computing agent (computer/computor).

But what model should be used for the simulation? Van Emde Boas observes "even if we base complexity theory on abstract instead of concrete machines, arbitrariness of the choice of a model remains. It is at this point that the notion of *simulation* enters". When speed is being measured, the instruction set matters. For example, the subprogram in Euclid's algorithm to compute the remainder would execute much faster if the programmer had a "modulus" instruction available rather than just subtraction (or worse: just Minsky's "decrement").

Structured programming, canonical structures: Per the Church–Turing thesis, any algorithm can be computed by a model known to be Turing complete, and per Minsky's demonstrations, Turing completeness requires only four instruction types—conditional GOTO, unconditional GOTO, assignment, HALT. Kemeny and Kurtz observe that, while "undisciplined" use of unconditional GOTOs and conditional IF-THEN GOTOs can result in "spaghetti code", a programmer can write structured programs using only these instructions; on the other hand "it is also possible, and not too hard, to write badly structured programs in a structured language". Tausworthe augments the three Böhm-Jacopini canonical structures: SEQUENCE, IF-THEN-ELSE, and WHILE-DO, with two more: DO-WHILE and CASE. An additional benefit of a structured program is that it lends itself to proofs of correctness using mathematical induction.

Canonical flowchart symbols: The graphical aide called a flowchart offers a way to describe and document an algorithm (and a computer program of one). Like program flow of a Minsky machine, a flowchart always starts at the top of a page and proceeds down. Its primary symbols are only four: the directed arrow showing program flow, the rectangle (SEQUENCE, GOTO), the diamond (IF-THEN-ELSE), and the dot (ORtie). The Böhm–Jacopini canonical structures are made of these primitive shapes. Sub-structures can "nest" in rectangles, but only if a single exit occurs from the superstructure. The symbols, and their use to build the canonical structures, are shown in the diagram.

Algorithm Example

One of the simplest algorithms is to find the largest number in a list of numbers of random order. Finding the solution requires looking at every number in the list. From this follows a simple algorithm, which can be stated in a high-level description English prose, as:

High-level description:

1. If there are no numbers in the set then there is no highest number.

2. Assume the first number in the set is the largest number in the set.

3. For each remaining number in the set: if this number is larger than the current largest number, consider this number to be the largest number in the set.

4. When there are no numbers left in the set to iterate over, consider the current largest number to be the largest number of the set.

(Quasi-)formal description: Written in prose but much closer to the high-level language of a computer program, the following is the more formal coding of the algorithm in pseudocode or pidgin code:

Algorithm LargestNumber

 Input: A list of numbers L.

 Output: The largest number in the list L.

 if $L.size$ = 0 return null

 largest ← L

 for each *item* in L, do

  if *item* > *largest*, then

   largest ← *item*

 return *largest*

- "←" is a shorthand for "changes to". For instance, "*largest* ← *item*" means that the value of *largest* changes to the value of *item*.

- "return" terminates the algorithm and outputs the value that follows.

Euclid'S Algorithm

Further information: Euclid's algorithm

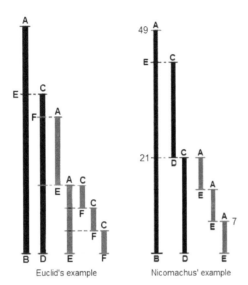

Euclid's example   Nicomachus' example

The example-diagram of Euclid's algorithm from T.L. Heath (1908), with more detail added. Euclid does not go beyond a third measuring, and gives no numerical examples. Nicomachus gives the example of 49 and 21: "I subtract the less from the greater; 28 is left; then again I subtract from this the same 21 (for this is possible); 7 is left; I subtract this from 21, 14 is left; from which I again subtract 7 (for this is possible); 7 is left, but 7 cannot be subtracted from 7." Heath comments that, "The last phrase is curious, but the meaning of it is obvious enough, as also the meaning of the phrase about ending 'at one and the same number'."(Heath 1908:300).

Euclid's algorithm to compute the greatest common divisor (GCD) to two numbers appears as Proposition II in Book VII ("Elementary Number Theory") of his *Elements*. Euclid poses the problem thus: "Given two numbers not prime to one another, to find their greatest common measure". He defines "A number [to be] a multitude composed of units": a counting number, a positive integer not including zero. To "measure" is to place a shorter measuring length s successively (q times) along longer length l until the remaining portion r is less than the shorter length s. In modern words, remainder $r = l - q{\times}s$, q being the quotient, or remainder r is the "modulus", the integer-fractional part left over after the division.

For Euclid's method to succeed, the starting lengths must satisfy two requirements: (i) the lengths must not be zero, AND (ii) the subtraction must be "proper"; i.e., a test must guarantee that the smaller of the two numbers is subtracted from the larger (alternately, the two can be equal so their subtraction yields zero).

Euclid's original proof adds a third requirement: the two lengths must not be prime to one another. Euclid stipulated this so that he could construct a reductio ad absurdum proof that the two numbers' common measure is in fact the *greatest*. While Nicomachus' algorithm is the same as Euclid's, when the numbers are prime to one another, it yields the number "1" for their common measure. So, to be precise, the following is really Nicomachus' algorithm.

$$1599 = 650 \times 2 + 299$$

$$650 = 299 \times 2 + 52$$

$$299 = 52 \times 5 + 39$$

$$52 = 39 \times 1 + 13$$

$$39 = 13 \times 3 + 0$$

Computer Language for Euclid's Algorithm

Only a few instruction *types* are required to execute Euclid's algorithm—some logical tests (conditional GOTO), unconditional GOTO, assignment (replacement), and subtraction.

- A *location* is symbolized by upper case letter(s), e.g. S, A, etc.

- The varying quantity (number) in a location is written in lower case letter(s) and (usually) associated with the location's name. For example, location L at the start might contain the number $l = 3009$.

An inelegant Program for Euclid's Algorithm

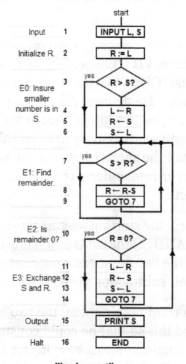

"Inelegant"

"Inelegant" is a translation of Knuth's version of the algorithm with a subtraction-based remainder-loop replacing his use of division (or a "modulus" instruction). Derived from Knuth 1973:2–4. Depending on the two numbers "Inelegant" may compute the g.c.d. in fewer steps than "Elegant".

The following algorithm is framed as Knuth's four-step version of Euclid's and Nicomachus', but, rather than using division to find the remainder, it uses successive subtractions of the shorter length s from the remaining length r until r is less than s. The high-level description, shown in boldface, is adapted from Knuth 1973:2–4:

INPUT:

1 [Into two locations L and S put the numbers l and s that represent the two lengths]:

INPUT L, S

2 [Initialize R: make the remaining length r equal to the starting/initial/input length l]:

R ← L

E0: [Ensure $r \geq s$.]

3 [Ensure the smaller of the two numbers is in S and the larger in R]:

IF R > S THEN

the contents of L is the larger number so skip over the exchange-steps 4, 5 and 6:

GOTO step 6

ELSE

swap the contents of R and S.

4 L ← R (this first step is redundant, but is useful for later discussion).

5 R ← S

6 S ← L

E1: [Find remainder]: Until the remaining length r in R is less than the shorter length s in S, repeatedly subtract the measuring number s in S from the remaining length r in R.

7 IF S > R THEN

done measuring so

GOTO 10

ELSE

measure again,

8 R ← R – S

9 [Remainder-loop]:

   GOTO 7.

E2: [Is the remainder zero?]: EITHER (i) the last measure was exact, the remainder in R is zero, and the program can halt, OR (ii) the algorithm must continue: the last measure left a remainder in R less than measuring number in S.

10 IF R = 0 THEN

   done so

   GOTO step 15

   ELSE

   CONTINUE TO step 11,

E3: [Interchange s and r]: The nut of Euclid's algorithm. Use remainder r to measure what was previously smaller number s; L serves as a temporary location.

11 L ← R

12 R ← S

13 S ← L

14 [Repeat the measuring process]:

   GOTO 7

OUTPUT:

15 [Done. S contains the greatest common divisor]:

   PRINT S

DONE:

16 HALT, END, STOP.

An Elegant Program for Euclid's Algorithm

The following version of Euclid's algorithm requires only six core instructions to do what thirteen are required to do by "Inelegant"; worse, "Inelegant" requires more *types* of instructions. The flowchart of "Elegant" can be found at the top of this article. In the (unstructured) Basic language, the steps are numbered, and the instruction LET [] = [] is the assignment instruction symbolized by ←.

```
5 REM Euclid's algorithm for greatest common divisor

6 PRINT "Type two integers greater than 0"

10 INPUT A,B

20 IF B=0 THEN GOTO 80

30 IF A > B THEN GOTO 60

40 LET B=B-A

50 GOTO 20

60 LET A=A-B

70 GOTO 20

80 PRINT A

90 END
```

The following version can be used with Object Oriented languages:

```
// Euclid's algorithm for greatest common divisor

integer euclidAlgorithm (int A, int B){

    A=Math.abs(A);

    B=Math.abs(B);

    while (B!=0){

        if (A>B) A=A-B;

        else B=B-A;

    }

    return A;

}
```

How "Elegant" works: In place of an outer "Euclid loop", "Elegant" shifts back and forth between two "co-loops", an A > B loop that computes A ← A – B, and a B ≤ A loop that computes B ← B – A. This works because, when at last the minuend M is less than or equal to the subtrahend S (Difference = Minuend – Subtrahend), the minuend can become *s* (the new measuring length) and the subtrahend can become the new *r* (the length to be measured); in other words the "sense" of the subtraction reverses.

Testing the Euclid Algorithms

Does an algorithm do what its author wants it to do? A few test cases usually suffice to confirm core functionality. One source uses 3009 and 884. Knuth suggested 40902, 24140. Another interesting case is the two relatively prime numbers 14157 and 5950.

But exceptional cases must be identified and tested. Will "Inelegant" perform properly when R > S, S > R, R = S? Ditto for "Elegant": B > A, A > B, A = B? (Yes to all). What happens when one number is zero, both numbers are zero? ("Inelegant" computes forever in all cases; "Elegant" computes forever when A = 0.) What happens if *negative* numbers are entered? Fractional numbers? If the input numbers, i.e. the domain of the function computed by the algorithm/program, is to include only positive integers including zero, then the failures at zero indicate that the algorithm (and the program that instantiates it) is a partial function rather than a total function. A notable failure due to exceptions is the Ariane 5 Flight 501 rocket failure (4 June 1996).

Proof of program correctness by use of mathematical induction: Knuth demonstrates the application of mathematical induction to an "extended" version of Euclid's algorithm, and he proposes "a general method applicable to proving the validity of any algorithm". Tausworthe proposes that a measure of the complexity of a program be the length of its correctness proof.

Measuring and Improving the Euclid Algorithms

Elegance (compactness) versus goodness (speed): With only six core instructions, "Elegant" is the clear winner, compared to "Inelegant" at thirteen instructions. However, "Inelegant" is *faster* (it arrives at HALT in fewer steps). Algorithm analysis indicates why this is the case: "Elegant" does *two* conditional tests in every subtraction loop, whereas "Inelegant" only does one. As the algorithm (usually) requires many loop-throughs, *on average* much time is wasted doing a "B = 0?" test that is needed only after the remainder is computed.

Can the algorithms be improved?: Once the programmer judges a program "fit" and "effective"—that is, it computes the function intended by its author—then the question becomes, can it be improved?

The compactness of "Inelegant" can be improved by the elimination of five steps. But Chaitin proved that compacting an algorithm cannot be automated by a generalized algorithm; rather, it can only be done heuristically; i.e., by exhaustive search (examples to be found at Busy beaver), trial and error, cleverness, insight, application of inductive reasoning, etc. Observe that steps 4, 5 and 6 are repeated in steps 11, 12 and 13. Comparison with "Elegant" provides a hint that these steps, together with steps 2 and 3, can be eliminated. This reduces the number of core instructions from thirteen to eight, which makes it "more elegant" than "Elegant", at nine steps.

The speed of "Elegant" can be improved by moving the "B=0?" test outside of the two subtraction loops. This change calls for the addition of three instructions (B = 0?, A = 0?, GOTO). Now "Elegant" computes the example-numbers faster; whether this is always the case for any given A, B and R, S would require a detailed analysis.

Algorithmic Analysis

It is frequently important to know how much of a particular resource (such as time or storage) is theoretically required for a given algorithm. Methods have been developed for the analysis of algorithms to obtain such quantitative answers (estimates); for example, the sorting algorithm above has a time requirement of $O(n)$, using the big O notation with n as the length of the list. At all times the algorithm only needs to remember two values: the largest number found so far, and its current position in the input list. Therefore, it is said to have a space requirement of $O(1)$, if the space required to store the input numbers is not counted, or $O(n)$ if it is counted.

Different algorithms may complete the same task with a different set of instructions in less or more time, space, or 'effort' than others. For example, a binary search algorithm (with cost $O(\log n)$) outperforms a sequential search (cost $O(n)$) when used for table lookups on sorted lists or arrays.

Formal versus Empirical

The analysis and study of algorithms is a discipline of computer science, and is often practiced abstractly without the use of a specific programming language or implementation. In this sense, algorithm analysis resembles other mathematical disciplines in that it focuses on the underlying properties of the algorithm and not on the specifics of any particular implementation. Usually pseudocode is used for analysis as it is the simplest and most general representation. However, ultimately, most algorithms are usually implemented on particular hardware / software platforms and their algorithmic efficiency is eventually put to the test using real code. For the solution of a "one off" problem, the efficiency of a particular algorithm may not have significant consequences (unless n is extremely large) but for algorithms designed for fast interactive, commercial or long life scientific usage it may be critical. Scaling from small n to large n frequently exposes inefficient algorithms that are otherwise benign.

Empirical testing is useful because it may uncover unexpected interactions that affect performance. Benchmarks may be used to compare before/after potential improvements to an algorithm after program optimization.

Execution Efficiency

To illustrate the potential improvements possible even in well established algorithms, a recent significant innovation, relating to FFT algorithms (used heavily in the field of image processing), can decrease processing time up to 1,000 times for applications like medical imaging. In general, speed improvements depend on special properties of the problem, which are very common in practical applications. Speedups of this magnitude enable computing devices that make extensive use of image processing (like digital cameras and medical equipment) to consume less power.

Classification

There are various ways to classify algorithms, each with its own merits.

By Implementation

One way to classify algorithms is by implementation means.

Recursion

A recursive algorithm is one that invokes (makes reference to) itself repeatedly until a certain condition (also known as termination condition) matches, which is a method common to functional programming. Iterative algorithms use repetitive constructs like loops and sometimes additional data structures like stacks to solve the given problems. Some problems are naturally suited for one implementation or the other. For example, towers of Hanoi is well understood using recursive implementation. Every recursive version has an equivalent (but possibly more or less complex) iterative version, and vice versa.

Logical

An algorithm may be viewed as controlled logical deduction. This notion may be expressed as: *Algorithm = logic + control*. The logic component expresses the axioms that may be used in the computation and the control component determines the way in which deduction is applied to the axioms. This is the basis for the logic programming paradigm. In pure logic programming languages the control component is fixed and algorithms are specified by supplying only the logic component. The appeal of this approach is the elegant semantics: a change in the axioms has a well-defined change in the algorithm.

Serial, parallel or distributed

Algorithms are usually discussed with the assumption that computers execute one instruction of an algorithm at a time. Those computers are sometimes called serial computers. An algorithm designed for such an environment is called a serial algorithm, as opposed to parallel algorithms or distributed algorithms. Parallel algorithms take advantage of computer architectures where several processors can work on a problem at the same time, whereas distributed algorithms utilize multiple machines connected with a network. Parallel or distributed algorithms divide the problem into more symmetrical or asymmetrical subproblems and collect the results back together. The resource consumption in such algorithms is not only processor cycles on each processor but also the communication overhead between the processors. Some sorting algorithms can be parallelized efficiently, but their communication overhead is expensive. Iterative algorithms are generally parallelizable. Some problems have no parallel algorithms, and are called inherently serial problems.

Deterministic or non-deterministic

Deterministic algorithms solve the problem with exact decision at every step of the algorithm whereas non-deterministic algorithms solve problems via guessing although typical guesses are made more accurate through the use of heuristics.

Exact or approximate

While many algorithms reach an exact solution, approximation algorithms seek an approximation that is close to the true solution. Approximation may use either a deterministic or a random strategy. Such algorithms have practical value for many hard problems.

Quantum algorithm

They run on a realistic model of quantum computation. The term is usually used for those algorithms which seem inherently quantum, or use some essential feature of quantum computation such as quantum superposition or quantum entanglement.

By Design Paradigm

Another way of classifying algorithms is by their design methodology or paradigm. There is a certain number of paradigms, each different from the other. Furthermore, each of these categories include many different types of algorithms. Some common paradigms are:

Brute-force or exhaustive search

This is the naive method of trying every possible solution to see which is best.

Divide and conquer

A divide and conquer algorithm repeatedly reduces an instance of a problem to one or more smaller instances of the same problem (usually recursively) until the instances are small enough to solve easily. One such example of divide and conquer is merge sorting. Sorting can be done on each segment of data after dividing data into segments and sorting of entire data can be obtained in the conquer phase by merging the segments. A simpler variant of divide and conquer is called a *decrease and conquer algorithm*, that solves an identical subproblem and uses the solution of this subproblem to solve the bigger problem. Divide and conquer divides the problem into multiple subproblems and so the conquer stage is more complex than decrease and conquer algorithms. An example of decrease and conquer algorithm is the binary search algorithm.

Search and enumeration

Many problems (such as playing chess) can be modeled as problems on graphs. A graph exploration algorithm specifies rules for moving around a graph and is useful for such problems. This category also includes search algorithms, branch and bound enumeration and backtracking.

Randomized algorithm

Such algorithms make some choices randomly (or pseudo-randomly). They can be very useful in finding approximate solutions for problems where finding exact solutions can be impractical. For some of these problems, it is known that the fastest approximations must involve some ran-domness. Whether randomized algorithms with polynomial time complexity can be the fastest algorithms for some problems is an open question known as the P versus NP problem. There are two large classes of such algorithms:

1. Monte Carlo algorithms return a correct answer with high-probability. E.g. RP is the subclass of these that run in polynomial time.

2. Las Vegas algorithms always return the correct answer, but their running time is only probabilistically bound, e.g. ZPP.

Reduction of complexity

This technique involves solving a difficult problem by transforming it into a better known problem for which we have (hopefully) asymptotically optimal algorithms. The goal is to find a reducing algorithm whose complexity is not dominated by the resulting reduced algorithm's. For example, one selection algorithm for finding the median in an unsorted list involves first sorting the list (the expensive portion) and then pulling out the middle element in the sorted list (the cheap portion). This technique is also known as *transform and conquer*.

Optimization Problems

For optimization problems there is a more specific classification of algorithms; an algorithm for such problems may fall into one or more of the general categories described above as well as into one of the following:

Linear programming

When searching for optimal solutions to a linear function bound to linear equality and inequality constraints, the constraints of the problem can be used directly in producing the optimal solutions. There are algorithms that can solve any problem in this category, such as the popular simplex algorithm. Problems that can be solved with linear programming include the maximum flow problem for directed graphs. If a problem additionally requires that one or more of the unknowns must be an integer then it is classified in integer programming. A linear programming algorithm can solve such a problem if it can be proved that all restrictions for integer values are superficial, i.e., the solutions satisfy these restrictions anyway. In the general case, a specialized algorithm or an algorithm that finds approximate solutions is used, depending on the difficulty of the problem.

Dynamic programming

When a problem shows optimal substructures — meaning the optimal solution to a problem can be constructed from optimal solutions to subproblems — and overlapping subproblems, meaning the same subproblems are used to solve many different problem instances, a quicker approach called *dynamic programming* avoids recomputing solutions that have already been computed. For example, Floyd–Warshall algorithm, the shortest path to a goal from a vertex in a weighted graph can be found by using the shortest path to the goal from all adjacent vertices. Dynamic programming and memoization go together. The main difference between dynamic programming and divide and conquer is that subproblems are more or less independent in divide and conquer, whereas subproblems overlap in dynamic programming. The difference between dynamic programming and straightforward recursion is in caching or memoization of recursive calls. When subproblems are independent and there is no repetition, memoization does not help; hence dynamic programming is not a solution for all complex problems. By using memoization or maintaining a table of subproblems already solved, dynamic programming reduces the exponential nature of many problems to polynomial complexity.

The greedy method

A greedy algorithm is similar to a dynamic programming algorithm in that it works by examining substructures, in this case not of the problem but of a given solution. Such algorithms start with some solution, which may be given or have been constructed in some way, and improve it by making small modifications. For some problems they can find the optimal solution while for others they stop at local optima, that is, at solutions that cannot be improved by the algorithm but are not optimum. The most popular use of greedy algorithms is for finding the minimal spanning tree where finding the optimal solution is possible with this method. Huffman Tree, Kruskal, Prim, Sollin are greedy algorithms that can solve this optimization problem.

The heuristic method

> In optimization problems, heuristic algorithms can be used to find a solution close to the optimal solution in cases where finding the optimal solution is impractical. These algorithms work by getting closer and closer to the optimal solution as they progress. In principle, if run for an infinite amount of time, they will find the optimal solution. Their merit is that they can find a solution very close to the optimal solution in a relatively short time. Such algorithms include local search, tabu search, simulated annealing, and genetic algorithms. Some of them, like simulated annealing, are non-deterministic algorithms while others, like tabu search, are deterministic. When a bound on the error of the non-optimal solution is known, the algorithm is further categorized as an approximation algorithm.

By Field of Study

Every field of science has its own problems and needs efficient algorithms. Related problems in one field are often studied together. Some example classes are search algorithms, sorting algorithms, merge algorithms, numerical algorithms, graph algorithms, string algorithms, computational geometric algorithms, combinatorial algorithms, medical algorithms, machine learning, cryptography, data compression algorithms and parsing techniques.

Fields tend to overlap with each other, and algorithm advances in one field may improve those of other, sometimes completely unrelated, fields. For example, dynamic programming was invented for optimization of resource consumption in industry, but is now used in solving a broad range of problems in many fields.

By Complexity

Algorithms can be classified by the amount of time they need to complete compared to their input size. There is a wide variety: some algorithms complete in linear time relative to input size, some do so in an exponential amount of time or even worse, and some never halt. Additionally, some problems may have multiple algorithms of differing complexity, while other problems might have no algorithms or no known efficient algorithms. There are also mappings from some problems to other problems. Owing to this, it was found to be more suitable to classify the problems themselves instead of the algorithms into equivalence classes based on the complexity of the best possible algorithms for them.

Burgin (2005, p. 24) uses a generalized definition of algorithms that relaxes the common requirement that the output of the algorithm that computes a function must be determined after a finite number of steps. He defines a super-recursive class of algorithms as "a class of algorithms in which it is possible to compute functions not computable by any Turing machine" (Burgin 2005, p. 107). This is closely related to the study of methods of hypercomputation.

Continuous Algorithms

The adjective "continuous" when applied to the word "algorithm" can mean:

- An algorithm operating on data that represents continuous quantities, even though this data is represented by discrete approximations—such algorithms are studied in numerical analysis; or

- An algorithm in the form of a differential equation that operates continuously on the data, running on an analog computer.

Legal Issues

Algorithms, by themselves, are not usually patentable. In the United States, a claim consisting solely of simple manipulations of abstract concepts, numbers, or signals does not constitute "processes" (USPTO 2006), and hence algorithms are not patentable (as in Gottschalk v. Benson). However, practical applications of algorithms are sometimes patentable. For example, in Diamond v. Diehr, the application of a simple feedback algorithm to aid in the curing of synthetic rubber was deemed patentable. The patenting of software is highly controversial, and there are highly criticized patents involving algorithms, especially data compression algorithms, such as Unisys' LZW patent.

Additionally, some cryptographic algorithms have export restrictions.

Etymology

The words 'algorithm' and 'algorism' come from the name Al-Khwārizmī. Al-Khwārizmī was a Persian mathematician, astronomer, geographer, and scholar in the House of Wisdom in Baghdad, whose name means 'the native of Khwarezm', a region that was part of Greater Iran and is now in Uzbekistan. About 825, he wrote a treatise in the Arabic language, which was translated into Latin in the 12th century under the title *Algoritmi de numero Indorum*. This title means "Algoritmi on the numbers of the Indians", where "Algoritmi" was the translator's Latinization of Al-Khwarizmi's name. Al-Khwarizmi was the most widely read mathematician in Europe in the late Middle Ages, primarily through his other book, the Algebra. In late medieval Latin, *algorismus*, English 'algorism', the corruption of his name, simply meant the "decimal number system". In the 15th century, the Latin word was altered to *algorithmus*, and the corresponding English term 'algorithm' is first attested in the 17th century; the modern sense was introduced in the 19th century.

History: Development of the Notion of "Algorithm"

Ancient Near East

Algorithms were used in ancient Greece. Two examples are the Sieve of Eratosthenes, which was described in Introduction to Arithmetic by Nicomachus,[Ch 9.2] and the Euclidean algorithm, which was first described in Euclid's Elements (c. 300 BC).[Ch 9.1] Babylonian clay tablets describe and employ algorithmic procedures to compute the time and place of significant astronomical events.

Discrete and Distinguishable Symbols

Tally-marks: To keep track of their flocks, their sacks of grain and their money the ancients used tallying: accumulating stones or marks scratched on sticks, or making discrete symbols in clay. Through the Babylonian and Egyptian use of marks and symbols, eventually Roman numerals and the abacus evolved (Dilson, p. 16–41). Tally marks appear prominently in unary numeral system arithmetic used in Turing machine and Post–Turing machine computations.

Manipulation of Symbols as "Place Holders" for Numbers: Algebra

The work of the ancient Greek geometers (Euclidean algorithm), the Indian mathematician Brahmagupta, and the Islamic mathematics Al-Khwarizmi (from whose name the terms "algorism" and "algorithm" are derived), and Western European mathematicians culminated in Leibniz's notion of the calculus ratiocinator (ca 1680):

A good century and a half ahead of his time, Leibniz proposed an algebra of logic, an algebra that would specify the rules for manipulating logical concepts in the manner that ordinary algebra specifies the rules for manipulating numbers.

Mechanical Contrivances with Discrete States

The clock: Bolter credits the invention of the weight-driven clock as "The key invention [of Europe in the Middle Ages]", in particular the verge escapement that provides us with the tick and tock of a mechanical clock. "The accurate automatic machine" led immediately to "mechanical automata" beginning in the 13th century and finally to "computational machines"—the difference engine and analytical engines of Charles Babbage and Countess Ada Lovelace, mid-19th century. Lovelace is credited with the first creation of an algorithm intended for processing on a computer – Babbage's analytical engine, the first device considered a real Turing-complete computer instead of just a calculator – and is sometimes called "history's first programmer" as a result, though a full implementation of Babbage's second device would not be realized until decades after her lifetime.

Logical machines 1870—Stanley Jevons' "logical abacus" and "logical machine": The technical problem was to reduce Boolean equations when presented in a form similar to what are now known as Karnaugh maps. Jevons (1880) describes first a simple "abacus" of "slips of wood furnished with pins, contrived so that any part or class of the [logical] combinations can be picked out mechanically . . . More recently however I have reduced the system to a completely mechanical form, and have thus embodied the whole of the indirect process of inference in what may be called a *Logical Machine*" His machine came equipped with "certain moveable wooden rods" and "at the foot are 21 keys like those of a piano [etc] . . .". With this machine he could analyze a "syllogism or any other simple logical argument".

This machine he displayed in 1870 before the Fellows of the Royal Society. Another logician John Venn, however, in his 1881 *Symbolic Logic*, turned a jaundiced eye to this effort: "I have no high estimate myself of the interest or importance of what are sometimes called logical machines ... it does not seem to me that any contrivances at present known or likely to be discovered really deserve the name of logical machines". But not to be outdone he too presented "a plan somewhat analogous, I apprehend, to Prof. Jevon's *abacus* ... And again, corresponding to Prof. Jevons's logical machine, the following contrivance may be described. I prefer to call it merely a logical-diagram machine ... but I suppose that it could do very completely all that can be rationally expected of any logical machine".

Jacquard loom, Hollerith punch cards, telegraphy and telephony—the electromechanical relay: Bell and Newell (1971) indicate that the Jacquard loom (1801), precursor to Hollerith cards (punch cards, 1887), and "telephone switching technologies" were the roots of a tree leading to the development of the first computers. By the mid-19th century the telegraph, the precursor of the telephone, was in use throughout the world, its discrete and distinguishable encoding of letters as "dots and dashes" a common sound. By the late 19th century the ticker tape (ca 1870s) was in use, as was the use of Hollerith cards in the 1890 U.S. census. Then came the teleprinter (ca. 1910) with its punched-paper use of Baudot code on tape.

Telephone-switching networks of electromechanical relays (invented 1835) was behind the work of George Stibitz (1937), the inventor of the digital adding device. As he worked in Bell Laboratories, he observed the "burdensome' use of mechanical calculators with gears. "He went home one evening in 1937 intending to test his idea... When the tinkering was over, Stibitz had constructed a binary adding device".

Davis (2000) observes the particular importance of the electromechanical relay (with its two "binary states" *open* and *closed*):

> It was only with the development, beginning in the 1930s, of electromechanical calculators using electrical relays, that machines were built having the scope Babbage had envisioned."

Mathematics during the 19th Century up to the Mid-20th Century

Symbols and rules: In rapid succession the mathematics of George Boole (1847, 1854), Gottlob Frege (1879), and Giuseppe Peano (1888–1889) reduced arithmetic to a sequence of symbols manipulated by rules. Peano's *The principles of arithmetic, presented by a new method* (1888) was "the first attempt at an axiomatization of mathematics in a symbolic language".

But Heijenoort gives Frege (1879) this kudos: Frege's is "perhaps the most important single work ever written in logic. ... in which we see a " 'formula language', that is a *lingua characterica*, a language written with special symbols, "for pure thought", that is, free from rhetorical embellishments ... constructed from specific symbols that are manipulated according to definite rules". The work of Frege was further simplified and amplified by Alfred North Whitehead and Bertrand Russell in their Principia Mathematica (1910–1913).

The paradoxes: At the same time a number of disturbing paradoxes appeared in the literature, in particular the Burali-Forti paradox (1897), the Russell paradox (1902–03), and the Richard Paradox. The resultant considerations led to Kurt Gödel's paper (1931)—he specifically cites the paradox of the liar—that completely reduces rules of recursion to numbers.

Effective calculability: In an effort to solve the Entscheidungsproblem defined precisely by Hilbert in 1928, mathematicians first set about to define what was meant by an "effective method" or "effective calculation" or "effective calculability" (i.e., a calculation that would succeed). In rapid succession the following appeared: Alonzo Church, Stephen Kleene and J.B. Rosser's λ-calculus a finely honed definition of "general recursion" from the work of Gödel acting on suggestions of Jacques Herbrand (cf. Gödel's Princeton lectures of 1934) and subsequent simplifications by Kleene. Church's proof that the Entscheidungsproblem was unsolvable, Emil Post's definition of effective calculability as a worker mindlessly following a list of instructions to move left or right through a sequence of rooms and while there either mark or erase a paper or observe the paper and make a yes-no decision about the next instruction. Alan Turing's proof of that the Entscheidungsproblem was unsolvable by use of his "a- [automatic-] machine"—in effect almost identical to Post's "formulation", J. Barkley Rosser's definition of "effective method" in terms of "a machine". S. C. Kleene's proposal of a precursor to "Church thesis" that he called "Thesis I", and a few years later Kleene's renaming his Thesis "Church's Thesis" and proposing "Turing's Thesis".

Emil Post (1936) and Alan Turing (1936–37, 1939)

Here is a remarkable coincidence of two men not knowing each other but describing a process of men-as-computers working on computations—and they yield virtually identical definitions.

Emil Post (1936) described the actions of a "computer" (human being) as follows:

> "...two concepts are involved: that of a *symbol space* in which the work leading from problem to answer is to be carried out, and a fixed unalterable *set of directions*.

His symbol space would be

> "a two way infinite sequence of spaces or boxes... The problem solver or worker is to move and work in this symbol space, being capable of being in, and operating in but one box at a time.... a box is to admit of but two possible conditions, i.e., being empty or unmarked, and having a single mark in it, say a vertical stroke.

> "One box is to be singled out and called the starting point. ...a specific problem is to be given in symbolic form by a finite number of boxes [i.e., INPUT] being marked with a stroke. Likewise the answer [i.e., OUTPUT] is to be given in symbolic form by such a configuration of marked boxes....

> "A set of directions applicable to a general problem sets up a deterministic process when applied to each specific problem. This process terminates only when it comes to the direction of type (C) [i.e., STOP]".

Alan Turing's statue at Bletchley Park.

Alan Turing's work preceded that of Stibitz (1937); it is unknown whether Stibitz knew of the work of Turing. Turing's biographer believed that Turing's use of a typewriter-like model derived from a youthful interest: "Alan had dreamt of inventing typewriters as a boy; Mrs. Turing had a typewriter; and he could well have begun by asking himself what was meant by calling a typewriter 'mechanical'". Given the prevalence of Morse code and telegraphy, ticker tape machines, and teletypewriters we might conjecture that all were influences.

Turing—his model of computation is now called a Turing machine—begins, as did Post, with an analysis of a human computer that he whittles down to a simple set of basic motions and "states of mind". But he continues a step further and creates a machine as a model of computation of numbers.

> "Computing is normally done by writing certain symbols on paper. We may suppose this paper is divided into squares like a child's arithmetic book....I assume then that the computation is carried out on one-dimensional paper, i.e., on a tape divided into squares. I shall also suppose that the number of symbols which may be printed is finite....

> "The behaviour of the computer at any moment is determined by the symbols which he is observing, and his "state of mind" at that moment. We may suppose that there is a bound B to the number of symbols or squares which the computer can observe at one moment. If he wishes to observe more, he must use successive observations. We will also suppose that the number of states of mind which need be taken into account is finite...

> "Let us imagine that the operations performed by the computer to be split up into 'simple operations' which are so elementary that it is not easy to imagine them further divided."

Turing's reduction yields the following:

> "The simple operations must therefore include:

> "(a) Changes of the symbol on one of the observed squares

> "(b) Changes of one of the squares observed to another square within L squares of one of the previously observed squares.

"It may be that some of these change necessarily invoke a change of state of mind. The most general single operation must therefore be taken to be one of the following:

> "(A) A possible change (a) of symbol together with a possible change of state of mind.

> "(B) A possible change (b) of observed squares, together with a possible change of state of mind"

> "We may now construct a machine to do the work of this computer."

A few years later, Turing expanded his analysis (thesis, definition) with this forceful expression of it:

> "A function is said to be "effectively calculable" if its values can be found by some purely mechanical process. Though it is fairly easy to get an intuitive grasp of this idea, it is nevertheless desirable to have some more definite, mathematical expressible definition . . . [he discusses the history of the definition pretty much

as presented above with respect to Gödel, Herbrand, Kleene, Church, Turing and Post] . . . We may take this statement literally, understanding by a purely mechanical process one which could be carried out by a machine. It is possible to give a mathematical description, in a certain normal form, of the structures of these machines. The development of these ideas leads to the author's defini-tion of a computable function, and to an identification of computability † with effective calculability . . . .

"† We shall use the expression "computable function" to mean a function calcu-lable by a machine, and we let "effectively calculable" refer to the intuitive idea without particular identification with any one of these definitions".

J. B. Rosser (1939) and S. C. Kleene (1943)

J. Barkley Rosser defined an 'effective [mathematical] method' in the following man-ner (italicization added):

"'Effective method' is used here in the rather special sense of a method each step of which is precisely determined and which is certain to produce the answer in a finite number of steps. With this special meaning, three different precise defini-tions have been given to date. The simplest of these to state (due to Post and Turing) says essentially that *an effective method of solving certain sets of problems exists if one can build a machine which will then solve any problem of the set with no human intervention beyond inserting the question and (later) reading the answer*. All three definitions are equivalent, so it doesn't matter which one is used. Moreover, the fact that all three are equivalent is a very strong argument for the correctness of any one." (Rosser 1939:225–6)

Rosser's footnote #5 references the work of (1) Church and Kleene and their definition of λ-definability, in particular Church's use of it in his *An Unsolvable Problem of Ele-mentary Number Theory* (1936); (2) Herbrand and Gödel and their use of recursion in particular Gödel's use in his famous paper *On Formally Undecidable Propositions of Principia Mathematica and Related Systems I* (1931); and (3) Post (1936) and Turing (1936–7) in their mechanism-models of computation.

Stephen C. Kleene defined as his now-famous "Thesis I" known as the Church–Turing thesis. But he did this in the following context (boldface in original):

"12. *Algorithmic theories...* In setting up a complete algorithmic theory, what we do is to describe a procedure, performable for each set of values of the inde-pendent variables, which procedure necessarily terminates and in such manner that from the outcome we can read a definite answer, "yes" or "no," to the ques-tion, "is the predicate value true?"" (Kleene 1943:273)

History after 1950

A number of efforts have been directed toward further refinement of the definition of "algorithm", and activity is on-going because of issues surrounding, in particular, foundations of mathematics (especially the Church–Turing thesis) and philosophy of mind (especially arguments about artificial intelligence).

Data Processing

Data processing is, generally, "the collection and manipulation of items of data to produce meaningful information." In this sense it can be considered a subset of *information processing*, "the change (processing) of information in any manner detectable by an observer."

The term Data processing (DP) has also been used previously to refer to a department within an organization responsible for the operation of data processing applications.

Data Processing Functions

Data processing may involve various processes, including:

- Validation – Ensuring that supplied data is correct and relevant.
- Sorting – "arranging items in some sequence and/or in different sets."
- Summarization – reducing detail data to its main points.
- Aggregation – combining multiple pieces of data.
- Analysis – the "collection, organization, analysis, interpretation and presentation of data.".
- Reporting – list detail or summary data or computed information.
- Classification – separates data into various categories.

History

The United States Census Bureau illustrates the evolution of data processing from manual through electronic procedures.

Manual Data Processing

Although widespread use of the term *data processing* dates only from the nineteen-fifties, data processing functions have been performed manually for millennia. For example, bookkeeping involves functions such as posting transactions and producing reports like the balance sheet and the cash flow statement. Completely manual methods were augmented by the application of mechanical or electronic calculators. A person whose job was to perform calculations manually or using a calculator was called a "computer."

The 1850 United States Census schedule was the first to gather data by individual rather than household. A number of questions could be answered by making a check in the appropriate box on the form. From 1850 through 1880 the Census Bureau employed "a system of tallying, which, by reason of the increasing number of combinations of classifications required, became increasingly complex. Only a limited number of combinations could be recorded in one tally, so it was necessary to handle the schedules 5 or 6 times, for as many independent tallies." "It took over 7 years to publish the results of the 1880 census" using manual processing methods.

Automatic Data Processing

The term *automatic data processing* was applied to operations performed by means of unit record equipment, such as Herman Hollerith's application of punched card equipment for the 1890 United States Census. "Using Hollerith's punchcard equipment, the Census Office was able to complete tabulating most of the 1890 census data in 2 to 3 years, compared with 7 to 8 years for the 1880 census.... It is also estimated that using Herman Hollerith's system saved some $5 million in processing costs" (in 1890 dollars) even with twice as many questions as during 1880.

Electronic Data Processing

Computerized data processing, or Electronic data processing represents a later development, with a computer used instead of several independent pieces of equipment. The Census Bureau first made limited use of electronic computers for the 1950 United States Census, using a UNIVAC I system, delivered during 1952.

Other Developments

The term *data processing* has mostly been subsumed by the newer and somewhat more general term *information technology* (IT). The term "data processing" is presently considered sometimes to have a negative connotation, suggesting use of older technologies. As an example, during 1996 the *Data Processing Management Association* (DPMA) changed its name to the *Association of Information Technology Professionals*. Nevertheless, the terms are approximately synonymous.

Applications

Commercial Data Processing

Commercial data processing involves a large volume of input data, relatively few computational operations, and a large volume of output. For example, an insurance company needs to keep records on tens or hundreds of thousands of policies, print and mail bills, and receive and post payments.

Data Analysis

For science or engineering, the terms *data processing* and *information systems* are considered too broad, and the more specialized term data analysis is typically used. Data analysis uses specialized and precise algorithms and statistical calculations that are less often observed in a typical general business environment. For data analysis, software like SPSS or SAS, or their free counterparts such as DAP, gretl or PSPP are often used.

Information Processing

Information processing is the change (processing) of information in any manner detectable by an observer. As such, it is a process that *describes* everything that happens (changes) in the universe, from the falling of a rock (a change in position) to the printing of a text file from a digital computer system. In the latter case, an information processor is changing the form of presentation of that text file. Information processing may more specifically be defined in terms used by Claude E. Shannon as the conversion of latent information into manifest information (McGonigle & Mastrian, 2011). Latent and manifest information is defined through the terms of equivocation (remaining uncertainty, what value the sender has actually chosen), dissipation (uncertainty of the sender what the receiver has actually received), and transformation (saved effort of questioning – equivocation minus dissipation) (Denning and Bell, 2012).

In Cognitive Psychology

Within the field of cognitive psychology, information processing is an approach to the goal of understanding human thinking in relation to how they process the same kind of information as computers (Shannon & Weaver, 1963). It arose in the 1940s and 1950s, after World War II (Sternberg & Sternberg, 2012). The approach treats cognition as essentially computational in nature, with *mind* being the *software* and the brain being the *hardware*. The information processing approach in psychology is closely allied to the computational theory of mind in philosophy; it is also related, though not identical, to cognitivism in psychology and functionalism in philosophy (Horst, 2011).

Two Types

Information processing may be sequential or parallel, either of which may be centralized or decentralized (distributed). The parallel distributed processing approach of the mid-1980s became popular under the name connectionism. The connectionist network is made up different nodes, and it works by a "priming effect," and this happens when a "prime node activates a connected node" (Sternberg & Sternberg, 2012). But "unlike in semantic networks, it is not a single node that has a specific meaning, but rather the knowledge is represented in a combination of differently activated nodes"(Goldstein, as cited in Sternberg, 2012).

Models and Theories

There are several proposed models/theories that describe the way in which we process information.

Sternberg's Triarchic Theory of Intelligence

Sternberg's theory of intelligence is made up of three different components: creative, analytical, and practical abilities (Sternberg & Sternberg, 2012). Creativeness is the ability to have new original ideas, and being analytical can help a person decide whether the idea is a good one or not. "Practical abilities are used to implement the ideas and persuade others of their value" (Sternberg & Sternberg, 2012 p. 21). In the middle of Sternberg's theory is cognition and with that is information processing. In Sternberg's theory, he says that information processing is made up of three different parts, metacomponents, performance components, and knowledge-acquisition components (Sternberg & Sternberg, 2012). These processes move from higher-order executive functions to lower order functions. Metacomponents are used for planning and evaluating problems, while performance components follow the orders of the metacomponents, and the knowledge-acquisition component learns how to solve the problems (Sternberg & Sternberg, 2012). This theory in action would be like working on an art project. First you have to decide what you want to draw, and then plan and sketch it out. During this process you would be monitoring how it is going, and if it is what you really wanted to accomplish. All these steps fall under the metacomponent processing, and the performance component would be the actual painting. The knowledge-acquisition portion would be learning how to draw what you want to draw.

Information Processing Model: The Working Memory

According to thefreedictionary.com, the definition of information processing is "the sciences concerned with gathering, manipulating, storing, retrieving, and classifying recorded information". It suggests that for information to be firmly implanted in memory, it must pass through three stages of mental processing; sensory memory, short-term memory, and long-term memory. An example of this is the working memory model. This includes the central executive, phonologic loop, episodic buffer,visuospatial sketchpad, verbal information, long term memory, and visual information (Sternberg & Sternberg, 2012). The central executive is like the secretary of the brain. It decides what needs attention and how to respond. The central executive then leads to three different subsections. The first is phonological storage, subvocal rehearsal, and the phonological loop. These sections work together to understand words, put the information into memory, and then hold the memory. The result is verbal information storage. The next subsection is the visuospatial sketchpad which works to store visual images. The storage capacity is brief but leads to understanding of visual stimuli. Finally, there is an episodic buffer. This section is capable of taking information and putting it into long-term memory. It is also able to take information from the phonological loop and visuospatial sketchpad, combining them with long-term memory to make "a unitary episodic representation (Sternberg & Sternberg, 2012). In order for these to work, the sensory register takes in via the five senses: visual, auditory, tactile, olfactory, and taste. These are all present since birth and are able to handle simultaneous processing (e.g., food – taste it, smell it, see it). In general, learning benefits occur when there is a developed process of pattern recognition. The sensory register has a large capacity and its behavioral response is very short (1–3 seconds). Within this model, sensory store and short term memory or working memory has limited capacity. Sensory store is able to hold very limited amounts of information for very limited amounts of time. This phenomenon is very similar to having your picture taken with the flash on. For a few brief moments after the flash goes off, the flash is still there. Soon after, though, it is gone and you would have never known it was there (Sternberg & Sternberg, 2012). Short term memory holds information for slightly longer periods of time, but still has a limited capacity. According to Linden (2007), "The capacity of STM had initially been estimated at "seven plus or minus two" items (Miller 1956), which fits the observation from neuropsychological testing that the average digit span of healthy adults is about seven (Cowan and others 2005). However, it emerged that these numbers of items can only be retained if they are grouped into so-called chunks, using perceptual or conceptual associations between individual stimuli." Its duration is of 5–20 seconds before it is out of the subject's mind. This occurs often with names of people newly introduced to. Images or information based on meaning are stored here as well, but it decays without rehearsal or repetition of such information. On the other hand, long-term memory has a potentially unlimited capacity (Sternberg & Sternberg, 2012) and its duration is indefinite. Although sometimes it is difficult to access, it encompasses everything learned until this point in time. One might become forgetful or feel as if the information is on the tip of the tongue.

Cognitive Development Theory

Another approach to viewing the ways in which information is processed in humans was suggested by Jean Piaget in what is called the *Piaget's Cognitive Development Theory* (Presnell, 1999). Piaget developed his model based on development and growth. He identified four different stages between different age brackets characterized by the type of information and by a distinctive thought process. The four stages are: the sensorimotor (from birth to 2 years), preoperational (2–6 years), concrete operational (6–11 years), and formal operational periods (11 years and older). During the sensorimotor stage, newborns and toddlers rely on their senses for information processing to which they respond with reflexes. In the preoperational stage, children learn through imitation and remain unable to take other people's point of view. The concrete operational stage is characterized by the developing ability to use logic and to consider multiple factors to solve a problem. The last stage is the formal operational, in which preadolescents and adolescents begin to understand abstract concepts and to develop the ability to create arguments and counter arguments.

Furthermore, adolescence is characterized by a series of changes in the biological, cognitive, and social realms. In the cognitive area, it is worth noting that the brain's prefrontal cortex as well as the limbic system undergoes important changes. The prefrontal cortex is the part of the brain that is active when engaged in complicated cognitive activities such as planning, generating goals and strategies, intuitive decision-making, and metacognition (thinking about thinking). This is consistent with Piaget's last stage of formal operations (McLeod, 2010). The prefrontal cortex becomes complete between adolescence and early adulthood. The limbic system is the part of the brain that modulates reward sensitivity based on changes in the levels of neurotransmitters (e.g., dopamine) and emotions.

In short, cognitive abilities vary according to our development and stages in life. It is at the adult stage that we are better able to be better planners, process and comprehend abstract concepts, and evaluate risks and benefits more aptly than an adolescent or child would be able to.

In Computing

In computing, information processing broadly refers to the use of algorithms to transform data—the defining activity of computers; indeed, a broad computing professional organization is known as the International Federation for Information Processing (IFIP). It is essentially synonymous with the terms data processing or computation, although with a more general connotation.

Information System

An information system (IS) is any organized system for the collection, organization, storage and communication of information. More specifically, it is the study of complementary networks that people and organizations use to collect, filter, process, create and distribute data.

A computer information system is a system composed of people and computers that processes or interprets information. The term is also sometimes used in more restricted senses to refer to only the software used to run a computerized database or to refer to only a computer system.

Information system is an academic study of systems with a specific reference to information and the complementary networks of hardware and software that people and organizations use to collect, filter, process, create and also distribute data. An emphasis is placed on an Information System having a definitive Boundary, Users, Processors, Stores, Inputs, Outputs and the aforementioned communication networks.

Any specific information system aims to support operations, management and decision-making. An information system is the information and communication technology (ICT) that an organization uses, and also the way in which people interact with this technology in support of business processes.

Some authors make a clear distinction between information systems, computer systems, and business processes. Information systems typically include an ICT component but are not purely concerned with ICT, focusing instead on the end use of information technology. Information systems are also different from business processes. Information systems help to control the performance of business processes.

Alter argues for advantages of viewing an information system as a special type of work system. A work system is a system in which humans or machines perform processes and activities using resources to produce specific products or services for customers. An information system is a work system whose activities are devoted to capturing, transmitting, storing, retrieving, manipulating and displaying information.

As such, information systems inter-relate with data systems on the one hand and activity systems on the other. An information system is a form of communication system in which data represent and are processed as a form of social memory. An information system can also be considered a semi-formal language which supports human decision making and action.

Information systems are the primary focus of study for organizational informatics.

Overview

Silver et al. (1995) provided two views on IS that includes software, hardware, data, people, and procedures. Zheng provided another system view of information system which also adds processes and essential system elements like environment, boundary, purpose, and interactions. The Association for Computing Machinery defines "Information systems specialists [as] focus[ing] on integrating information technology solutions and business processes to meet the information needs of businesses and other enterprises."

There are various types of information systems, for example: transaction processing systems, decision support systems, knowledge management systems, learning management systems, database management systems, and office information systems. Critical to most information systems are information technologies, which are typically designed to enable humans to perform tasks for which the human brain is not well suited, such as: handling large amounts of information, performing complex calculations, and controlling many simultaneous processes.

Information technologies are a very important and malleable resource available to executives. Many companies have created a position of chief information officer (CIO) that sits on the executive board with the chief executive officer (CEO), chief financial officer (CFO), chief operating officer (COO), and chief technical officer (CTO). The CTO may also serve as CIO, and vice versa. The chief information security officer (CISO) focuses on information security management.

The six components that must come together in order to produce an information system are:

1. Hardware: The term hardware refers to machinery. This category includes the computer itself, which is often referred to as the central processing unit (CPU), and all of its support equipments. Among the support equipments are input and output devices, storage devices and communications devices.

2. Software: The term software refers to computer programs and the manuals (if any) that support them. Computer programs are machine-readable instructions that direct the circuitry within the hardware parts of the system to function in ways that produce useful information from data. Programs are generally stored on some input / output medium, often a disk or tape.

3. Data: Data are facts that are used by programs to produce useful information. Like programs, data are generally stored in machine-readable form on disk or tape until the computer needs them.

4. Procedures: Procedures are the policies that govern the operation of a computer system. "Procedures are to people what software is to hardware" is a common analogy that is used to illustrate the role of procedures in a system.

5. People: Every system needs people if it is to be useful. Often the most overlooked element of the system are the people, probably the component that most influence the success or failure of information systems. This includes "not only the users, but those who operate and service the computers, those who maintain the data, and those who support the network of computers." <Kroenke, D. M. (2015). MIS Essentials. Pearson Education>

6. Feedback: it is another component of the IS, that defines that an IS may be provided with a feedback (Although this component isn't necessary to function).

Data is the bridge between hardware and people. This means that the data we collect is only data, until we involve people. At that point, data is now information.

Types of Information System

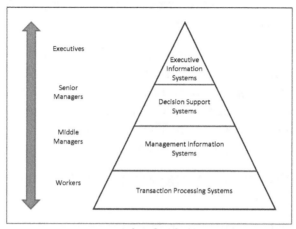

A four level

The "classic" view of Information systems found in the textbooks in the 1980s was of a pyramid of systems that reflected the hierarchy of the organization, usually transaction processing systems at the bottom of the pyramid, followed by management information systems, decision support systems, and ending with executive information systems at the top. Although the pyramid model remains useful, since it was first formulated a number of new technologies have been developed and new categories of information systems have emerged, some of which no longer fit easily into the original pyramid model.

Some examples of such systems are:

- data warehouses
- enterprise resource planning
- enterprise systems
- expert systems
- search engines
- geographic information system
- global information system
- office automation.

A computer(-based) information system is essentially an IS using computer technology to carry out some or all of its planned tasks. The basic components of computer-based information systems are:

- *Hardware*- these are the devices like the monitor, processor, printer and keyboard, all of which work together to accept, process, show data and information.

- *Software*- are the programs that allow the hardware to process the data.

- *Databases*- are the gathering of associated files or tables containing related data.

- *Networks*- are a connecting system that allows diverse computers to distribute resources.

- *Procedures*- are the commands for combining the components above to process information and produce the preferred output.

The first four components (hardware, software, database, and network) make up what is known as the information technology platform. Information technology workers could then use these components to create information systems that watch over safety measures, risk and the management of data. These actions are known as information technology services.

Certain information systems support parts of organizations, others support entire organizations, and still others, support groups of organizations. Recall that each department or functional area within an organization has its own collection of application programs, or information systems. These functional area information systems (FAIS) are supporting pillars for more general IS namely, business intelligence systems and dashboards. As the name suggest, each FAIS support a particular function within the organization, e.g.: accounting IS, finance IS, production/operation management (POM) IS, marketing IS, and human resources IS. In finance and accounting, managers use IT systems to forecast revenues and business activity, to determine the best sources and uses of funds, and to perform audits to ensure that the organization is fundamentally sound and that all financial reports and documents are accurate. Other types of organizational information systems are FAIS, Transaction processing systems, enterprise resource planning, office automation system, management information system, decision support system, expert system, executive dashboard, supply chain management system, and electronic commerce system. Dashboards are a special form of IS that support all managers of the organization. They provide rapid access to timely information and direct access to structured information in the form of reports. Expert systems attempt to duplicate the work of human experts by applying reasoning capabilities, knowledge, and expertise within a specific domain.

Information System Development

Information technology departments in larger organizations tend to strongly influence the development, use, and application of information technology in the organizations. A series of methodologies and processes can be used to develop and use an information system. Many developers now use an engineering approach such as the system development life cycle (SDLC), which is a systematic procedure of developing an information system through stages that occur in sequence. Recent research aims at enabling and measuring the ongoing, collective development of such systems within an organization by the entirety of human actors themselves. An information system can be developed in house (within the organization) or outsourced. This can be accomplished by outsourcing certain components or the entire system. A specific case is the geographical distribution of the development team (offshoring, global information system).

A computer-based information system, following a definition of Langefors, is a technologically implemented medium for:

- recording, storing, and disseminating linguistic expressions,

- as well as for drawing conclusions from such expressions.

Geographic information systems, land information systems, and disaster information systems are examples of emerging information systems, but they can be broadly considered as spatial information systems. System development is done in stages which include:

- Problem recognition and specification

- Information gathering

- Requirements specification for the new system

- System design

- System construction

- System implementation

- Review and maintenance.

As an Academic Discipline

The field of study called *information systems* encompasses a variety of topics including systems analysis and design, computer networking, information security, database management and decision support systems. *Information management* deals with the practical and theoretical problems of collecting and analyzing information in a business function area including business productivity tools, applications programming and implementation, electronic commerce, digital media production, data mining, and decision support. *Communications and networking* deals with the telecommunication technologies. Information systems bridges business and computer science using the theoretical foundations of information and computation to study various business models and related algorithmic processes on building the IT systems within a computer science discipline. Computer information system(s) (CIS) is a field studying computers and algorithmic processes, including their principles, their software and hardware designs, their applications, and their impact on society, whereas IS emphasizes functionality over design.

Several IS scholars have debated the nature and foundations of Information Systems which has its roots in other reference disciplines such as Computer Science, Engineering, Mathematics, Management Science, Cybernetics, and others. Information systems also can be defined as a collection of hardware, software, data, people and procedures that work together to produce quality information.

Differentiating IS from Related Disciplines

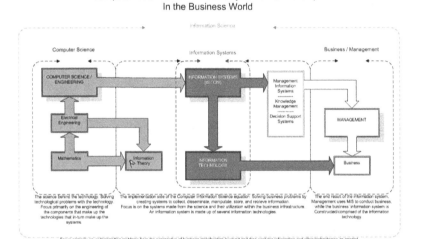

Information Systems relationship to Information Technology, Computer Science, Information Science, and Business.

Similar to computer science, other disciplines can be seen as both related and foundation disciplines of IS. The domain of study of IS involves the study of theories and practices related to the social and technological phenomena, which determine the development, use, and effects of information systems in organization and society. But, while there may be considerable overlap of the disciplines at the boundaries, the disciplines are still differentiated by the focus, purpose, and orientation of their activities.

In a broad scope, the term *Information Systems* is a scientific field of study that addresses the range of strategic, managerial, and operational activities involved in the gathering, processing, storing, distributing, and use of information and its associated technologies in society and organizations. The term information systems is also used to describe an organizational function that applies IS knowledge in industry, government agencies, and not-for-profit organizations. *Information Systems* often refers to the interaction between algorithmic processes and technology. This interaction can occur within or across organizational boundaries. An information system is the technology an organization uses and also the way in which the organizations interact with the technology and the way in which the technology works with the organization's business processes. Information systems are distinct from information technology (IT) in that an information system has an information technology component that interacts with the processes' components.

One problem with that approach is that it prevents the IS field from being interested in non-organizational use of ICT, such as in social networking, computer gaming, mobile personal usage, etc. A different way of differentiating the IS field from its neighbours is to ask, "Which aspects of reality are most meaningful in the IS field and other fields?" This approach, based on philosophy, helps to define not just the focus, purpose and orientation, but also the dignity, destiny and responsibility of the field among other fields. *International Journal of Information Management*, 30, 13-20.

Career Pathways

Information Systems have a number of different areas of work:

- IS strategy
- IS management
- IS development
- IS iteration
- IS organization

There is a wide variety of career paths in the information systems discipline. "Workers with specialized technical knowledge and strong communications skills will have the best prospects. Workers with management skills and an understanding of business practices and principles will have excellent opportunities, as companies are increasingly looking to technology to drive their revenue."

Information technology is important to the operation of contemporary businesses, it offers many employment opportunities. The information systems field includes the people in organizations who design and build information systems, the people who use those systems, and the people responsible for managing those systems. The demand for traditional IT staff such as programmers, business analysts, systems analysts, and designer is significant. Many well-paid jobs exist in areas of Information technology. At the top of the list is the chief information officer (CIO).

The CIO is the executive who is in charge of the IS function. In most organizations, the

CIO works with the chief executive officer (CEO), the chief financial officer (CFO), and other senior executives. Therefore, he or she actively participates in the organization's strategic planning process.

Research

Information systems research is generally interdisciplinary concerned with the study of the effects of information systems on the behavior of individuals, groups, and organizations. Hevner et al. (2004) categorized research in IS into two scientific paradigms including *behavioral science* which is to develop and verify theories that explain or predict human or organizational behavior and *design science* which extends the boundaries of human and organizational capabilities by creating new and innovative artifacts.

Salvatore March and Gerald Smith proposed a framework for researching different aspects of Information Technology including outputs of the research (research outputs) and activities to carry out this research (research activities). They identified research outputs as follows:

1. *Constructs* which are concepts that form the vocabulary of a domain. They constitute a conceptualization used to describe problems within the domain and to specify their solutions.

2. A *model* which is a set of propositions or statements expressing relationships among constructs.

3. A *method* which is a set of steps (an algorithm or guideline) used to perform a task. Methods are based on a set of underlying constructs and a representation (model) of the solution space.

4. An *instantiation* is the realization of an artifact in its environment.

Also research activities including:

1. *Build* an artifact to perform a specific task.

2. *Evaluate* the artifact to determine if any progress has been achieved.

3. Given an artifact whose performance has been evaluated, it is important to determine why and how the artifact worked or did not work within its environment. Therefore, *theorize* and *justify* theories about IT artifacts.

Although Information Systems as a discipline has been evolving for over 30 years now, the core focus or identity of IS research is still subject to debate among scholars. There are two main views around this debate: a narrow view focusing on the IT artifact as the core subject matter of IS research, and a broad view that focuses on the interplay between social and technical aspects of IT that is embedded into a dynamic evolving context. A third view calls on IS scholars to pay balanced attention to both the IT artifact and its context.

Since the study of information systems is an applied field, industry practitioners expect information systems research to generate findings that are immediately applicable in practice. This is not always the case however, as information systems researchers often explore behavioral issues in much more depth than practitioners would expect them to do. This may render information systems research results difficult to understand, and has led to criticism.

In the last ten years the business trend is represented by the considerable increasing of Information Systems Function (ISF) role, especially with regard the enterprise strategies and operations supporting. It became a key-factor to increase productivity and to support new value creation. To study an information system itself, rather than its effects, information systems models are used, such as EATPUT.

The international body of Information Systems researchers, the Association for Information Systems (AIS), and its Senior Scholars Forum Subcommittee on Journals (23 April 2007), proposed a 'basket' of journals that the AIS deems as 'excellent', and nominated: Management Information Systems Quarterly (MISQ), Information Systems Research (ISR), Journal of the Association for Information Systems (JAIS), Journal of Management Information Systems (JMIS), European Journal of Information Systems (EJIS), and Information Systems Journal (ISJ).

A number of annual information systems conferences are run in various parts of the world, the majority of which are peer reviewed. The AIS directly runs the International Conference on Information Systems (ICIS) and the Americas Conference on Information Systems (AMCIS), while AIS affiliated conferences include the Pacific Asia Conference on Information Systems (PACIS), European Conference on Information Systems (ECIS), the Mediterranean Conference on Information Systems (MCIS), the International Conference on Information Resources Management (Conf-IRM) and the Wuhan International Conference on E-Business (WHICEB). AIS chapter conferences include Australasian Conference on Information Systems (ACIS), Information Systems Research Conference in Scandinavia (IRIS), Information Systems International Conference (ISICO), Conference of the Italian Chapter of AIS (itAIS), Annual Mid-Western AIS Conference (MWAIS) and Annual Conference of the Southern AIS (SAIS). EDSIG , which is the special interest group on education of the AITP , organizes the Conference on Information Systems and Computing Education and the Conference on Information Systems Applied Research which are both held annually in November.

The Impact on Economic Models

- Microeconomic theory model

- Transaction cost theory

- Agency theory

Information Management

Information management (IM) concerns a cycle of organisational activity: the acquisition of information from one or more sources, the custodianship and the distribution of that information to those who need it, and its ultimate disposition through archiving or deletion.

This cycle of organisational involvement with information involves a variety of stakeholders: for example those who are responsible for assuring the quality, accessibility and utility of acquired information, those who are responsible for its safe storage and disposal, and those who need it for decision making. Stakeholders might have rights to originate, change, distribute or delete information according to organisational information management policies.

Information management embraces all the generic concepts of management, including: planning, organizing, structuring, processing, controlling, evaluation and reporting of information activities, all of which is needed in order to meet the needs of those with organisational roles or functions that depend on information.

Information management is closely related to, and overlaps with, the management of *data*, *systems*, *technology*, *processes* and – where the availability of information is critical to organisational success – *strategy*. This broad view of the realm of information management contrasts with the earlier, more traditional view, that the life cycle of managing information is an operational matter that requires specific procedures, organisational capabilities and standards that deal with information as a product or a service.

History

Emergent Ideas Out of Data Management

In the 1970s the management of information largely concerned matters closer to what would now be called data management: punched cards, magnetic tapes and other record-keeping media, involving a life cycle of such formats requiring origination, distribution, backup, maintenance and disposal. At this time the huge potential of information technology began to be recognised: for example a single chip storing a whole book, or electronic mail moving messages instantly around the world, remarkable ideas at the time. With the proliferation of information technology and the extending reach of information systems in the 1980s and 1990s, information management took on a new form. Progressive businesses such as British Petroleum transformed the vocabulary of what was then "IT management", so that "systems analysts" became "business analysts", "monopoly supply" became a mixture of "insourcing" and "outsourcing", and the large IT function was transformed into "lean teams" that began to allow some agility in the processes that harness information for business benefit. The scope of senior management interest in information at British Petroleum extended from the creation of value through improved business processes, based upon the effective management of information, permitting the implementation of appropriate information systems (or "applications") that were operated on IT infrastructure that was outsourced. In this way, information management was no longer a simple job that could be performed by anyone who had nothing else to do, it became highly strategic and a matter for senior management attention. An understanding of the technologies involved, an ability to manage information systems projects and business change well, and a willingness to align technology and business strategies all became necessary.

Positioning Information Management in the Bigger Picture

In the transitional period leading up to the strategic view of information management, Venkatraman (a strong advocate of this process of transition and transformation, proffered a simple arrangement of ideas that succinctly brought data management, information management and knowledge management together) argued that:

- Data that is maintained in IT infrastructure has to be *interpreted* in order to render information.

- The information in our information systems has to be *understood* in order to emerge as knowledge.

- Knowledge allows managers to *take effective decisions*.

- Effective decisions have to lead to *appropriate actions*.

- Appropriate actions are expected to deliver *meaningful results*.

This is often referred to as the DIKAR model: Data, Information, Knowledge, Action and Result, it gives a strong clue as to the layers involved in aligning technology and organisational strategies, and it can be seen as a pivotal moment in changing attitudes to information management. The recognition that information management is an investment that must deliver meaningful results is important to all modern organisations that depend on information and good decision making for their success.

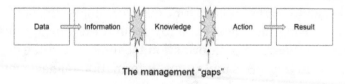

The management "gaps"

This simple model summarises a presentation by Venkatraman in 1996, as reported by Ward and Peppard (2002, page 207).

Some Theoretical Background

Behavioural and Organisational Theories

Clearly, good information management is crucial to the smooth working of organisa-tions, and although there is no commonly accepted theory of information management *per se*, behavioural and organisational theories help. Following the behavioural science theory of management, mainly developed at Carnegie Mellon University and promi-nently supported by March and Simon, most of what goes on in modern organizations is actually information handling and decision making. One crucial factor in informa-tion handling and decision making is an individuals' ability to process information and to make decisions under limitations that might derive from the context: a person's age, the situational complexity, or a lack of requisite quality in the information that is at hand – all of which is exacerbated by the rapid advance of technology and the new kinds of system that it enables, especially as the social web emerges as a phenomenon that business cannot ignore. And yet, well before there was any general recognition of the importance of information management in organisations, March and Simon ar-gued that organizations have to be considered as cooperative systems, with a high level of information processing and a vast need for decision making at various levels. In-stead of using the model of the "economic man", as advocated in classical theory they proposed "administrative man" as an alternative, based on their argumentation about the cognitive limits of rationality. Additionally they proposed the notion of satisficing, which entails searching through the available alternatives until an acceptability thresh-old is met - another idea that still has currency.

Economic Theory

In addition to the organisational factors mentioned by March and Simon, there are other issues that stem from economic and environmental dynamics. There is the cost of collecting and evaluating the information needed to take a decision, including the time and effort required. The transaction cost associated with information processes can be high. In particular, established organizational rules and procedures can prevent the taking of the most appropriate decision, leading to sub-optimum outcomes . This is an issue that has been presented as a major problem with bureaucratic organizations that lose the economies of strategic change because of entrenched attitudes.

Strategic Information Management

Background

According to the Carnegie Mellon School an organization's ability to process information is at the core of organizational and managerial competency, and an organization's strategies must be designed to improve information processing capability and as information sys-tems that provide that capability became formalised and automated, competencies were severely tested at many levels. It was recognised that organisations needed to be able to

learn and adapt in ways that were never so evident before and academics began to organise and publish definitive works concerning the strategic management of information, and
information systems. Concurrently, the ideas of business process management and knowledge management although much of the optimistic early thinking about business process
redesign has since been discredited in the information management literature.

Aligning Technology and Business Strategy with Information Management

Venkatraman has provided a simple view of the requisite capabilities of an organisation
that wants to manage information well – the DIKAR model. He also worked with others
to understand how technology and business strategies could be appropriately aligned in
order to identify specific capabilities that are needed. This work was paralleled by other
writers in the world of consulting, practice and academia.

A Contemporary Portfolio Model for Information

Bytheway has collected and organised basic tools and techniques for information management in a single volume. At the heart of his view of information management is a
portfolio model that takes account of the surging interest in external sources of information and the need to organise un-structured information external so as to make it
useful (see the figure).

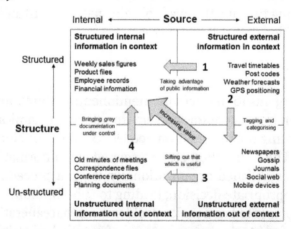

This portfolio model organizes issues of internal and external sourcing and management of information, that may be either structured or unstructured.

Such an information portfolio as this shows how information can be gathered and use-
fully organised, in four stages:

Stage 1: Taking advantage of public information: recognise and adopt well-structured
external schemes of reference data, such as post codes, weather data, GPS positioning
data and travel timetables, exemplified in the personal computing press.

Stage 2: Tagging the noise on the world wide web: use existing schemes such as post codes and GPS data or more typically by adding "tags", or construct a formal ontology that provides structure. Shirky provides an overview of these two approaches.

Stage 3: Sifting and analysing: in the wider world the generalised ontologies that are under development extend to hundreds of entities and hundreds of relations between them and provide the means to elicit meaning from large volumes of data. Structured data in databases works best when that structure reflects a higher-level information model – an ontology, or an entity-relationship model.

Stage 4: Structuring and archiving: with the large volume of data available from sources such as the social web and from the miniature telemetry systems used in personal health management, new ways to archive and then trawl data for meaningful information. Map-reduce methods, originating from functional programming, are a more recent way of eliciting information from large archival datasets that is becoming interesting to regular businesses that have very large data resources to work with, but it requires advanced multi-processor resources.

Competencies to Manage Information Well

The Information Management Body of Knowledge was made available on the world wide web in 2004 and sets out to show that the required management competencies to derive real benefits from an investment in information are complex and multi-layered. The framework model that is the basis for understanding competencies comprises six "knowledge" areas and four "process" areas:

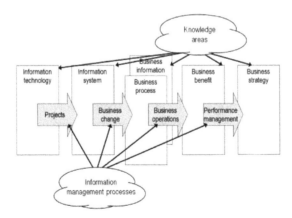

This framework is the basis of organising the "Information Management Body of Knowledge" first made available in 2004. This version is adapted by the addition of "Business information" in 2014.

The Information Management Knowledge Areas:

The IMBOK is based on the argument that there are six areas of required management competency, two of which ("business process management" and "business information management") are very closely related.

- Information technology: The pace of change of technology and the pressure to constantly acquire the newest technological products can undermine the stability of the infrastructure that supports systems, and thereby optimises business processes and delivers benefits. It is necessary to manage the "supply side" and recognise that technology is, increasingly, becoming a commodity.

- Information system: While historically information systems were developed in-house, over the years it has become possible to acquire most of the software systems that an organisation needs from the software package industry. However, there is still the potential for competitive advantage from the implementation of new systems ideas that deliver to the strategic intentions of organisations.

- Business processes and Business information: Information systems are applied to business processes in order to improve them, and they bring data to the business that becomes useful as business information. Business process management is still seen as a relatively new idea because it is not universally adopted, and it has been difficult in many cases; business *information* management is even more of a challenge.

- Business benefit: What are the benefits that we are seeking? It is necessary not only to be brutally honest about what *can* be achieved, but also to ensure the active management and assessment of benefit delivery. Since the emergence and popularisation of the Balanced scorecard there has been huge interest in business performance management but not much serious effort has been made to relate business performance management to the benefits of information technology investments and the introduction of new information systems until the turn of the millennium.

- Business strategy: Although a long way from the workaday issues of managing information in organisations, strategy in most organisations simply has to be informed by information technology and information systems opportunities, whether to address poor performance or to improve differentiation and competitiveness. Strategic analysis tools such as the value chain and critical success factor analysis are directly dependent on proper attention to the information that is (or could be) managed

The Information Management Processes:

Even with full capability and competency within the six knowledge areas, it is argued that things can still go wrong. The problem lies in the migration of ideas and information management value from one area of competency to another. Summarising what Bytheway explains in some detail (and supported by selected secondary references):

- Projects: Information technology is without value until it is engineered into information systems that meet the needs of the business by means of good project management.

- Business change: The best information systems succeed in delivering benefits through the achievement of change within the business systems, but people do not appreciate change that makes new demands upon their skills in the ways that new information systems often do. Contrary to common expectations, there is some evidence that the public sector has succeeded with information technology induced business change.

- Business operations: With new systems in place, with business processes and business information improved, and with staff finally ready and able to work with new processes, then the business can get to work, even when new systems extend far beyond the boundaries of a single business.

- Performance management: Investments are no longer solely about financial results, financial success must be balanced with internal efficiency, customer satisfaction, and with organisational learning and development.

Summary

There are always many ways to see a business, and the information management viewpoint is only one way. It is important to remember that other areas of business activity will also contribute to strategy – it is not only good information management that moves a business forwards. Corporate governance, human resource management, product development and marketing will all have an important role to play in strategic ways, and we must not see one domain of activity alone as the sole source of strategic success. On the other hand, corporate governance, human resource management, product development and marketing are all dependent on effective information management, and so in the final analysis our competency to manage information well, on the broad basis that is offered here, can be said to be predominant.

Operationalising Information Management

Managing Requisite Change

Organizations are often confronted with many information management challenges and issues at the operational level, especially when organisational change is engendered. The novelty of new systems architectures and a lack of experience with new styles of information management requires a level of organisational change management that is notoriously difficult to deliver. As a result of a general organisational reluctance to change, to enable new forms of information management, there might be (for example): a shortfall in the requisite resources, a failure to acknowledge new classes of information and the new procedures that use them, a lack of support from senior management leading to a loss of strategic vision, and even political manoeuvring that undermines the operation of the whole organisation. However, the implementation of new forms of information management should normally lead to operational benefits.

The Early Work of Galbraith

In early work, taking an information processing view of organisation design, Jay Galbraith has identified five tactical areas to increase information processing capacity and reduce the need for information processing.

- Developing, implementing, and monitoring all aspects of the "environment" of an organization.

- Creation of slack resources so as to decrease the load on the overall hierarchy of resources and to reduce information processing relating to overload.

- Creation of self-contained tasks with defined boundaries and that can achieve proper closure, and with all the resources at hand required to perform the task.

- Recognition of lateral relations that cut across functional units, so as to move decision power to the process instead of fragmenting it within the hierarchy.

- Investment in vertical information systems that route information flows for a specific task (or set of tasks) in accordance to the applied business logic.

The Matrix Organisation

The lateral relations concept leads to an organizational form that is different from the simple hierarchy, the "matrix organization". This brings together the vertical (hierarchical) view of an organisation and the horizontal (product or project) view of the work that it does visible to the outside world. The creation of a matrix organization is one management response to a persistent fluidity of external demand, avoiding multifarious and spurious responses to episodic demands that tend to be dealt with individually.

Information Theory

Information theory studies the quantification, storage, and communication of information. It was originally proposed by Claude E. Shannon in 1948 to find fundamental limits on signal processing and communication operations such as data compression, in a landmark paper entitled "A Mathematical Theory of Communication". Now this theory has found applications in many other areas, including statistical inference, natural language processing, cryptography, neurobiology, the evolution and function of molecular codes, model selection in ecology, thermal physics, quantum computing, linguistics, plagiarism detection, pattern recognition, and anomaly detection.

A key measure in information theory is "entropy". Entropy quantifies the amount of uncertainty involved in the value of a random variable or the outcome of a random process. For example, identifying the outcome of a fair coin flip (with two equally likely outcomes) provides less information (lower entropy) than specifying the outcome from a roll of a die (with six equally likely outcomes). Some other important measures in information theory are mutual information, channel capacity, error exponents, and relative entropy.

Applications of fundamental topics of information theory include lossless data compression (e.g. ZIP files), lossy data compression (e.g. MP3s and JPEGs), and channel coding (e.g. for Digital Subscriber Line (DSL)).

The field is at the intersection of mathematics, statistics, computer science, physics, neurobiology, and electrical engineering. Its impact has been crucial to the success of the Voyager missions to deep space, the invention of the compact disc, the feasibility of mobile phones, the development of the Internet, the study of linguistics and of human perception, the understanding of black holes, and numerous other fields. Important sub-fields of information theory include source coding, channel coding, algorithmic complexity theory, algorithmic information theory, information-theoretic security, and measures of information.

Overview

Information theory studies the transmission, processing, utilization, and extraction of information. Abstractly, information can be thought of as the resolution of uncertainty. In the case of communication of information over a noisy channel, this abstract concept was made concrete in 1948 by Claude Shannon in his paper "A Mathematical Theory of Communication", in which "information" is thought of as a set of possible messages, where the goal is to send these messages over a noisy channel, and then to have the receiver reconstruct the message with low probability of error, in spite of the channel noise. Shannon's main result, the noisy-channel coding theorem showed that, in the limit of many channel uses, the rate of information that is asymptotically achievable is equal to the channel capacity, a quantity dependent merely on the statistics of the channel over which the messages are sent.

Information theory is closely associated with a collection of pure and applied disciplines that have been investigated and reduced to engineering practice under a variety of rubrics throughout the world over the past half century or more: adaptive systems, anticipatory systems, artificial intelligence, complex systems, complexity science, cybernetics, informatics, machine learning, along with systems sciences of many descriptions. Information theory is a broad and deep mathematical theory, with equally broad and deep applications, amongst which is the vital field of coding theory.

Coding theory is concerned with finding explicit methods, called *codes*, for increasing the efficiency and reducing the error rate of data communication over noisy channels to near the Channel capacity. These codes can be roughly subdivided into data compression (source coding) and error-correction (channel coding) techniques. In the latter case, it took many years to find the methods Shannon's work proved were possible. A third class of information theory codes are cryptographic algorithms (both codes and ciphers). Concepts, methods and results from coding theory and information theory are widely used in cryptography and cryptanalysis.

Information theory is also used in information retrieval, intelligence gathering, gambling, statistics, and even in musical composition.

Historical Background

The landmark event that established the discipline of information theory, and brought it to immediate worldwide attention, was the publication of Claude E. Shannon's classic paper "A Mathematical Theory of Communication" in the *Bell System Technical Journal* in July and October 1948.

Prior to this paper, limited information-theoretic ideas had been developed at Bell Labs, all implicitly assuming events of equal probability. Harry Nyquist's 1924 paper, *Certain Factors Affecting Telegraph Speed*, contains a theoretical section quantifying "intelligence" and the "line speed" at which it can be transmitted by a communication system, giving the relation $W = K \log m$ (recalling Boltzmann's constant), where W is the speed of transmission of intelligence, m is the number of different voltage levels to choose from at each time step, and K is a constant. Ralph Hartley's 1928 paper, *Transmission of Information*, uses the word *information* as a measurable quantity, reflecting the receiver's ability to distinguish one sequence of symbols from any other, thus quantifying information as $H = \log S^n = n \log S$, where S was the number of possible symbols, and n the number of symbols in a transmission. The unit of information was therefore the decimal digit, much later renamed the hartley in his honour as a unit or scale or measure of information. Alan Turing in 1940 used similar ideas as part of the statistical analysis of the breaking of the German second world war Enigma ciphers.

Much of the mathematics behind information theory with events of different probabilities were developed for the field of thermodynamics by Ludwig Boltzmann and J. Willard Gibbs. Connections between information-theoretic entropy and thermodynamic entropy, including the important contributions by Rolf Landauer in the 1960s, are explored in *Entropy in thermodynamics and information theory*.

In Shannon's revolutionary and groundbreaking paper, the work for which had been substantially completed at Bell Labs by the end of 1944, Shannon for the first time introduced the qualitative and quantitative model of communication as a statistical process underlying information theory, opening with the assertion that

"The fundamental problem of communication is that of reproducing at one point, either exactly or approximately, a message selected at another point."

With it came the ideas of

- the information entropy and redundancy of a source, and its relevance through the source coding theorem;

- the mutual information, and the channel capacity of a noisy channel, including the promise of perfect loss-free communication given by the noisy-channel coding theorem;

- the practical result of the Shannon–Hartley law for the channel capacity of a Gaussian channel; as well as

- the bit—a new way of seeing the most fundamental unit of information.

Quantities of Information

Information theory is based on probability theory and statistics. Information theory often concerns itself with measures of information of the distributions associated with random variables. Important quantities of information are entropy, a measure of information in a single random variable, and mutual information, a measure of information in common between two random variables. The former quantity is a property of the probability distribution of a random variable and gives a limit on the rate at which data generated by independent samples with the given distribution can be reliably compressed. The latter is a property of the joint distribution of two random variables, and is the maximum rate of reliable communication across a noisy channel in the limit of long block lengths, when the channel statistics are determined by the joint distribution.

The choice of logarithmic base in the following formulae determines the unit of information entropy that is used. A common unit of information is the bit, based on the binary logarithm. Other units include the nat, which is based on the natural logarithm, and the hartley, which is based on the common logarithm.

In what follows, an expression of the form $p \log p$ is considered by convention to be equal to zero whenever $p = 0$. This is justified because $\lim_{p \to 0+} p \log p = 0$ for any logarithmic base.

Entropy of an Information Source

Based on the probability mass function of each source symbol to be communicated, the Shannon entropy H, in units of bits (per symbol), is given by

$$H = -\sum_i p_i \log_2(p_i)$$

where p_i is the probability of occurrence of the i-th possible value of the source symbol. This equation gives the entropy in the units of "bits" (per symbol) because it uses a logarithm of base 2, and this base-2 measure of entropy has sometimes been called the "shannon" in his honor. Entropy is also commonly computed using the natural logarithm (base e, where e is Euler's number), which produces a measurement of entropy in "nats" per symbol and sometimes simplifies the analysis by avoiding the need to include extra constants in the formulas. Other bases are also possible, but less commonly used. For example, a logarithm of base $2^8 = 256$ will produce a measurement in bytes per symbol, and a logarithm of base 10 will produce a measurement in decimal digits (or hartleys) per symbol.

Intuitively, the entropy H_X of a discrete random variable X is a measure of the amount of *uncertainty* associated with the value of X when only its distribution is known.

The entropy of a source that emits a sequence of N symbols that are independent and identically distributed (iid) is $N \cdot H$ bits (per message of N symbols). If the source data symbols are identically distributed but not independent, the entropy of a message of length N will be less than $N \cdot H$.

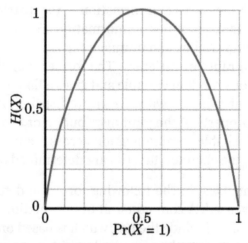

The entropy of a Bernoulli trial as a function of success probability, often called the **binary entropy function**, $H_b(p)$. The entropy is maximized at 1 bit per trial when the two possible outcomes are equally probable, as in an unbiased coin toss.

Suppose one transmits 1000 bits (0s and 1s). If the value of each of these bits is known to the receiver (has a specific value with certainty) ahead of transmission, it is clear that no information is transmitted. If, however, each bit is independently equally likely to be 0 or 1, 1000 shannons of information (more often called bits) have been transmitted. Between these two extremes, information can be quantified as follows. If $\mathbb{X}$ is the set of all messages $\{x_1, ..., x_n\}$ that X could be, and $p(x)$ is the probability of some $x \in \mathbb{X}$, then the entropy, H, of X is defined:

$$H(X) = \mathbb{E}_X[I(x)] = -\sum_{x \in \mathbb{X}} p(x) \log p(x).$$

(Here, $I(x)$ is the self-information, which is the entropy contribution of an individual message, and $\mathbb{E}_X$ is the expected value.) A property of entropy is that it is maximized when all the messages in the message space are equiprobable $p(x) = 1/n$; i.e., most unpredictable, in which case $H(X) = \log n$.

The special case of information entropy for a random variable with two outcomes is the binary entropy function, usually taken to the logarithmic base 2, thus having the shannon (Sh) as unit:

$$H_b(p) = -p \log_2 p - (1-p) \log_2 (1-p)$$

Joint Entropy

The joint entropy of two discrete random variables X and Y is merely the entropy of their pairing: (X, Y). This implies that if X and Y are independent, then their joint entropy is the sum of their individual entropies.

For example, if (X, Y) represents the position of a chess piece — X the row and Y the column, then the joint entropy of the row of the piece and the column of the piece will be the entropy of the position of the piece.

$$H(X,Y) = \mathbb{E}_{X,Y}[-\log p(x,y)] = -\sum_{x,y} p(x,y) \log p(x,y)$$

Despite similar notation, joint entropy should not be confused with cross entropy.

Conditional Entropy (Equivocation)

The conditional entropy or conditional uncertainty of X given random variable Y (also called the equivocation of X about Y) is the average conditional entropy over Y:

$$H(X|Y) = \mathbb{E}_Y[H(X|y)] = -\sum_{y \in Y} p(y) \sum_{x \in X} p(x|y) \log p(x|y) = -\sum_{x,y} p(x,y) \log \frac{p(x,y)}{p(y)}.$$

Because entropy can be conditioned on a random variable or on that random variable being a certain value, care should be taken not to confuse these two definitions of conditional entropy, the former of which is in more common use. A basic property of this form of conditional entropy is that:

$$H(X|Y) = H(X,Y) - H(Y).$$

Mutual Information (Transinformation)

Mutual information measures the amount of information that can be obtained about one random variable by observing another. It is important in communication where it can be used to maximize the amount of information shared between sent and received signals. The mutual information of X relative to Y is given by:

$$I(X;Y) = \mathbb{E}_{X,Y}[SI(x,y)] = \sum_{x,y} p(x,y) \log \frac{p(x,y)}{p(x)p(y)}$$

where SI (*Specific mutual Information*) is the pointwise mutual information.

A basic property of the mutual information is that

$$I(X;Y) = H(X) - H(X \mid Y).$$

That is, knowing Y, we can save an average of $I(X; Y)$ bits in encoding X compared to not knowing Y.

Mutual information is symmetric:

$$I(X;Y) = I(Y;X) = H(X) + H(Y) - H(X,Y).$$

Mutual information can be expressed as the average Kullback–Leibler divergence (information gain) between the posterior probability distribution of X given the value of Y and the prior distribution on X:

$$I(X;Y) = \mathbb{E}_{p(y)}[D_{KL}(p(X \mid Y = y) \| p(X))].$$

In other words, this is a measure of how much, on the average, the probability distribution on X will change if we are given the value of Y. This is often recalculated as the divergence from the product of the marginal distributions to the actual joint distribution:

$$I(X;Y) = D_{KL}(p(X,Y) \| p(X)p(Y)).$$

Mutual information is closely related to the log-likelihood ratio test in the context of contingency tables and the multinomial distribution and to Pearson's χ^2 test: mutual information can be considered a statistic for assessing independence between a pair of variables, and has a well-specified asymptotic distribution.

Kullback–Leibler Divergence (Information Gain)

The Kullback–Leibler divergence (or information divergence, information gain, or relative entropy) is a way of comparing two distributions: a "true" probability distribution $p(X)$, and an arbitrary probability distribution $q(X)$. If we compress data in a manner that assumes $q(X)$ is the distribution underlying some data, when, in reality, $p(X)$ is the correct distribution, the Kullback–Leibler divergence is the number of average additional bits per datum necessary for compression. It is thus defined

$$D_{KL}(p(X) \| q(X)) = \sum_{x \in X} -p(x) \log q(x) - \sum_{x \in X} -p(x) \log p(x) = \sum_{x \in X} p(x) \log \frac{p(x)}{q(x)}.$$

Although it is sometimes used as a 'distance metric', KL divergence is not a true metric since it is not symmetric and does not satisfy the triangle inequality (making it a semi-quasimetric).

Another interpretation of the KL divergence is the "unnecessary surprise" introduced by a prior from the truth: suppose a number X is about to be drawn randomly from a discrete set with probability distribution $p(x)$. If Alice knows the true distribution $p(x)$, while Bob believes (has a prior) that the distribution is $q(x)$, then Bob will be more surprised than Alice, on average, upon seeing the value of X. The KL divergence is the (objective) expected value of Bob's (subjective) surprisal minus Alice's surprisal, measured in bits if the *log* is in base 2. In this way, the extent to which Bob's prior is "wrong" can be quantified in terms of how "unnecessarily surprised" it's expected to make him.

Other Quantities

Other important information theoretic quantities include Rényi entropy (a generalization of entropy), differential entropy (a generalization of quantities of information to continuous distributions), and the conditional mutual information.

Coding Theory

A picture showing scratches on the readable surface of a CD-R. Music and data CDs are coded using error correcting codes and thus can still be read even if they have minor scratches using error detection and correction.

Coding theory is one of the most important and direct applications of information theory. It can be subdivided into source coding theory and channel coding theory. Using a statistical description for data, information theory quantifies the number of bits needed to describe the data, which is the information entropy of the source.

- Data compression (source coding): There are two formulations for the compression problem:

1. lossless data compression: the data must be reconstructed exactly;

2. lossy data compression: allocates bits needed to reconstruct the data, within a specified fidelity level measured by a distortion function. This subset of Information theory is called rate–distortion theory.

- Error-correcting codes (channel coding): While data compression removes as much redundancy as possible, an error correcting code adds just the right kind of redundancy (i.e., error correction) needed to transmit the data efficiently and faithfully across a noisy channel.

This division of coding theory into compression and transmission is justified by the information transmission theorems, or source–channel separation theorems that justify the use of bits as the universal currency for information in many contexts. However, these theorems only hold in the situation where one transmitting user wishes to communicate to one receiving user. In scenarios with more than one transmitter (the multiple-access channel), more than one receiver (the broadcast channel) or intermediary "helpers" (the relay channel), or more general networks, compression followed by transmission may no longer be optimal. Network information theory refers to these multi-agent communication models.

Source Theory

Any process that generates successive messages can be considered a **source** of information. A memoryless source is one in which each message is an independent identically distributed random variable, whereas the properties of ergodicity and stationarity impose less restrictive constraints. All such sources are stochastic. These terms are well studied in their own right outside information theory.

Rate

Information **rate** is the average entropy per symbol. For memoryless sources, this is merely the entropy of each symbol, while, in the case of a stationary stochastic process, it is

$$r = \lim_{n \to \infty} H(X_n \mid X_{n-1}, X_{n-2}, X_{n-3}, \ldots);$$

that is, the conditional entropy of a symbol given all the previous symbols generated. For the more general case of a process that is not necessarily stationary, the *average rate* is

$$r = \lim_{n \to \infty} \frac{1}{n} H(X_1, X_2, \ldots X_n);$$

that is, the limit of the joint entropy per symbol. For stationary sources, these two expressions give the same result.

It is common in information theory to speak of the "rate" or "entropy" of a language. This is appropriate, for example, when the source of information is English prose. The rate of a source of information is related to its redundancy and how well it can be compressed, the subject of source coding.

Channel Capacity

Communications over a channel—such as an ethernet cable—is the primary motivation of information theory. As anyone who's ever used a telephone (mobile or landline) knows, however, such channels often fail to produce exact reconstruction of a signal; noise, periods of silence, and other forms of signal corruption often degrade quality. How much information can one hope to communicate over a noisy (or otherwise imperfect) channel?

Consider the communications process over a discrete channel. A simple model of the process is shown below:

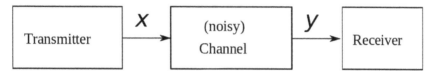

Here X represents the space of messages transmitted, and Y the space of messages received during a unit time over our channel. Let $p(y|x)$ be the conditional probability distribution function of Y given X. We will consider $p(y|x)$ to be an inherent fixed property of our communications channel (representing the nature of the **noise** of our channel). Then the joint distribution of X and Y is completely determined by our channel and by our choice of $f(x)$, the marginal distribution of messages we choose to send over the channel. Under these constraints, we would like to maximize the rate of information, or the signal, we can communicate over the channel. The appropriate measure for this is the mutual information, and this maximum mutual information is called the channel capacity and is given by:

$$C = \max_{f} I(X;Y).$$

This capacity has the following property related to communicating at information rate R (where R is usually bits per symbol). For any information rate $R < C$ and coding error $\varepsilon > 0$, for large enough N, there exists a code of length N and rate $\geq$ R and a decoding algorithm, such that the maximal probability of block error is $\leq \varepsilon$; that is, it is always possible to transmit with arbitrarily small block error. In addition, for any rate $R > C$, it is impossible to transmit with arbitrarily small block error.

Channel coding is concerned with finding such nearly optimal codes that can be used to transmit data over a noisy channel with a small coding error at a rate near the channel capacity.

Capacity of Particular Channel Models

- A continuous-time analog communications channel subject to Gaussian noise.

- A binary symmetric channel (BSC) with crossover probability p is a binary input, binary output channel that flips the input bit with probability p. The BSC has a capacity of $1 - H_b(p)$ bits per channel use, where H_b is the binary entropy function to the base 2 logarithm:

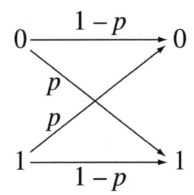

- A binary erasure channel (BEC) with erasure probability p is a binary input, ternary output channel. The possible channel outputs are 0, 1, and a third symbol 'e' called an erasure. The erasure represents complete loss of information about an input bit. The capacity of the BEC is $1 - p$ bits per channel use.

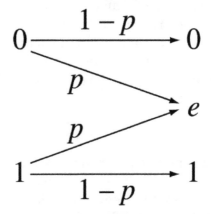

Applications to Other Fields

Intelligence Uses and Secrecy Applications

Information theoretic concepts apply to cryptography and cryptanalysis. Turing's information unit, the ban, was used in the Ultra project, breaking the German Enigma machine code and hastening the end of World War II in Europe. Shannon himself defined an important concept now called the unicity distance. Based on the redundancy of the plaintext, it attempts to give a minimum amount of ciphertext necessary to ensure unique decipherability.

Information theory leads us to believe it is much more difficult to keep secrets than it might first appear. A brute force attack can break systems based on asymmetric key algorithms or on most commonly used methods of symmetric key algorithms (sometimes called secret key algorithms), such as block ciphers. The security of all such methods currently comes from the assumption that no known attack can break them in a practical amount of time.

Information theoretic security refers to methods such as the one-time pad that are not vulnerable to such brute force attacks. In such cases, the positive conditional mutual information between the plaintext and ciphertext (conditioned on the key) can ensure proper transmission, while the unconditional mutual information between the plaintext and ciphertext remains zero, resulting in absolutely secure communications. In other words, an eavesdropper would not be able to improve his or her guess of the plaintext by gaining knowledge of the ciphertext but not of the key. However, as in any other cryptographic system, care must be used to correctly apply even information-theoretically secure methods; the Venona project was able to crack the one-time pads of the Soviet Union due to their improper reuse of key material.

Pseudorandom Number Generation

Pseudorandom number generators are widely available in computer language libraries and application programs. They are, almost universally, unsuited to cryptographic use as they do not evade the deterministic nature of modern computer equipment and software. A class of improved random number generators is termed cryptographically secure pseudorandom number generators, but even they require random seeds external to the software to work as intended. These can be obtained via extractors, if done carefully. The measure of sufficient randomness in extractors is min-entropy, a value related to Shannon entropy through Rényi entropy; Rényi entropy is also used in evaluating randomness in cryptographic systems. Although related, the distinctions among these measures mean that a random variable with high Shannon entropy is not necessarily satisfactory for use in an extractor and so for cryptography uses.

Seismic Exploration

One early commercial application of information theory was in the field of seismic oil exploration. Work in this field made it possible to strip off and separate the unwanted noise from the desired seismic signal. Information theory and digital signal processing offer a major improvement of resolution and image clarity over previous analog methods.

Semiotics

Concepts from information theory such as redundancy and code control have been used by semioticians such as Umberto Eco and Rossi-Landi to explain ideology as a form of message transmission whereby a dominant social class emits its message by using signs that exhibit a high degree of redundancy such that only one message is decoded among a selection of competing ones.

Miscellaneous Applications

Information theory also has applications in gambling and investing, black holes, bio-informatics.

Information Technology

Information technology (IT) is the application of computers and internet to store, re-trieve, transmit, and manipulate data, or information, often in the context of a busi-ness or other enterprise. IT is considered a subset of information and communications technology (ICT). In 2012, Zuppo proposed an ICT hierarchy where each hierarchy level "contain some degree of commonality in that they are related to technologies that facilitate the transfer of information and various types of electronically mediated com-munications." Business/IT was one level of the ICT hierarchy.

The term is commonly used as a synonym for computers and computer networks, but it also encompasses other information distribution technologies such as television and telephones. Several industries are associated with information technology, including computer hardware, software, electronics, semiconductors, internet, telecom equip-ment, engineering, healthcare, e-commerce, and computer services.[a]

Humans have been storing, retrieving, manipulating, and communicating information since the Sumerians in Mesopotamia developed writing in about 3000 BC, but the term *information technology* in its modern sense first appeared in a 1958 article published in the *Harvard Business Review*; authors Harold J. Leavitt and Thomas L. Whisler commented that "the new technology does not yet have a single established name. We shall call it information technology (IT)." Their definition consists of three categories: techniques for processing, the application of statistical and mathematical methods to decision-making, and the simulation of higher-order thinking through computer pro-grams.

Based on the storage and processing technologies employed, it is possible to distin-guish four distinct phases of IT development: pre-mechanical (3000 BC – 1450 AD), mechanical (1450–1840), electromechanical (1840–1940), electronic (1940–present), and moreover, IT as a service. This article focuses on the most recent period (electron-ic), which began in about 1940.

History of Computer Technology

Devices have been used to aid computation for thousands of years, probably initially in the form of a tally stick. The Antikythera mechanism, dating from about the beginning of the first century BC, is generally considered to be the earliest known mechanical an-alog computer, and the earliest known geared mechanism. Comparable geared devices did not emerge in Europe until the 16th century, and it was not until 1645 that the first mechanical calculator capable of performing the four basic arithmetical operations was developed.

Zuse Z3 replica on display at Deutsches Museum in Munich. The Zuse Z3 is the first programmable computer.

Electronic computers, using either relays or valves, began to appear in the early 1940s. The electromechanical Zuse Z3, completed in 1941, was the world's first programmable computer, and by modern standards one of the first machines that could be considered a complete computing machine. Colossus, developed during the Second World War to decrypt German messages was the first electronic digital computer. Although it was programmable, it was not general-purpose, being designed to perform only a single task. It also lacked the ability to store its program in memory; programming was carried out using plugs and switches to alter the internal wiring. The first recognisably modern electronic digital stored-program computer was the Manchester Small-Scale Experimental Machine (SSEM), which ran its first program on 21 June 1948.

The development of transistors in the late 1940s at Bell Laboratories allowed a new generation of computers to be designed with greatly reduced power consumption. The first commercially available stored-program computer, the Ferranti Mark I, contained 4050 valves and had a power consumption of 25 kilowatts. By comparison the first transistorised computer, developed at the University of Manchester and operational by November 1953, consumed only 150 watts in its final version.

Data Processing

Data Storage

Early electronic computers such as Colossus made use of punched tape, a long strip of paper on which data was represented by a series of holes, a technology now obsolete. Electronic data storage, which is used in modern computers, dates from World War

II, when a form of delay line memory was developed to remove the clutter from radar signals, the first practical application of which was the mercury delay line. The first random-access digital storage device was the Williams tube, based on a standard cathode ray tube, but the information stored in it and delay line memory was volatile in that it had to be continuously refreshed, and thus was lost once power was removed. The earliest form of non-volatile computer storage was the magnetic drum, invented in 1932 and used in the Ferranti Mark 1, the world's first commercially available general-purpose electronic computer.

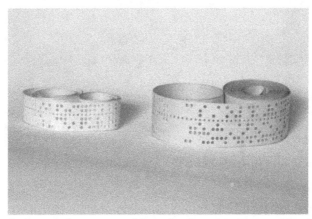

Punched tapes that were used in early computers to represent data.

IBM introduced the first hard disk drive in 1956, as a component of their 305 RAMAC computer system. Most digital data today is still stored magnetically on hard disks, or optically on media such as CD-ROMs. Until 2002 most information was stored on analog devices, but that year digital storage capacity exceeded analog for the first time. As of 2007 almost 94% of the data stored worldwide was held digitally: 52% on hard disks, 28% on optical devices and 11% on digital magnetic tape. It has been estimated that the worldwide capacity to store information on electronic devices grew from less than 3 exabytes in 1986 to 295 exabytes in 2007, doubling roughly every 3 years.

Databases

Database management systems emerged in the 1960s to address the problem of storing and retrieving large amounts of data accurately and quickly. One of the earliest such systems was IBM's Information Management System (IMS), which is still widely deployed more than 40 years later. IMS stores data hierarchically, but in the 1970s Ted Codd proposed an alternative relational storage model based on set theory and predicate logic and the familiar concepts of tables, rows and columns. The first commercially available relational database management system (RDBMS) was available from Oracle in 1980.

All database management systems consist of a number of components that together allow the data they store to be accessed simultaneously by many users while maintaining its integrity. A characteristic of all databases is that the structure of the data they contain is defined and stored separately from the data itself, in a database schema.

The extensible markup language (XML) has become a popular format for data representation in recent years. Although XML data can be stored in normal file systems, it is commonly held in relational databases to take advantage of their "robust implementation verified by years of both theoretical and practical effort". As an evolution of the Standard Generalized Markup Language (SGML), XML's text-based structure offers the advantage of being both machine and human-readable.

Data Retrieval

The relational database model introduced a programming-language independent Structured Query Language (SQL), based on relational algebra.

The terms "data" and "information" are not synonymous. Anything stored is data, but it only becomes information when it is organized and presented meaningfully. Most of the world's digital data is unstructured, and stored in a variety of different physical formats[b] even within a single organization. Data warehouses began to be developed in the 1980s to integrate these disparate stores. They typically contain data extracted from various sources, including external sources such as the Internet, organized in such a way as to facilitate decision support systems (DSS).

Data Transmission

Data transmission has three aspects: transmission, propagation, and reception. It can be broadly categorized as broadcasting, in which information is transmitted unidirectionally downstream, or telecommunications, with bidirectional upstream and downstream channels.

XML has been increasingly employed as a means of data interchange since the early 2000s, particularly for machine-oriented interactions such as those involved in web-oriented protocols such as SOAP, describing "data-in-transit rather than ... data-at-rest". One of the challenges of such usage is converting data from relational databases into XML Document Object Model (DOM) structures.

Data Manipulation

Hilbert and Lopez identify the exponential pace of technological change (a kind of Moore's law): machines' application-specific capacity to compute information per capita roughly doubled every 14 months between 1986 and 2007; the per capita capacity of the world's general-purpose computers doubled every 18 months during the same two decades; the global telecommunication capacity per capita doubled every 34 months; the world's storage capacity per capita required roughly 40 months to double (every 3 years); and per capita broadcast information has doubled every 12.3 years.

Massive amounts of data are stored worldwide every day, but unless it can be analysed and presented effectively it essentially resides in what have been called data tombs: "data archives that are seldom visited". To address that issue, the field of data mining – "the process of discovering interesting patterns and knowledge from large amounts of data" – emerged in the late 1980s.

Perspective

Academic Perspective

In an academic context, the Association for Computing Machinery defines IT as "undergraduate degree programs that prepare students to meet the computer technology needs of business, government, healthcare, schools, and other kinds of organizations .... IT specialists assume responsibility for selecting hardware and software products appropriate for an organization, integrating those products with organizational needs and infrastructure, and installing, customizing, and maintaining those applications for the organization's computer users."

Commercial and Employment Perspective

In a business context, the Information Technology Association of America has defined information technology as "the study, design, development, application, implementation, support or management of computer-based information systems". The responsibilities of those working in the field include network administration, software development and installation, and the planning and management of an organization's technology life cycle, by which hardware and software are maintained, upgraded and replaced.

The business value of information technology lies in the automation of business processes, provision of information for decision making, connecting businesses with their customers, and the provision of productivity tools to increase efficiency.

Worldwide IT spending forecast (billions of U.S. dollars)		
Category	**2014 spending**	**2015 spending**
Devices	685	725
	140	144
Data center systems	321	344
	967	1,007
Telecom services	1,635	1,668
Total	3,748	3,888

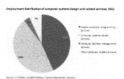

Employment distribution of computer systems design and related services, 2011

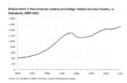

Employment in the computer systems and design related services industry, in thousands, 1990-2011

Occupational growth and wages in computer systems design and related services, 2010-2020

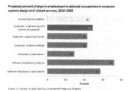

Projected percent change in employment in selected occupations in computer systems design and related services, 2010-2020

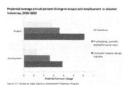

Projected average annual percent change in output and employment in selected industries, 2010-2020

Ethical Perspective

The field of information ethics was established by mathematician Norbert Wiener in the 1940s. Some of the ethical issues associated with the use of information technology include:

- Breaches of copyright by those downloading files stored without the permission of the copyright holders

- Employers monitoring their employees' emails and other Internet usage

- Unsolicited emails

- Hackers accessing online databases

- Web sites installing cookies or spyware to monitor a user's online activities

References

- Laplante, Phillip (2007). What Every Engineer Should Know about Software Engineering. Boca Raton: CRC. ISBN 978-0-8493-7228-5. Retrieved 2011-01-21.

- Bell, C. Gordon and Newell, Allen (1971), Computer Structures: Readings and Examples, Mc-Graw–Hill Book Company, New York. ISBN 0-07-004357-4.

- Bellah, Robert Neelly (1985). Habits of the Heart: Individualism and Commitment in American Life. Berkeley: University of California Press. ISBN 978-0-520-25419-0.

- Scott, Michael L. (2009). Programming Language Pragmatics (3rd ed.). Morgan Kaufmann Publishers/Elsevier. ISBN 978-0-12-374514-9.

- van Heijenoort, Jean (2001). From Frege to Gödel, A Source Book in Mathematical Logic, 1879–1931 ((1967) ed.). Harvard University Press, Cambridge, MA. ISBN 0-674-32449-8., 3rd edition 1976[?], ISBN 0-674-32449-8.

- Hodges, Andrew (1983). Alan Turing: The Enigma ((1983) ed.). Simon and Schuster, New York. ISBN 0-671-49207-1., ISBN 0-671-49207-1.

- Illingworth, Valerie (11 December 1997). Dictionary of Computing. Oxford Paperback Reference (4th ed.). Oxford University Press. p. 241. ISBN 9780192800466.

- D'Atri A., De Marco M., Casalino N. (2008). "Interdisciplinary Aspects of Information Systems Studies", Physica-Verlag, Springer, Germany, pp. 1–416, doi:10.1007/978-3-7908-2010-2 ISBN 978-3-7908-2009-6

- F. Rieke; D. Warland; R Ruyter van Steveninck; W Bialek (1997). Spikes: Exploring the Neural Code. The MIT press. ISBN 978-0262681087.

- Fazlollah M. Reza (1994) [1961]. An Introduction to Information Theory. Dover Publications, Inc., New York. ISBN 0-486-68210-2.

- Jerry D. Gibson (1998). Digital Compression for Multimedia: Principles and Standards. Morgan Kaufmann. ISBN 1-55860-369-7.

Informatics: An Overview

Informatics concerns itself with information and computer information systems. Informatics has many branches, such as computer science, information technology and statistics. This chapter on informatics offers an insightful focus, keeping in mind the complex subject matter.

Informatics

Informatics is the science of information and computer information systems. As an academic field it involves the practice of information processing, and the engineering of information systems. The field considers the interaction between humans and information alongside the construction of interfaces, organisations, technologies and systems. It also develops its own conceptual and theoretical foundations and utilizes foundations developed in other fields. As such, the field of informatics has great breadth and encompasses many individual specializations, including disciplines of computer science, information systems, information technology and statistics. Since the advent of computers, individuals and organizations increasingly process information digitally. This has led to the study of informatics with computational, mathematical, biological, cognitive and social aspects, including study of the social impact of information technologies.

Etymology

In 1956 the German computer scientist Karl Steinbuch coined the word *Informatik* by publishing a paper called *Informatik: Automatische Informationsverarbeitung* ("Informatics: Automatic Information Processing"). The English term *Informatics* is sometimes understood as meaning the same as computer science. The German word *Informatik* is usually translated to English as *computer science.*

The French term *informatique* was coined in 1962 by Philippe Dreyfus together with various translations—informatics (English), also proposed independently and simultaneously by Walter F. Bauer and associates who co-founded *Informatics Inc.*, and *informatica* (Italian, Spanish, Romanian, Portuguese, Dutch), referring to the application of computers to store and process information.

The term was coined as a combination of "information" and "automatic" to describe the science of automating information interactions. The morphology—*informat*-ion +

-ics—uses "the accepted form for names of sciences, as conics, linguistics, optics, or matters of practice, as economics, politics, tactics", and so, linguistically, the meaning extends easily to encompass both the science of information and the practice of information processing.

History

This new term was adopted across Western Europe, and, except in English, developed a meaning roughly translated by the English 'computer science', or 'computing science'. Mikhailov advocated the Russian term *informatika* (1966), and the English *informatics* (1967), as names for the *theory of scientific information*, and argued for a broader meaning, including study of the use of information technology in various communities (for example, scientific) and of the interaction of technology and human organizational structures.

> *Informatics is the discipline of science which investigates the structure and properties (not specific content) of scientific information, as well as the regularities of scientific information activity, its theory, history, methodology and organization.*

Usage has since modified this definition in three ways. First, the restriction to scientific information is removed, as in business informatics or legal informatics. Second, since most information is now digitally stored, computation is now central to informatics. Third, the representation, processing and communication of information are added as objects of investigation, since they have been recognized as fundamental to any scientific account of information. Taking *information* as the central focus of study distinguishes *informatics* from *computer science*. Informatics includes the study of biological and social mechanisms of information processing whereas computer science focuses on the digital computation. Similarly, in the study of representation and communication, informatics is indifferent to the substrate that carries information. For example, it encompasses the study of communication using gesture, speech and language, as well as digital communications and networking.

In the English-speaking world the term *informatics* was first widely used in the compound medical informatics, taken to include "the cognitive, information processing, and communication tasks of medical practice, education, and research, including information science and the technology to support these tasks". Many such compounds are now in use; they can be viewed as different areas of "*applied informatics*". Indeed, "In the U.S., however, informatics is linked with applied computing, or computing in the context of another domain."

Informatics encompasses the study of systems that represent, process, and communicate information. However, the theory of computation in the specific discipline of theoretical computer science, which evolved from Alan Turing, studies the notion of a complex system regardless of whether or not information actually exists. Since both fields process information, there is some disagreement among scientists as to field hierarchy; for example Arizona State University attempted to adopt a broader definition of informatics to even encompass cognitive science at the launch of its School of Computing and Informatics in September 2006.

A broad interpretation of *informatics*, as "the study of the structure, algorithms, behaviour, and interactions of natural and artificial computational systems," was introduced by the University of Edinburgh in 1994 when it formed the grouping that is now its School of Informatics. This meaning is now (2006) increasingly used in the United Kingdom.

The 2008 Research Assessment Exercise, of the UK Funding Councils, includes a new, *Computer Science and Informatics,* unit of assessment (UoA), whose scope is described as follows:

> *The UoA includes the study of methods for acquiring, storing, processing, communicating and reasoning about information, and the role of interactivity in natural and artificial systems, through the implementation, organisation and use of computer hardware, software and other resources. The subjects are characterised by the rigorous application of analysis, experimentation and design.*

Academic Schools and Departments

Academic research in the informatics area can be found in a number of disciplines such as computer science, information technology, Information and Computer Science, information system, business information management and health informatics.

In France, the first degree level qualifications in Informatics (computer science) appeared in the mid-1960s.

In English-speaking countries, the first example of a degree level qualification in Informatics occurred in 1982 when Plymouth Polytechnic (now the University of Plymouth) offered a four-year BSc(Honours) degree in Computing and Informatics – with an initial intake of only 35 students. The course still runs today making it the longest available qualification in the subject.

At the Indiana University School of Informatics (Bloomington, Indianapolis and Southeast), informatics is defined as "the art, science and human dimensions of information technology" and "the study, application, and social consequences of technology." It is also defined in Informatics 101, Introduction to Informatics as "the application of information technology to the arts, sciences, and professions." These definitions are widely accepted in the United States, and differ from British usage in omitting the study of natural computation.

Texas Woman's University places its informatics degrees in its department of Mathematics and Computer Science within the College of Arts & Sciences, though it offers interdisciplinary Health Informatics degrees. Informatics is presented in a generalist framework, as evidenced by their definition of informatics ("Using technology and data analytics to derive meaningful information from data for data and decision driven practice in user centered systems"), though TWU is also known for its nursing and health informatics programs.

At the University of California, Irvine Department of Informatics, informatics is defined as "the interdisciplinary study of the design, application, use and impact of information technology. The discipline of informatics is based on the recognition that the design of this technology is not solely a technical matter, but must focus on the relationship between the technology and its use in real-world settings. That is, informatics designs solutions in context, and takes into account the social, cultural and organizational settings in which computing and information technology will be used."

At the University of Michigan, Ann Arbor Informatics interdisciplinary major, informatics is defined as "the study of information and the ways information is used by and affects human beings and social systems. The major involves coursework from the College of Literature, Science and the Arts, where the Informatics major is housed, as well as the School of Information and the College of Engineering. Key to this growing field is that it applies both technological and social perspectives to the study of information. Michigan's interdisciplinary approach to teaching Informatics gives a solid grounding in contemporary computer programming, mathematics, and statistics, combined with study of the ethical and social science aspects of complex information systems. Experts in the field help design new information technology tools for specific scientific, business, and cultural needs." Michigan offers four curricular tracks within the informatics degree to provide students with increased expertise. These four track topics include:

- *Internet Informatics*: An applied track in which students experiment with technologies behind Internet-based information systems and acquire skills to map problems to deployable Internet-based solutions. This track will replace Computational Informatics in Fall 2013.

- Data Mining & Information Analysis: Integrates the collection, analysis, and visualization of complex data and its critical role in research, business, and government to provide students with practical skills and a theoretical basis for approaching challenging data analysis problems.

- *Life Science Informatics*: Examines artificial information systems, which has helped scientists make great progress in identifying core components of organisms and ecosystems.

- Social Computing: Advances in computing have created opportunities for studying patterns of social interaction and developing systems that act as introducers, recommenders, coordinators, and record-keepers. Students, in this track, craft, evaluate, and refine social software computer applications for engaging technology in unique social contexts. This track will be phased out in Fall 2013 in favor of the new bachelor of science in information. This will be the first undergraduate degree offered by the School of Information since its founding in 1996. The School of Information already contains a Master's program, Doctorate program, and a professional master's program in conjunction with the School of Public Health. The BS in Information at the University of Michigan will be the first curriculum program of its kind in the United States, with the first graduating class to emerge in 2015. Students will be able to apply for this unique degree in 2013 for the 2014 Fall semester; the new degree will be a stem off of the most popular Social Computing track in the current Informatics interdisciplinary major in LSA. Applications will be open to upper-classmen, juniors and seniors, along with a variety of information classes available for first and second year students to gauge interest and value in the specific sector of study. The degree was approved by the University on June 11, 2012. Along with a new degree in the School of Information, there has also been the first and only chapter of an Informatics Professional Fraternity, Kappa Theta Pi, chartered in Fall 2012.

At the University of Washington, Seattle Informatics Undergraduate Program, Informatics is an undergraduate program offered by the Information School. Bachelor of Science in Informatics is described as "[a] program that focuses on computer systems from a user-centered perspective and studies the structure, behavior and interactions of natural and artificial systems that store, process and communicate information. Includes instruction in information sciences, human computer interaction, information system analysis and design, telecommunications structure and information architecture and management." Washington offers three degree options as well as a custom track.

- Human-Computer Interaction: The iSchool's work in human-computer interaction (HCI) strives to make information and computing useful, usable, and accessible to all. The Informatics HCI option allows one to blend your technical skills and expertise with a broader perspective on how design and development work impacts users. Courses explore the design, construction, and evaluation of interactive technologies for use by individuals, groups, and organizations, and the social implications of these systems. This work encompasses user interfaces, accessibility concerns, new design techniques and methods for interactive systems and collaboration. Coursework also examines the values implicit in the design and development of technology.

- Information Architecture: Information architecture (IA) is a crucial component in the development of successful Web sites, software, intranets, and online communities. Architects structure the underlying information and its presentation in a logical and intuitive way so that people can put information to use. As an Informatics major with an IA option, one will master the skills needed to organize and label information for improved navigation and search. One will build frameworks to effectively collect, store and deliver information. One will also learn to design the databases and XML storehouses that drive complex and interactive websites, including the navigation, content layout, personalization, and transactional features of the site.

- Information Assurance and Cybersecurity: Information Assurance and Cybersecurity (IAC) is the practice of creating and managing safe and secure systems. It is crucial for organizations public and private, large and small. In the IAC option, one will be equipped with the knowledge to create, deploy, use, and manage systems that preserve individual and organizational privacy and security. This tri-campus concentration leverages the strengths of the Information School, the Computing and Software Systems program at UW Bothell, and the Institute of Technology at UW Tacoma. After a course in the technical, policy, and management foundations of IAC, one may take electives at any campus to learn such specialties as information assurance policy, secure coding, or networking and systems administration.

- Custom (Student-Designed Concentration): Students may choose to develop their own concentration, with approval from the academic adviser. Student-designed concentrations are created out of a list of approved courses and also result in the Bachelor of Science degree.

Organizational Informatics

One of the most significant areas of application of informatics is that of organizational informatics. Organizational informatics is fundamentally interested in the application of information, information systems and ICT within organisations of various forms including private sector, public sector and voluntary sector organisations. As such, organisational informatics can be seen to be sub-category of social informatics and a super-category of business informatics.

Theories of socio-technical Systems

Theories about Socio-Technical Systems include: Functionalism/ Transaction economics, Socio-Technical Interaction Networks/Infrastructure, Media, Information Societies, and Ethics/Values.

Functionalism/transaction Economics

Functionalism is defined as the impact new technologies have. Technologies are able to supply new functions or even revise preexisting functions. The main impact of these technologies is seen in the change that they provide and the new things that are possible with these changes. These changes also come with a grain of salt because of the costs that come along with these changes. Looking at the costs and benefits, transaction economics, is extremely critical in the study of the impact of a technology. The difference in costs that is given is equal to the impact of using the new technology. New technologies have made a lot of the tasks done on a daily basis a lot more cost efficient.

Socio-technical Networks/infrastructure

Socio-technical interaction network (STIN) is a network that includes people, equipment, data, diverse resources, documents, messages, legal arrangements, enforcement mechanisms and resource flows. STINs are embedded in all of the ICT (Information Communication Technology) that are used today. The bases of these STINs are known as infrastructure. Infrastructure is known as the basic physical and organization structures that are essential to the operation of an enterprise This infrastructure offers solutions that may occur in STINs. Infrastructure is also often not visible and for that reason it is taken for granted. However, infrastructure is extremely important.

Business informatics

Business informatics (BI) or organizational informatics is a discipline combining information technology (IT), informatics and management concepts. The BI discipline was created in Germany, from the concept of "Wirtschaftsinformatik". It is an established, successful academic discipline including bachelor, master and diploma programs in Austria, Belgium, France, Germany, Ireland, The Netherlands, Russia, Sweden, Switzerland, Turkey and is establishing in an increasing number of other countries as well as Australia or Mexico. BI integrates core elements from the disciplines of business administration, information systems and computer science into one field.

Business Informatics as an Integrative Discipline

BI shows many similarities to information systems (IS), which is a well established discipline originating from North America. However, there are a few differences that make business informatics a unique own discipline:

1. Business informatics includes information technology, like the relevant portions of applied computer science, to a larger extent than information systems does.

2. Business informatics includes significant construction and implementation oriented elements. I.e. one major focus lies in the development of solutions for business problems rather than the ex post investigation of their impact.

Information systems (IS) focuses on empirically explaining phenomena of the real world. IS has been said to have an "explanation-oriented" focus in contrast to the "solution-oriented" focus that dominates BI. IS researchers make an effort to explain phenomena of acceptance and influence of IT in organizations and the society applying an empirical approach. In order to do that usually qualitative and quantitative empirical studies are conducted and evaluated. In contrast to that, BI researchers mainly focus on the creation of IT solutions for challenges they have observed or assumed.

Tight integration between research and teaching following the Humboldtian ideal is another goal in business informatics. Insights gained in actual research projects become part of the curricula quite fast because most researchers are also lecturers at the same time. The pace of scientific and technological progress in BI is quite rapid, therefore subjects taught are under permanent reconsideration and revision. In its evolution, the BI discipline is fairly young. Therefore, significant hurdles have to be overcome in order to further establish its vision.

Urban Informatics

Urban informatics refers to the study of people creating, applying and using information and communication technology and data in the context of cities and urban environments. Various definitions are available, some provided in the Definitions section. Urban informatics is a trans-disciplinary field of research and practice that draws on three broad domains: people, place and technology.

- People can refer to city residents, citizens, community groups, from various socio-cultural backgrounds, as well as the social dimensions of non-profit organisations and businesses. The social research domains that urban informatics draws from include urban sociology, media studies, communication studies, cultural studies, city planning and others.

- Place can refer to distinct urban sites, locales and habitats, as well as to larger scale geographic entities such as neighbourhoods, public space, suburbs, regions, or peri-urban areas. The place or spatial research domains entail urban studies, architecture, urban design, urban planning, geography, and others.

- Technology can refer to various types of information and communication technology and ubiquitous computing / urban computing technology such as mobile phones, wearable devices, urban screens, media façades, sensors, and other Internet of Things devices. The technology research domains span informatics, computer science, software engineering, human-computer interaction, and others.

In addition to geographic data / spatial data, most common sources of data relevant to urban informatics can be divided into three broad categories: government data (census data, open data, etc.); personal data (social media, quantified self data, etc.), and; sensor data (transport, surveillance, CCTV, Internet of Things devices, etc.).

Although first mentions of the term date back as early as 1987, urban informatics did not emerge as a notable field of research and practice until 2006. Since then, the emergence and growing popularity of ubiquitous computing, open data and big data analytics, as well as smart cities contributed to a surge in interest in urban informatics, not just from academics but also from industry and city governments seeking to explore and apply the possibilities and opportunities of urban informatics.

Research and development work in urban informatics has targeted various concerns, issues, applications and domains, including public engagement and activism, citizen science and participatory sensing, environmental sustainability, food and urban agriculture, libraries and coworking spaces, urban design and planning, city safety and security, transport and mobility.

Definitions

Many definitions of urban informatics have been published and can be found online. The descriptions provided by Townsend in his foreword and by Foth in his preface to the "Handbook of Research on Urban Informatics" emphasize two key aspects: (1) the new possibilities (including real-time data) for both citizens and city administrations afforded by ubiquitous computing, and (2) the convergence of physical and digital aspects of the city.

"Urban informatics is the study, design, and practice of urban experiences across different urban contexts that are created by new opportunities of real-time, ubiquitous technology and the augmentation that mediates the physical and digital layers of people networks and urban infrastructures."

— Foth, Choi, Satchell, 2011, Urban Informatics

Although closely related, Foth differentiates urban informatics from the field of urban computing by suggesting that the former focusses more on the social and human implications of technology in cities (similar to the community and social emphases of how community informatics and social informatics are defined), and the latter focusses more on technology and computing. Urban informatics emphasises the relationship between urbanity, as expressed through the many dimensions of urban life, and technology.

Later, with the increasing popularity of commercial opportunities under the label of smart city and big data, subsequent definitions became narrow and limited in defining urban informatics mainly as big data analytics for efficiency and productivity gains in city contexts – unless the arts and social sciences are added to the interdisciplinary mix. This specialisation within urban informatics is sometimes referred to as 'data-driven, networked urbanism' or urban science. Three examples:

"The use of information and communications technology to better understand metropolitan needs, challenges, and opportunities."

—McKinsey on Society, 2012, Emerging Trends in Urban Informatics

"Urban informatics uses data to better understand how cities work. This understanding can remedy a wide range of issues affecting the everyday lives of citizens and the long-term health and efficiency of cities – from morning commutes to emergency preparedness to air quality."

—Center for Urban Science and Progress, 2013, What is Urban Informatics?

"Urban informatics, understood as the capture of the soundings produced by all of a city's connected devices and the application of data from those devices analysed in various ways."

—Thrift, 2014, The Promise of Urban Informatics: Some Speculations

This narrow view prominent in the new field of urban science was met with criticism by many scholars and commentators calling for a broader perspective that included not just the views of city officials but citizens. They suggested a shift in focus from the smart city to smart citizens. Michael Batty included both aspects – the narrow focus on data analysis and the wider focus on citizen participation and engagement – in his definition of urban informatics:

"Urban Informatics is loosely defined as the application of computers to the functioning of cities. In its narrower focus, it pertains to the ways in which computers are being embedded into cities as hardware and as software so that the routine functions can be made more efficient, not only through automated responses but through the data that such computation generates which is central to policy analysis. This narrow focus is on control. In its wider focus, it is concerned with the use of computers and communications to enable services to be delivered across many domains and to enable populations to engage and interact in policy issues that require citizen participation."

—Batty, 2013, Urban Informatics and Big Data

History

One of the first occurrences of the term can be found in Mark E. Hepworth's 1987 article "The Information City", which mentions the term "urban informatics" on page 261, however, Hepworth's overall discussion is more concerned with the broader notion of "informatics planning." Considering the article pre-dates the advent of ubiquitous computing and urban computing, it does contain some visionary thoughts about major changes on the horizon brought about by information and communication technology and the impact on cities.

On 12 September 2003, The Feature published an article by Howard Rheingold titled, "Cities, Swarms, Cell Phones: The Birth of Urban Informatics." In this article, Rheingold refers to Anthony Townsend as an "urban informatician and wireless activist."

The Urban Informatics Research Lab was founded at Queensland University of Technology in 2006, the first research group explicitly named to reflect its dedication to the study of urban informatics. The first edited book on the topic, the "Handbook of Research on Urban Informatics", published in 2009., brought together researchers and scholars from three broad domains: people, place, and technology, or; the social, the spatial, and the technical.

There were many precursors to this transdisciplinarity of "people, place, and technology." From an architecture, planning and design background, there is the work of the late William J. Mitchell, Dean of the MIT School of Architecture and Planning, and author of the 1995 book "City of Bits: Space, Place, and the Infobahn." Mitchell was influential in suggesting a profound relationship between place and technology at a time when mainstream interest was focused on the promise of the Information Superhighway and what Frances Cairncross called the "Death of Distance." Rather than a decline in the significance of place through services such as telecommuting, distance education, e-commerce, the physical / tangible layers of the city started to mix with the digital layers of the internet and online communications. Aspects of this trend have been studied under the terms community informatics and community network.

One of the first texts that systematically examined the impact of information technologies on the spatial and social evolution of cities is Telecommunications and the City: Electronic Spaces, Urban Places, by Stephen Graham and Simon Marvin. The relationship between cities and the internet was further expanded upon in a volume edited by Stephen Graham entitled "Cybercities Reader" and by various authors in the 2006 book "Networked Neighbourhoods: The Connected Community in Context" edited by Patrick Purcell. Furthermore, early contributions influencing the urban informatics discourse have been published in the Situated Technologies Pamphlet Series that contains nine issues published by the Architectural League of New York between 2007 and 2012. Additionally, contributions from architecture, design and planning scholars are contained in the 2007 journal special issue on "Space, Sociality, and Pervasive Computing" published in the journal Environment and Planning B: Planning and Design, 34(3), guest edited by the late Bharat Dave, as well as in the 2008 book "Augmented Urban Spaces: Articulating the Physical and Electronic City" edited by Alessandro Aurigi and Fiorella De Cindio, based on contributions to the Digital Cities 4 workshop held in conjunction with the Communities and Technologies (C&T) conference 2005 in Milan, Italy.

The first prominent and explicit use of the term urban informatics in the sociology and media studies literature appears in the 2007 special issue "Urban Informatics: Software, Cities and the New Cartographies of Knowing Capitalism" published in the journal Information, Communication & Society, 10(6), guest edited by Ellison, Burrows, & Parker. Later on, in 2013, Burrows and Beer argued that the socio-technical transformations described by research studies conducted in the field of urban informatics give reason for sociologists more broadly to not only question epistemological and methodological norms and practices but also to rethink spatial assumptions.

In computer science, the sub-domains of human-computer interaction, ubiquitous computing, and urban computing, provided early contributions that influenced the emerging field of urban informatics. Examples include the Digital Cities workshop series, Greenfield's 2006 book "Everyware: The Dawning Age of Ubiquitous Computing" as well as the 2006 special issue "Urban Computing: Navigating Space and Context" published in the IEEE journal Computer, 39(9), guest edited by Shklovski & Chang, and the 2007 special issue "Urban Computing" published in the IEEE journal Pervasive Computing, 6(3), guest edited by Kindberg, Chalmers, & Paulos.

Digital Cities Workshop Series

The Digital Cities Workshop Series started in 1999 and is the longest running academic workshop series that has focused on, and profoundly influenced the field of urban informatics. The first two workshops in 1999 and 2001 were both held in Kyoto, Japan, with subsequent workshops since 2003 held in conjunction with the biennial International Conference on Communities and Technologies (C&T).

Each Digital Cities workshop proceedings have become the basis for key anthologies listed below, which in turn have also been formative to a diverse set of emerging fields, including urban informatics, urban computing, smart cities, pervasive computing, internet of things, media architecture, urban interaction design, and urban science.

Workshop	Location	Resulting Anthology
Digital Cities 1	Kyoto, Japan, 1999	Ishida, T., & Isbister, K. (Eds.). (2000). Digital Cities: Technologies, Experiences, and Future Perspectives (Lecture Notes in Computer Science No. 1765). Heidelberg, Germany: Springer.
Digital Cities 2	Kyoto, Japan, 2001	Tanabe, M., van den Besselaar, P., & Ishida, T. (Eds.) (2002). Digital Cities 2: Computational and Sociological Approaches (Lecture Notes in Computer Science No. 2362). Heidelberg, Germany: Springer.
Digital Cities 3	C&T 2003, Amsterdam, NL	Van den Besselaar, P., & Koizumi, S. (Eds.) (2005). Digital Cities 3: Information Technologies for Social Capital (Lecture Notes in Computer Science No. 3081). Heidelberg, Germany: Springer.
Digital Cities 4	C&T 2005, Milan, Italy	Aurigi, A., & De Cindio, F. (Eds.) (2008). Augmented Urban Spaces: Articulating the Physical and Electronic City. Aldershot, UK: Ashgate.

Digital Cities 5	C&T 2007, Michigan, U.S.	Foth, M. (Ed.) (2009). Handbook of Research on Urban Informatics: The Practice and Promise of the Real-Time City. Hershey, PA: Information Science Reference, IGI Global.
Digital Cities 6	C&T 2009, PennState, U.S.	Foth, M., Forlano, L., Satchell, C., & Gibbs, M. (Eds.) (2011). From Social Butterfly to Engaged Citizen: Urban Informatics, Social Media, Ubiquitous Computing, and Mobile Technology to Support Citizen Engagement. Cambridge, MA: MIT Press.
Digital Cities 7	C&T 2011, Brisbane, Australia	Foth, M., Brynskov, M., & Ojala, T. (Eds.) (2015). Citizen's Right to the Digital City: Urban Interfaces, Activism, and Placemaking. Singapore: Springer.
Digital Cities 8	C&T 2013, Munich, Germany	Foth, M., Brynskov, M., & Ojala, T. (Eds.) (2015). Citizen's Right to the Digital City: Urban Interfaces, Activism, and Placemaking. Singapore: Springer.
Digital Cities 9	C&T 2015, Limerick, Ireland	de Lange, M., & de Waal, M. (2017, forthcoming). The Hackable City: Digital Media & Collaborative Citymaking in the Network Society.
Digital Cities 10	C&T 2017, Troyes, France	TBC

Research Centres

A July 2015 report published by the New York University's Rudin Center for Transportation Policy and Management and the Data & Society Research Institute contains a timeline of research centres that focus on urban informatics and related research. Additional entries shown in the table below have been sourced from an additional timeline compiled by the UrbanIxD (Urban Interaction Design) project. This timeline was publicly displayed as part of the City | Data | Future exhibition at the Media Architecture Biennale 2014 in Aarhus, Denmark, on 19 November 2014.

Year	Research Centres
1995	UCL Centre for Advanced Spatial Analysis, University College London
2003	Smart Cities Program, MIT Media Lab, Massachusetts Institute of Technology
2004	MIT Senseable City Lab, Massachusetts Institute of Technology
2005	Urban Scaling Working Group, Santa Fee Institute
2006	Urban Informatics Research Lab, Queensland University of Technology
2007	The Mobile City, The Netherlands
2010	Future Cities Laboratory, ETH Zürich
2011	Boston Area Research Initiative, Radcliffe Institute for Advanced Study, Harvard University
2012	Center for Urban Science and Progress, New York University

2012	Intel Collaborative Research Institute for Sustainable and Connected Cities (ICRI Cities), Imperial College and University College London
2012	Urban Center for Computation and Data, University of Chicago and Argonne National Laboratory
2013	MediaLab-Prado, Madrid
2013	Programmable City Project, Maynooth University
2013	Amsterdam Institute for Advanced Metropolitan Solutions, TU Delft
2014	Warwick Institute for the Science of Cities, University of Warwick
2014	Urban Big Data Centre, University of Glasgow
2014	City Sciences, Universidad Politécnica de Madrid
2014	Metro21, Carnegie Mellon University
2015	Urban Informatics Program, Northeastern University

Methods

The diverse range of people, groups and organisations involved in urban informatics is reflective of the diversity of methods being used in its pursuit and practice. As a result, urban informatics borrows from a wide range of methodologies across the social sciences, humanities, arts, design, architecture, planning (including geographic information systems), and technology (in particular computer science, pervasive computing, and ubiquitous computing), and applies those to the urban domain. Examples include:

- action research and participatory action research
- big data analytics and urban science
- critical theory
- cultural mapping
- grounded theory
- interaction design
- participatory design
- spatial analysis including urban modelling, complex urban systems analysis, geographic information systems, space syntax analysis
- user-centred design

Conferences and Workshops

- Digital Cities workshop series, 1999-
- LSE Cities Urban Age conference series, 2005-
- MediaCity, 2006-

- Media Architecture Biennale, 2007-

- Engaging Data: First International Forum on the Application and Management of Personal Electronic Information, 2009 (Boston, MA, USA)

- First International Workshop on the Urban Internet of Things, 2010 (Tokyo, Japan)

- International Workshop on Pervasive Urban Applications (PURBA), 2011-

- International Symposium on Pervasive Displays (PerDis), 2012-

- When the City Meets the Citizen workshop, 2012-2013

- Symposium on Urban Informatics: Exploring Smarter Cities, 2013 (Drexel University, PA, USA)

- FutureEverything: Future Cities, 2013 (Manchester, UK)

- UrbanIxD Summer School: Designing Interactions in the Networked City, 2013 (Split, Croatia)

- Workshop on Understanding the City with Urban Informatics (UCUI), 2015 (Melbourne, Australia)

- Smart Cities: Designing Places & Urban Mentalities Summer School, 2016 (Vienna, Austria)

Astroinformatics

Astroinformatics is an interdisciplinary field of study involving the combination of astronomy, data science, informatics, and information/communications technologies.

Background

Astroinformatics is primarily focused on developing the tools, methods, and applications of computational science, data science, and statistics for research and education in data-oriented astronomy. Early efforts in this direction included data discovery, metadata standards development, data modeling, astronomical data dictionary development, data access, information retrieval, data integration, and data mining in the astronomical Virtual Observatory initiatives. Further development of the field, along with astronomy community endorsement, was presented to the National Research Council (United States) in 2009 in the Astroinformatics "State of the Profession" Position Paper for the 2010 Astronomy and Astrophysics Decadal Survey. That position paper provided the basis for the subsequent more detailed exposition of the field in the Informatics Journal paper Astroinformatics: Data-Oriented Astronomy Research and Education.

Astroinformatics as a distinct field of research was inspired by work in the fields of Bioinformatics and Geoinformatics, and through the eScience work of Jim Gray (computer scientist) at Microsoft Research, whose legacy was remembered and continued through the Jim Gray eScience Awards.

Though the primary focus of Astroinformatics is on the large worldwide distributed collection of digital astronomical databases, image archives, and research tools, the field recognizes the importance of legacy data sets as well—using modern technologies to preserve and analyze historical astronomical observations. Some Astroinformatics practitioners help to digitize historical and recent astronomical observations and images in a large database for efficient retrieval through web-based interfaces. Another aim is to help develop new methods and software for astronomers, as well as to help facilitate the process and analysis of the rapidly growing amount of data in the field of astronomy.

Astroinformatics is described as the Fourth Paradigm of astronomical research. There are many research areas involved with astroinformatics, such as data mining, machine learning, statistics, visualization, scientific data management, and semantic science. Data mining and machine learning play significant roles in Astroinformatics as a scientific research discipline due to their focus on "knowledge discovery from data" (KDD) and "learning from data".

The amount of data collected form astronomical sky surveys has grown from gigabytes to terabytes throughout the past decade and is predicted to grow in the next decade into hundreds of petabytes with the Large Synoptic Survey Telescope and into the exabytes with the Square Kilometre Array. This plethora of new data both enables and challenges effective astronomical research. Therefore, new approaches are required. In part, due to this data-driven science is becoming a recognized academic discipline. Consequently, astronomy (and other scientific disciplines) are developing sub-disciplines information and data intensive to an extent that these sub-disciplines are now becoming (or have already become) stand alone research disciplines and full-fledged academic programs. While many institutes of education do not boast an astroinformatics program, the most likely will in the near future.

Informatics has been recently defined as "the use of digital data, information, and related services for research and knowledge generation". However the usual, or commonly used definition is "informatics is the discipline of organizing, accessing, integrating, and mining data from multiple sources for discovery and decision support." Therefore, the discipline of astroinformatics includes many naturally-related specialties including data modeling, data organization, etc. It may also include transformation and normalization methods for data integration and information visualization, as well as knowledge extraction, indexing techniques, information retrieval and data mining methods. Classification schemes (e.g., taxonomies, ontologies, folksonomies, and/or collaborative tagging) plus Astrostatistics will also be heavily involved. Citizen science projects (such as Galaxy Zoo) also contribute highly valued novelty discovery, feature meta-tagging, and object characterization within large astronomy data sets. All of these specialties enable scientific discovery across varied massive data collections, collaborative research, and data re-use, in both research and learning environments.

In 2012, two position papers were presented to the Council of the American Astronomical Society that led to the establishment of formal working groups in Astroinformatics and Astrostatistics for the profession of astronomy within the USA and elsewhere.

Astroinformatics provides a natural context for the integration of education and research. The experience of research can now be implemented within the classroom to establish and grow Data Literacy through the easy re-use of data. It also has many other uses, such as repurposing archival data for new projects, literature-data links, intelligent retrieval of information, and many others.

Conferences

Year	Place	Link
2016	Sorrento, Italy	
2015	Dubrovnik, Dalmatia	
2014	University of Chile	
2013	Australia Telescope National Facility, CSIRO	
2012	Microsoft Research	
2011	Sorrento, Italy	
2010	Caltech	

Bioinformatics

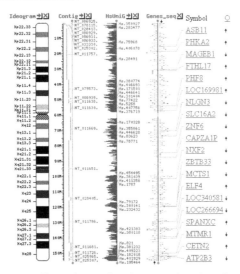

Map of the human X chromosome (from the National Center for Biotechnology Information website).

Bioinformatics is an interdisciplinary field that develops methods and software tools for understanding biological data. As an interdisciplinary field of science, bioinformatics combines computer science, statistics, mathematics, and engineering to analyze and interpret biological data. Bioinformatics has been used for *in silico* analyses of biological queries using mathematical and statistical techniques.

Bioinformatics is both an umbrella term for the body of biological studies that use computer programming as part of their methodology, as well as a reference to specific analysis "pipelines" that are repeatedly used, particularly in the field of genomics. Common uses of bioinformatics include the identification of candidate genes and nucleotides (SNPs). Often, such identification is made with the aim of better understanding the genetic basis of disease, unique adaptations, desirable properties (esp. in agricultural species), or differences between populations. In a less formal way, bioinformatics also tries to understand the organisational principles within nucleic acid and protein sequences.

Introduction

Bioinformatics has become an important part of many areas of biology. In experimental molecular biology, bioinformatics techniques such as image and signal processing allow extraction of useful results from large amounts of raw data. In the field of genetics and genomics, it aids in sequencing and annotating genomes and their observed mutations. It plays a role in the text mining of biological literature and the development of biological and gene ontologies to organize and query biological data. It also plays a role in the analysis of gene and protein expression and regulation. Bioinformatics tools aid in the comparison of genetic and genomic data and more generally in the understanding of evolutionary aspects of molecular biology. At a more integrative level, it helps analyze and catalogue the biological pathways and networks that are an important part of systems biology. In structural biology, it aids in the simulation and modeling of DNA, RNA, proteins as well as biomolecular interactions.

History

Historically, the term *bioinformatics* did not mean what it means today. Paulien Hogeweg and Ben Hesper coined it in 1970 to refer to the study of information processes in biotic systems. This definition placed bioinformatics as a field parallel to biophysics (the study of physical processes in biological systems) or biochemistry (the study of chemical processes in biological systems).

Sequences

$$5'ATGACGTGGGGA3'$$
$$3'TACTGCACCCCT5'$$

Sequences of genetic material are frequently used in bioinformatics and are easier to manage using computers than manually.

Computers became essential in molecular biology when protein sequences became available after Frederick Sanger determined the sequence of insulin in the early 1950s. Comparing multiple sequences manually turned out to be impractical. A pioneer in the field was Margaret Oakley Dayhoff, who has been hailed by David Lipman, director of the National Center for Biotechnology Information, as the "mother and father of bioinformatics." Dayhoff compiled one of the first protein sequence databases, initially published as books and pioneered methods of sequence alignment and molecular evolution. Another early contributor to bioinformatics was Elvin A. Kabat, who pioneered biological sequence analysis in 1970 with his comprehensive volumes of antibody sequences released with Tai Te Wu between 1980 and 1991.

Goals

To study how normal cellular activities are altered in different disease states, the biological data must be combined to form a comprehensive picture of these activities. Therefore, the field of bioinformatics has evolved such that the most pressing task now involves the analysis and interpretation of various types of data. This includes nucleotide and amino acid sequences, protein domains, and protein structures. The actual process of analyzing and interpreting data is referred to as computational biology. Important sub-disciplines within bioinformatics and computational biology include:

- Development and implementation of computer programs that enable efficient access to, use and management of, various types of information

- Development of new algorithms (mathematical formulas) and statistical measures that assess relationships among members of large data sets. For example, there are methods to locate a gene within a sequence, to predict protein structure and/or function, and to cluster protein sequences into families of related sequences.

The primary goal of bioinformatics is to increase the understanding of biological processes. What sets it apart from other approaches, however, is its focus on developing and applying computationally intensive techniques to achieve this goal. Examples include: pattern recognition, data mining, machine learning algorithms, and visualization. Major research efforts in the field include sequence alignment, gene finding, genome assembly, drug design, drug discovery, protein structure alignment, protein structure prediction, prediction of gene expression and protein–protein interactions, genome-wide association studies, the modeling of evolution and cell division/mitosis.

Bioinformatics now entails the creation and advancement of databases, algorithms, computational and statistical techniques, and theory to solve formal and practical problems arising from the management and analysis of biological data.

Over the past few decades, rapid developments in genomic and other molecular research technologies and developments in information technologies have combined to produce a tremendous amount of information related to molecular biology. Bioinformatics is the name given to these mathematical and computing approaches used to glean understanding of biological processes.

Common activities in bioinformatics include mapping and analyzing DNA and protein sequences, aligning DNA and protein sequences to compare them, and creating and viewing 3-D models of protein structures.

Relation to other Fields

Bioinformatics is a science field that is similar to but distinct from biological computation and computational biology. Biological computation uses bioengineering and biology to build biological computers, whereas bioinformatics uses computation to better understand biology. Bioinformatics and computational biology have similar aims and approaches, but they differ in scale: bioinformatics organizes and analyzes basic biological data, whereas computational biology builds theoretical models of biological systems, just as mathematical biology does with mathematical models.

Analyzing biological data to produce meaningful information involves writing and running software programs that use algorithms from graph theory, artificial intelligence, soft computing, data mining, image processing, and computer simulation. The algorithms in turn depend on theoretical foundations such as discrete mathematics, control theory, system theory, information theory, and statistics.

Sequence Analysis

```
A5ASC3.1   14 SIKLWPPSQTTRLLLVERMANNLST..PSIFTRK..YGSLSKEEARENAKQIEEVACSTANQ.....HYEKEPDGDGGSAVQLYAKECSKLILEVLK 101
B4F917.1   13 SIKLWPPSESTRIMLVDRMTNNLST..ESIFSRK..YRLLGKQEAHENAKTIEELCFALADE.....HFREEPDGDGSSAVQLYAKETSKMMLEVLK 100
A9S1V2.1   23 VFKLWPPSQGTREAVRQKMALKLSS..ACFESQS..FARIELADAQEHARAIEEVAFGAAQE.....ADSGGDKTGSAVVMVYAKHASKLMLETLR 109
B9GSN7.1   13 SVKLWPPGQSTRLMLVERMTKNFIT..PSFISRK..YGLLSKEEAEEDAKKIEEVAFAAANQ.....HYEKQPDGDGSSAVQIYAKESSRLMLEVLK 100
Q8H056.1   30 SFSIWPPTQRTRDAVVRRLVDTLGG..DTILCKR..YGAVPAADAEPAARGIEAEAFDAAAA..SGEAAATASVEEGIKALQLYSKEVSRRLLDFVK 120
Q0D4Z3.2   44 SLSIWPPSQRTRDAVVRRLVQTLVA..PSILSQR..YGAVPEAEAGRAAAAVEAEAYAAVTES.SSAAAAPASVEDGIEVLQAYSKEVSRRLLELAK 135
B9MVW8.1   56 SFSIWPPTQRTRDAIISRLIETLST..TSVLSKR..YGTIPKEEASEASRRIEEEAFSGAST.......VASSEKDGLEVLQLYSKEISKRMLETVK 141
Q0IYC5.1   29 SFAVWPPTRRTRDAVVRRLVAVLSGDTTTALRKRYRYGAVPAADAERAARAVEAQAFDAASA...SSSSSSSVEDGIETLQLYSREVSNRLLAFVR 121
A9NWJ46.1  13 SIKLWPPSESTRLMLVERMTDNLSS..VSFFSRK..YGLLSKEEAAENAKRIEETAFLAAND....HEAKEPNLDDSSVVQFYAREASKLMLEALK 100
Q9C500.1   57 SLRIWPPTQKTRDAVLNRLIETLST..ESILSKR..YGTLKSDDATTVAKLIEEEAYGVASN......AVSSDDDGIKILELYSKEISKRMLESVK 142
Q2HRI7.1   25 NYSIWPPKQRTRDAVKNRLIETLST..PSVLTKR..YGTMSADEASAAAIQIEDEAFSVANA.......SSSTSNDNVTILEVYSKEISKRMIETVK 110
Q9M7N3.1   28 SFKIWPPTREAVVRRLVETLTS..QSVLSKR..YGVIPEEDATSAARIIEEEAFSVASV.ASAASTGGRPEDEWIEVLHIYSQEIXQRVVESAK 119
Q9M7N6.1   25 SFSIWPPTQRTRDAVINRLIESLST..PSILSKR..YGTLPQDEASETARLIEEEAFAAAGS.......TASDADDGIEILQVYSKEISKRMIDTVK 110
Q9LE82.1   14 SVKMWPPSKSTRLMLVERMTKNITT..PSIFSRK..YGLLSVEEAEQDAKRIEDLAFATANK.....HFQNEPDGDGTSAVHVYAKESSKLMLDVIK 101
Q9M651.2   13 SIKLWPPSLPTRKALIERITNNFSS..KTIFTEK..YGSLTKDQATENAKRIEDIAFSTANQ.....QFEREPDGDGGSAVQLYAKECSKLILEVLK 100
B9R748.1   48 SLSIWPPTQRTRDAVITRLIETLSS..PSVLSKR..YGTISHDEAESAARRIEDEAFGVANT.......ATSAEDDGLEILQLYSKEISRRMLDTVK 133
```

The sequences of different genes or proteins may be aligned side-by-side to measure their similarity. This alignment compares protein sequences containing WPP domains.

Since the Phage Φ-X174 was sequenced in 1977, the DNA sequences of thousands of organisms have been decoded and stored in databases. This sequence information is analyzed to determine genes that encode proteins, RNA genes, regulatory sequences, structural motifs, and repetitive sequences. A comparison of genes within a species or between different species can show similarities between protein functions, or relations between species (the use of molecular systematics to construct phylogenetic trees). With the growing amount of data, it long ago became impractical to analyze DNA sequences manually. Today, computer programs such as BLAST are used daily to search sequences from more than 260 000 organisms, containing over 190 billion nucleotides. These programs can compensate for mutations (exchanged, deleted or inserted bases) in the DNA sequence, to identify sequences that are related, but not identical. A variant of this sequence alignment is used in the sequencing process itself. The so-called shotgun sequencing technique (which was used, for example, by The Institute for Genomic Research (TIGR) to sequence the first bacterial genome, *Haemophilus influenzae*) does not produce entire chromosomes. Instead it generates the sequences of many thousands of small DNA fragments (ranging from 35 to 900 nucleotides long, depending on the sequencing technology). The ends of these fragments overlap and, when aligned properly by a genome assembly program, can be used to reconstruct the complete genome. Shotgun sequencing yields sequence data quickly, but the task of assembling the fragments can be quite complicated for larger genomes. For a genome as large as the human genome, it may take many days of CPU time on large-memory, multiprocessor computers to assemble the fragments, and the resulting assembly usually contains numerous gaps that must be filled in later. Shotgun sequencing is the method of choice for virtually all genomes sequenced today, and genome assembly algorithms are a critical area of bioinformatics research.

Following the goals that the Human Genome Project left to achieve after its closure in 2003, a new project developed by the National Human Genome Research Institute in the U.S appeared. The so-called ENCODE project is a collaborative data collection of the functional elements of the human genome that uses next-generation DNA-sequencing technologies and genomic tiling arrays, technologies able to generate automatically large amounts of data with lower research costs but with the same quality and viability.

Another aspect of bioinformatics in sequence analysis is annotation. This involves computational gene finding to search for protein-coding genes, RNA genes, and other functional sequences within a genome. Not all of the nucleotides within a genome are part of genes. Within the genomes of higher organisms, large parts of the DNA do not serve any obvious purpose.

Genome Annotation

In the context of genomics, annotation is the process of marking the genes and other biological features in a DNA sequence. This process needs to be automated because most genomes are too large to annotate by hand, not to mention the desire to annotate as many genomes as possible, as the rate of sequencing has ceased to pose a bottleneck. Annotation is made possible by the fact that genes have recognisable start and stop regions, although the exact sequence found in these regions can vary between genes.

The first genome annotation software system was designed in 1995 by Owen White, who was part of the team at The Institute for Genomic Research that sequenced and analyzed the first genome of a free-living organism to be decoded, the bacterium *Haemophilus influenzae*. White built a software system to find the genes (fragments of genomic sequence that encode proteins), the transfer RNAs, and to make initial assignments of function to those genes. Most current genome annotation systems work similarly, but the programs available for analysis of genomic DNA, such as the GeneMark program trained and used to find protein-coding genes in *Haemophilus influenzae*, are constantly changing and improving.

Computational Evolutionary Biology

Evolutionary biology is the study of the origin and descent of species, as well as their change over time. Informatics has assisted evolutionary biologists by enabling researchers to:

- trace the evolution of a large number of organisms by measuring changes in their DNA, rather than through physical taxonomy or physiological observations alone,

- more recently, compare entire genomes, which permits the study of more complex evolutionary events, such as gene duplication, horizontal gene transfer, and the prediction of factors important in bacterial speciation,

- build complex computational population genetics models to predict the outcome of the system over time

- track and share information on an increasingly large number of species and organisms

Future work endeavours to reconstruct the now more complex tree of life.

The area of research within computer science that uses genetic algorithms is sometimes confused with computational evolutionary biology, but the two areas are not necessarily related.

Comparative Genomics

The core of comparative genome analysis is the establishment of the correspondence between genes (orthology analysis) or other genomic features in different organisms. It is these intergenomic maps that make it possible to trace the evolutionary processes responsible for the divergence of two genomes. A multitude of evolutionary events acting at various organizational levels shape genome evolution. At the lowest level, point mutations affect individual nucleotides. At a higher level, large chromosomal segments undergo duplication, lateral transfer, inversion, transposition, deletion and insertion. Ultimately, whole genomes are involved in processes of hybridization, polyploidization and endosymbiosis, often leading to rapid speciation. The complexity of genome evolution poses many exciting challenges to developers of mathematical models and algorithms, who have recourse to a spectra of algorithmic, statistical and mathematical techniques, ranging from exact, heuristics, fixed parameter and approximation algorithms for problems based on parsimony models to Markov Chain Monte Carlo algorithms for Bayesian analysis of problems based on probabilistic models.

Many of these studies are based on the homology detection and protein families computation.

Pan Genomics

Pan genomics is a concept introduced in 2005 by Tettelin and Medini which eventually took root in bioinformatics. Pan genome is the complete gene repertoire of a particular taxonomic group: although initially applied to closely related strains of a species, it can be applied to a larger context like genus, phylum etc. It is divided in two parts- The Core genome: Set of genes common to all the genomes under study (These are often housekeeping genes vital for survival) and The Dispensable/Flexible Genome: Set of genes not present in all but one or some genomes under study. a bioinformatics tool BPGA can be used to characterize the Pan Genome of bacterial species.

Genetics of Disease

With the advent of next-generation sequencing we are obtaining enough sequence data to map the genes of complex diseases such as diabetes, infertility, breast cancer or Alzheimer's Disease. Genome-wide association studies are a useful approach to pinpoint the mutations responsible for such complex diseases. Through these studies, thousands of DNA variants have been identified that are associated with similar diseases and traits. Furthermore, the possibility for genes to be used at prognosis, diagnosis or treatment is one of the most essential applications. Many studies are discussing both the promising ways to choose the genes to be used and the problems and pitfalls of using genes to predict disease presence or prognosis.

Analysis of Mutations in Cancer

In cancer, the genomes of affected cells are rearranged in complex or even unpredictable ways. Massive sequencing efforts are used to identify previously unknown point mutations in a variety of genes in cancer. Bioinformaticians continue to produce specialized automated systems to manage the sheer volume of sequence data produced, and they create new algorithms and software to compare the sequencing results to the growing collection of human genome sequences and germline polymorphisms. New physical detection technologies are employed, such as oligonucleotide microarrays to identify chromosomal gains and losses (called comparative genomic hybridization), and single-nucleotide polymorphism arrays to detect known *point mutations*. These detection methods simultaneously measure several hundred thousand sites throughout the genome, and when used in high-throughput to measure thousands of samples, generate terabytes of data per experiment. Again the massive amounts and new types of data generate new opportunities for bioinformaticians. The data is often found to contain considerable variability, or noise, and thus Hidden

Markov model and change-point analysis methods are being developed to infer real copy number changes.

With the breakthroughs that this next-generation sequencing technology is providing to the field of Bioinformatics, cancer genomics could drastically change. These new methods and software allow bioinformaticians to sequence many cancer genomes quickly and affordably. This could create a more flexible process for classifying types of cancer by analysis of cancer driven mutations in the genome. Furthermore, tracking of patients while the disease progresses may be possible in the future with the sequence of cancer samples.

Another type of data that requires novel informatics development is the analysis of lesions found to be recurrent among many tumors.

Gene and Protein Expression

Analysis of Gene Expression

The expression of many genes can be determined by measuring mRNA levels with multiple techniques including microarrays, expressed cDNA sequence tag (EST) sequencing, serial analysis of gene expression (SAGE) tag sequencing, massively parallel signature sequencing (MPSS), RNA-Seq, also known as "Whole Transcriptome Shotgun Sequencing" (WTSS), or various applications of multiplexed in-situ hybridization. All of these techniques are extremely noise-prone and/or subject to bias in the biological measurement, and a major research area in computational biology involves developing statistical tools to separate signal from noise in high-throughput gene expression studies. Such studies are often used to determine the genes implicated in a disorder: one might compare microarray data from cancerous epithelial cells to data from non-cancerous cells to determine the transcripts that are up-regulated and down-regulated in a particular population of cancer cells.

Analysis of Protein Expression

Protein microarrays and high throughput (HT) mass spectrometry (MS) can provide a snapshot of the proteins present in a biological sample. Bioinformatics is very much involved in making sense of protein microarray and HT MS data; the former approach faces similar problems as with microarrays targeted at mRNA, the latter involves the problem of matching large amounts of mass data against predicted masses from protein sequence databases, and the complicated statistical analysis of samples where multiple, but incomplete peptides from each protein are detected.

Analysis of Regulation

Regulation is the complex orchestration of events by which a signal, potentially an extracellular signal such as a hormone, eventually leads to an increase or decrease in the activity of one or more proteins. Bioinformatics techniques have been applied to explore various steps in this process.

For example, gene expression can be regulated by nearby elements in the genome. Promoter analysis involves the identification and study of sequence motifs in the DNA surrounding the coding region of a gene. These motifs influence the extent to which that region is transcribed into mRNA. Enhancer elements far away from the promoter can also regulate gene expression, through three-dimensional looping interactions. These interactions can be determined by bioinformatic analysis of chromosome conformation capture experiments.

Expression data can be used to infer gene regulation: one might compare microarray data from a wide variety of states of an organism to form hypotheses about the genes involved in each state. In a single-cell organism, one might compare stages of the cell cycle, along with various stress conditions (heat shock, starvation, etc.). One can then apply clustering algorithms to that expression data to determine which genes are co-expressed. For example, the upstream regions (promoters) of co-expressed genes can be searched for over-represented regulatory elements. Examples of clustering algorithms applied in gene clustering are k-means clustering, self-organizing maps (SOMs), hierarchical clustering, and consensus clustering methods.

Analysis of Nuclear Organization

Data from high-throughput chromosome conformation capture experiments, such as Hi-C (experiment) and ChIA-PET, can provide information on the spatial proximity of DNA loci. Anaylsis of these experiments can determine the three-dimensional structure and nuclear organization of chromatin. Bioinformatic challenges in this field include partitioning the genome into domains, such as Topologically Associating Domains (TADs), that are organised together in three-dimensional space.

Structural Bioinformatics

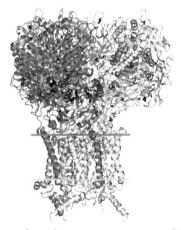

3-dimensional protein structures such as this one are common subjects in bioinformatic analyses.

Protein structure prediction is another important application of bioinformatics. The amino acid sequence of a protein, the so-called primary structure, can be easily determined from the sequence on the gene that codes for it. In the vast majority of cases, this primary structure uniquely determines a structure in its native environment. (Of course, there are exceptions, such as the bovine spongiform encephalopathy – a.k.a. Mad Cow Disease – prion.) Knowledge of this structure is vital in understanding the function of the protein. Structural information is usually classified as one of *secondary*, *tertiary* and *quaternary* structure. A viable general solution to such predictions remains an open problem. Most efforts have so far been directed towards heuristics that work most of the time.

One of the key ideas in bioinformatics is the notion of homology. In the genomic branch of bioinformatics, homology is used to predict the function of a gene: if the sequence of gene *A*, whose function is known, is homologous to the sequence of gene *B,* whose function is unknown, one could infer that B may share A's function. In the structural branch of bioinformatics, homology is used to determine which parts of a protein are important in structure formation and interaction with other proteins. In a technique called homology modeling, this information is used to predict the structure of a protein once the structure of a homologous protein is known. This currently remains the only way to predict protein structures reliably.

One example of this is the similar protein homology between hemoglobin in humans and the hemoglobin in legumes (leghemoglobin). Both serve the same purpose of transporting oxygen in the organism. Though both of these proteins have completely different amino acid sequences, their protein structures are virtually identical, which reflects their near identical purposes.

Other techniques for predicting protein structure include protein threading and *de novo* (from scratch) physics-based modeling.

Network and Systems Biology

Network analysis seeks to understand the relationships within biological networks such as metabolic or protein–protein interaction networks. Although biological networks can be constructed from a single type of molecule or entity (such as genes), network biology often attempts to integrate many different data types, such as proteins, small molecules, gene expression data, and others, which are all connected physically, functionally, or both.

Systems biology involves the use of computer simulations of cellular subsystems (such as the networks of metabolites and enzymes that comprise metabolism, signal transduction pathways and gene regulatory networks) to both analyze and visualize the complex connections of these cellular processes. Artificial life or virtual evolution attempts to understand evolutionary processes via the computer simulation of simple (artificial) life forms.

Molecular Interaction Networks

Interactions between proteins are frequently visualized and analyzed using networks. This network is made up of protein–protein interactions from *Treponema pallidum*, the causative agent of syphilis and other diseases.

Tens of thousands of three-dimensional protein structures have been determined by X-ray crystallography and protein nuclear magnetic resonance spectroscopy (protein NMR) and a central question in structural bioinformatics is whether it is practical to predict possible protein–protein interactions only based on these 3D shapes, without performing protein–protein interaction experiments. A variety of methods have been developed to tackle the protein–protein docking problem, though it seems that there is still much work to be done in this field.

Other interactions encountered in the field include Protein–ligand (including drug) and protein–peptide. Molecular dynamic simulation of movement of atoms about rotatable bonds is the fundamental principle behind computational algorithms, termed docking algorithms, for studying molecular interactions.

Others

Literature Analysis

The growth in the number of published literature makes it virtually impossible to read every paper, resulting in disjointed sub-fields of research. Literature analysis aims to employ computational and statistical linguistics to mine this growing library of text resources. For example:

- Abbreviation recognition – identify the long-form and abbreviation of biological terms

- Named entity recognition – recognizing biological terms such as gene names

- Protein–protein interaction – identify which proteins interact with which proteins from text

The area of research draws from statistics and computational linguistics.

High-throughput Image Analysis

Computational technologies are used to accelerate or fully automate the processing, quantification and analysis of large amounts of high-information-content biomedical imagery. Modern image analysis systems augment an observer's ability to make measurements from a large or complex set of images, by improving accuracy, objectivity, or speed. A fully developed analysis system may completely replace the observer. Although these systems are not unique to biomedical imagery, biomedical imaging is becoming more important for both diagnostics and research. Some examples are:

- high-throughput and high-fidelity quantification and sub-cellular localization (high-content screening, cytohistopathology, Bioimage informatics)

- morphometrics

- clinical image analysis and visualization

- determining the real-time air-flow patterns in breathing lungs of living animals

- quantifying occlusion size in real-time imagery from the development of and recovery during arterial injury

- making behavioral observations from extended video recordings of laboratory animals

- infrared measurements for metabolic activity determination

- inferring clone overlaps in DNA mapping, e.g. the Sulston score

High-throughput Single Cell Data Analysis

Computational techniques are used to analyse high-throughput, low-measurement single cell data, such as that obtained from flow cytometry. These methods typically involve finding populations of cells that are relevant to a particular disease state or experimental condition.

Biodiversity Informatics

Biodiversity informatics deals with the collection and analysis of biodiversity data, such as taxonomic databases, or microbiome data. Examples of such analyses include phylogenetics, niche modelling, species richness mapping, or species identification tools.

Databases

Databases are essential for bioinformatics research and applications. Many databases exist, covering various information types: for example, DNA and protein sequences, molecular structures, phenotypes and biodiversity. Databases may contain empirical data (obtained directly from experiments), predicted data (obtained from analysis), or, most commonly, both. They may be specific to a particular organism, pathway or molecule of interest. Alternatively, they can incorporate data compiled from multiple other databases. These databases vary in their format, way of accession and whether they are public or not.

Some of the most commonly used databases are listed below. For a more comprehensive list, please check the link at the beginning of the subsection.

- Used in Motif Finding: GenomeNet MOTIF Search

- Used in Gene Ontology: ToppGene FuncAssociate, Enrichr, GATHER

- Used in finding Protein Structures/Family: Pfam

- Used for Next Generation Sequencing: Sequence Read Archive

- Used in Gene Expression Analysis: GEO, ArrayExpress

- Used in Network Analysis: Interaction Analysis Databases(BioGRID, MINT, HPRD, Curated Human Signaling Network), Functional Networks (STRING, KEGG)

- Used in design of synthetic genetic circuits: GenoCAD

Software and tools

Software tools for bioinformatics range from simple command-line tools, to more complex graphical programs and standalone web-services available from various bioinformatics companies or public institutions.

Open-source Bioinformatics Software

Many free and open-source software tools have existed and continued to grow since the 1980s. The combination of a continued need for new algorithms for the analysis of emerging types of biological readouts, the potential for innovative *in silico* experiments, and freely available open code bases have helped to create opportunities for all research groups to contribute to both bioinformatics and the range of open-source software available, regardless of their funding arrangements. The open source tools often act as incubators of ideas, or community-supported plug-ins in commercial applications. They may also provide *de facto* standards and shared object models for assisting with the challenge of bioinformation integration.

The range of open-source software packages includes titles such as Bioconductor, BioPerl, Biopython, BioJava, BioJS, BioRuby, Bioclipse, EMBOSS, .NET Bio, Orange with its bioinformatics add-on, Apache Taverna, UGENE and GenoCAD. To maintain this tradition and create further opportunities, the non-profit Open Bioinformatics Foundation have supported the annual Bioinformatics Open Source Conference (BOSC) since 2000.

An alternative method to build public bioinformatics databases is to use the MediaWiki engine with the *WikiOpener* extension. This system allows the database to be accessed and updated by all experts in the field.

Web services in Bioinformatics

SOAP- and REST-based interfaces have been developed for a wide variety of bioinformatics applications allowing an application running on one computer in one part of the world to use algorithms, data and computing resources on servers in other parts of the world. The main advantages derive from the fact that end users do not have to deal with software and database maintenance overheads.

Basic bioinformatics services are classified by the EBI into three categories: SSS (Sequence Search Services), MSA (Multiple Sequence Alignment), and BSA (Biological Sequence Analysis). The availability of these service-oriented bioinformatics resources demonstrate the applicability of web-based bioinformatics solutions, and range from a collection of standalone tools with a common data format under a single, standalone or web-based interface, to integrative, distributed and extensible bioinformatics workflow management systems.

Bioinformatics Workflow Management Systems

A Bioinformatics workflow management system is a specialized form of a workflow management system designed specifically to compose and execute a series of computational or data manipulation steps, or a workflow, in a Bioinformatics application. Such systems are designed to

- provide an easy-to-use environment for individual application scientists themselves to create their own workflows

- provide interactive tools for the scientists enabling them to execute their workflows and view their results in real-time

- simplify the process of sharing and reusing workflows between the scientists.

- enable scientists to track the provenance of the workflow execution results and the workflow creation steps.

Some of the platforms giving this service: Galaxy, Kepler, Taverna, UGENE, Anduril.

Education Platforms

Software platforms designed to teach bioinformatics concepts and methods include Rosalind and online courses offered through the Swiss Institute of Bioinformatics Training Portal. The Canadian Bioinformatics Workshops provides videos and slides from training workshops on their website under a Creative Commons license. The 4273π project or 4273pi project also offers open source educational materials for free. The course runs on low cost raspberry pi computers and has been used to teach adults and school pupils. 4273π is actively developed by a consortium of academics and research staff who have run research level bioinformatics using raspberry pi computers and the 4273π operating system.

MOOC platforms also provide online certifications in bioinformatics and related disciplines, including Coursera's Bioinformatics Specialization (UC San Diego) and Genomic Data Science Specialization (Johns Hopkins) as well as EdX's Data Analysis for Life Sciences XSeries (Harvard).

Conferences

There are several large conferences that are concerned with bioinformatics. Some of the most notable examples are Intelligent Systems for Molecular Biology (ISMB), European Conference on Computational Biology (ECCB), and Research in Computational Molecular Biology (RECOMB).

References

- Beynon-Davies P. (2002). Information Systems: an introduction to informatics in Organisations. Palgrave, Basingstoke, UK. ISBN 0-333-96390-3

- Kitchin, Rob; Dodge, Martin (2011). Code/Space: Software and Everyday Life. Cambridge, MA: MIT Press. ISBN 9780262042482.

- Foth, Marcus; Brynskov, Martin; Ojala, Timo (2015). Citizen's Right to the Digital City: Urban Interfaces, Activism, and Placemaking. Singapore: Springer. ISBN 9789812879172.

- Choi, Jaz Hee-jeong; Foth, Marcus; Hearn, Greg (2014). Eat, Cook, Grow: Mixing Human-Computer Interactions with Human-Food Interactions. Cambridge, Mass.: MIT Press. ISBN 978-0-262-02685-7.

- Bilandzic, Mark; Foth, Marcus (2017). "Designing hubs for connected learning: social, spatial and technological insights from Coworking, Hackerspaces and Meetup groups". In Carvalho, Lucila; Goodyear, Peter; de Laat, Maarten. Place-Based Spaces for Networked Learning. Abingdon, UK: Routledge. ISBN 978-1-138-85086-6.

- Foth, Marcus (2009). Handbook of Research on Urban Informatics: The Practice and Promise of the Real-Time City. Hershey, PA: Information Science Reference. ISBN 978-1-60566-152-0

- Hemment, Drew; Townsend, Anthony (2013). Smart Citizens (PDF). Manchester, UK: FutureEverything. ISBN 978-0-9568958-7-5. Retrieved 28 July 2016.

- Cairncross, Frances (1997). The Death of Distance: How the Communications Revolution will Change our Lives. Boston, Mass.: Harvard Business School Press. ISBN 978-0-87584-806-8.

- Aurigi, Alessandro; De Cindio, Fiorella (2008). Augmented Urban Spaces: Articulating the Physical and Electronic City. Aldershot, UK: Ashgate. ISBN 978-0-7546-7149-7.

- Greenfield, Adam (2006). Everyware: The Dawning Age of Ubiquitous Computing. San Francisco, US: New Riders. ISBN 0321384016.

- Hearn, Greg; Tacchi, Jo; Foth, Marcus; Lennie, June (2009). Action Research and New Media: Concepts, Methods, and Cases. Cresskill, NJ: Hampton Press. ISBN 978-1-57273-866-9.

- Moshfeghi, Yashar (2015). Proceedings of the ACM First International Workshop on Understanding the City with Urban Informatics. New York, NY: ACM. ISBN 978-1-4503-3786-1. Retrieved 15 Sep 2016.

- Gordon, Eric; Silva, Adriana de Souza e (2011). Net Locality: Why Location Matters in a Networked World. Chichester, West Sussex, UK: Wiley-Blackwell. ISBN 978-1-4051-8060-3.

- Townsend, Anthony M. (2013). Smart Cities: Big Data, Civic Hackers, and the Quest for a New Utopia. New York, NY: W. W. Norton & Company, Inc. ISBN 978-0-393-08287-6.

Various Applications of Information and Computer Science

The intelligence exhibited by machines is called artificial intelligence, a machine is considered to be intelligent if it is a flexible agent that perceives its environment and maximizing its possibilities of achieving a goal. It also gives a brief detail on robotics and systems development life cycle. The aspects elucidated in this chapter are of vital importance to the field of information and computer science.

Artificial Intelligence

Artificial intelligence (AI) is intelligence exhibited by machines. In computer science, an ideal "intelligent" machine is a flexible rational agent that perceives its environment and takes actions that maximize its chance of success at some goal. Colloquially, the term "artificial intelligence" is applied when a machine mimics "cognitive" functions that humans associate with other human minds, such as "learning" and "problem solving". As machines become increasingly capable, facilities once thought to require intelligence are removed from the definition. For example, optical character recognition is no longer perceived as an exemplar of "artificial intelligence" having become a routine technology. Capabilities still classified as AI include advanced Chess and Go systems and self-driving cars.

AI research is divided into subfields that focus on specific problems or on specific approaches or on the use of a particular tool or towards satisfying particular applications.

The central problems (or goals) of AI research include reasoning, knowledge, planning, learning, natural language processing (communication), perception and the ability to move and manipulate objects. General intelligence is among the field's long-term goals. Approaches include statistical methods, computational intelligence, soft computing (e.g. machine learning), and traditional symbolic AI. Many tools are used in AI, including versions of search and mathematical optimization, logic, methods based on probability and economics. The AI field draws upon computer science, mathematics, psychology, linguistics, philosophy, neuroscience and artificial psychology.

The field was founded on the claim that human intelligence "can be so precisely described that a machine can be made to simulate it." This raises philosophical arguments about the nature of the mind and the ethics of creating artificial beings endowed with human-like intelligence, issues which have been explored by myth, fiction and philosophy since antiquity. Attempts to create artificial intelligence has experienced many setbacks, including the ALPAC report of 1966, the abandonment of perceptrons in 1970, the Lighthill Report of 1973 and the collapse of the Lisp machine market in 1987. In the twenty-first century AI techniques became an essential part of the technology industry, helping to solve many challenging problems in computer science.

History

While the concept of artificial beings (some of which are capable of thought) appeared as storytelling devices in antiquity, the idea of actually trying to build a machine to perform useful reasoning may have begun with Ramon Lull (c. 1300 CE). The first known calculating machine was built around 1623 by scientist Wilhelm Schickard. Gottfried Leibniz then built a crude variant, intended to perform operations on concepts rather than numbers. Since the 19th century, artificial beings are common in fiction, as in Mary Shelley's *Frankenstein* or Karel Čapek's *R.U.R. (Rossum's Universal Robots)*.

Mechanical or "formal" reasoning began with philosophers and mathematicians in antiquity. In the 19th century, George Boole refined those ideas into propositional logic and Gottlob Frege developed a notational system for mechanical reasoning (a *"predicate calculus"*). Around the 1940s, Alan Turing's theory of computation suggested that a machine, by shuffling symbols as simple as "0" and "1", could simulate any conceivable act of mathematical deduction. This insight, that digital computers can simulate any process of formal reasoning, is known as the Church–Turing thesis. Along with concurrent discoveries in neurology, information theory and cybernetics, this led researchers to consider the possibility of building an electronic brain. The first work that is now generally recognized as AI was McCullough and Pitts' 1943 formal design for Turing-complete "artificial neurons".

The field of AI research was founded at a conference at Dartmouth College in 1956. The attendees, including John McCarthy, Marvin Minsky, Allen Newell, Arthur Samuel and Herbert Simon, became the leaders of AI research. They and their students wrote programs that were, to most people, simply astonishing: computers were winning at checkers, solving word problems in algebra, proving logical theorems and speaking English. By the middle of the 1960s, research in the U.S. was heavily funded by the Department of Defense and laboratories had been established around the world. AI's founders were optimistic about the future: Herbert Simon predicted that "machines will be capable, within twenty years, of doing any work a man can do". Marvin Minsky agreed, writing that "within a generation ... the problem of creating 'artificial intelligence' will substantially be solved".

They failed to recognize the difficulty of some of the remaining tasks. Progress slowed and in 1974, in response to the criticism of Sir James Lighthill and ongoing pressure from the US Congress to fund more productive projects, both the U.S. and British governments cut off exploratory research in AI. The next few years would later be called an "AI winter", a period when funding for AI projects was hard to find.

In the early 1980s, AI research was revived by the commercial success of expert systems, a form of AI program that simulated the knowledge and analytical skills of human experts. By 1985 the market for AI had reached over a billion dollars. At the same time, Japan's fifth generation computer project inspired the U.S and British governments to restore funding for academic research. However, beginning with the collapse of the Lisp Machine market in 1987, AI once again fell into disrepute, and a second, longer-lasting hiatus began.

In the late 1990s and early 21st century, AI began to be used for logistics, data mining, medical diagnosis and other areas. The success was due to increasing computational power, greater emphasis on solving specific problems, new ties between AI and other fields and a commitment by researchers to mathematical methods and scientific standards. Deep Blue became the first computer chess-playing system to beat a reigning world chess champion, Garry Kasparov on 11 May 1997.

Advanced statistical techniques (loosely known as deep learning), access to large amounts of data and faster computers enabled advances in machine learning and perception. By the mid 2010s, machine learning applications were used throughout the world. In a *Jeopardy!* quiz show exhibition match, IBM's question answering system, Watson, defeated the two greatest Jeopardy champions, Brad Rutter and Ken Jennings, by a significant margin. The Kinect, which provides a 3D body–motion interface for the Xbox 360 and the Xbox One use algorithms that emerged from lengthy AI research as do intelligent personal assistants in smartphones. In March 2016, AlphaGo won 4 out of 5 games of Go in a match with Go champion Lee Sedol, becoming the first computer Go-playing system to beat a professional Go player without handicaps.

Research

Goals

The general problem of simulating (or creating) intelligence has been broken down into sub-problems. These consist of particular traits or capabilities that researchers expect an intelligent system to display. The traits described below have received the most attention.

Deduction, Reasoning, Problem Solving

Early researchers developed algorithms that imitated step-by-step reasoning that humans use when they solve puzzles or make logical deductions (reason). By the late 1980s and 1990s, AI research had developed methods for dealing with uncertain or incomplete information, employing concepts from probability and economics.

For difficult problems, algorithms can require enormous computational resources—most experience a "combinatorial explosion": the amount of memory or computer time required becomes astronomical for problems of a certain size. The search for more efficient problem-solving algorithms is a high priority.

Human beings ordinarily use fast, intuitive judgments rather than step-by-step deduction that early AI research was able to model. AI has progressed using "sub-symbolic" problem solving: embodied agent approaches emphasize the importance of sensorimotor skills to higher reasoning; neural net research attempts to simulate the structures inside the brain that give rise to this skill; statistical approaches to AI mimic the human ability to guess.

Knowledge Representation

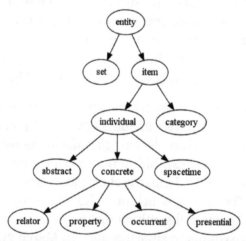

An ontology represents knowledge as a set of concepts within a domain
and the relationships between those concepts.

Knowledge representation and knowledge engineering are central to AI research. Many of the problems machines are expected to solve will require extensive knowledge about the world. Among the things that AI needs to represent are: objects, properties, categories and relations between objects; situations, events, states and time; causes and effects; knowledge about knowledge (what we know about what other people know); and many other, less well researched domains. A representation of "what exists" is an ontology: the set of objects, relations, concepts and so on that the machine knows about. The most general are called upper ontologies, which attempt to provide a foundation for all other knowledge.

Among the most difficult problems in knowledge representation are:

Default reasoning and the qualification problem

> Many of the things people know take the form of "working assumptions." For
> example, if a bird comes up in conversation, people typically picture an animal

that is fist sized, sings, and flies. None of these things are true about all birds. John McCarthy identified this problem in 1969 as the qualification problem: for any commonsense rule that AI researchers care to represent, there tend to be a huge number of exceptions. Almost nothing is simply true or false in the way that abstract logic requires. AI research has explored a number of solutions to this problem.

The breadth of commonsense knowledge

The number of atomic facts that the average person knows is astronomical. Research projects that attempt to build a complete knowledge base of commonsense knowledge (e.g., Cyc) require enormous amounts of laborious ontological engineering—they must be built, by hand, one complicated concept at a time. A major goal is to have the computer understand enough concepts to be able to learn by reading from sources like the Internet, and thus be able to add to its own ontology.

The subsymbolic form of some commonsense knowledge

Much of what people know is not represented as "facts" or "statements" that they could express verbally. For example, a chess master will avoid a particular chess position because it "feels too exposed" or an art critic can take one look at a statue and instantly realize that it is a fake. These are intuitions or tendencies that are represented in the brain non-consciously and sub-symbolically. Knowledge like this informs, supports and provides a context for symbolic, conscious knowledge. As with the related problem of sub-symbolic reasoning, it is hoped that situated AI, computational intelligence, or statistical AI will provide ways to represent this kind of knowledge.

Planning

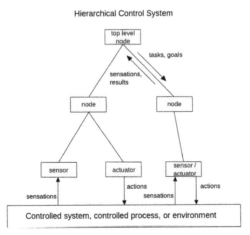

A hierarchical control system is a form of control system in which a set of devices and governing software is arranged in a hierarchy.

Intelligent agents must be able to set goals and achieve them. They need a way to visualize the future (they must have a representation of the state of the world and be able to make predictions about how their actions will change it) and be able to make choices that maximize the utility (or "value") of the available choices.

In classical planning problems, the agent can assume that it is the only thing acting on the world and it can be certain what the consequences of its actions may be. However, if the agent is not the only actor, it must periodically ascertain whether the world matches its predictions and it must change its plan as this becomes necessary, requiring the agent to reason under uncertainty.

Multi-agent planning uses the cooperation and competition of many agents to achieve a given goal. Emergent behavior such as this is used by evolutionary algorithms and swarm intelligence.

Learning

Machine learning is the study of computer algorithms that improve automatically through experience and has been central to AI research since the field's inception.

Unsupervised learning is the ability to find patterns in a stream of input. Supervised learning includes both classification and numerical regression. Classification is used to determine what category something belongs in, after seeing a number of examples of things from several categories. Regression is the attempt to produce a function that describes the relationship between inputs and outputs and predicts how the outputs should change as the inputs change. In reinforcement learning the agent is rewarded for good responses and punished for bad ones. The agent uses this sequence of rewards and punishments to form a strategy for operating in its problem space. These three types of learning can be analyzed in terms of decision theory, using concepts like utility. The mathematical analysis of machine learning algorithms and their performance is a branch of theoretical computer science known as computational learning theory.

Within developmental robotics, developmental learning approaches were elaborated for lifelong cumulative acquisition of repertoires of novel skills by a robot, through autonomous self-exploration and social interaction with human teachers, and using guidance mechanisms such as active learning, maturation, motor synergies, and imitation.

Natural Language Processing (Communication)

Natural language processing gives machines the ability to read and understand the languages that humans speak. A sufficiently powerful natural language processing system would enable natural language user interfaces and the acquisition of knowledge directly from human-written sources, such as newswire texts. Some straightforward applications of natural language processing include information retrieval, text mining, question answering and machine translation.

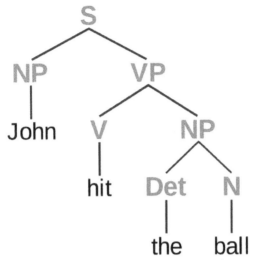

A parse tree represents the syntactic structure of a sentence according to some formal grammar.

A common method of processing and extracting meaning from natural language is through semantic indexing. Increases in processing speeds and the drop in the cost of data storage makes indexing large volumes of abstractions of the user's input much more efficient.

Perception

Machine perception is the ability to use input from sensors (such as cameras, microphones, tactile sensors, sonar and others more exotic) to deduce aspects of the world. Computer vision is the ability to analyze visual input. A few selected subproblems are speech recognition, facial recognition and object recognition.

Motion and Manipulation

The field of robotics is closely related to AI. Intelligence is required for robots to be able to handle such tasks as object manipulation and navigation, with sub-problems of localization (knowing where you are, or finding out where other things are), mapping (learning what is around you, building a map of the environment), and motion planning (figuring out how to get there) or path planning (going from one point in space to another point, which may involve compliant motion – where the robot moves while maintaining physical contact with an object).

Long-term Goals

Among the long-term goals in the research pertaining to artificial intelligence are: (1) Social intelligence, (2) Creativity, and (3) General intelligence.

Social Intelligence

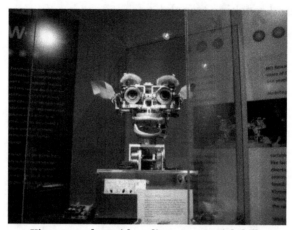

Kismet, a robot with rudimentary social skills

Affective computing is the study and development of systems and devices that can recognize, interpret, process, and simulate human affects. It is an interdisciplinary field spanning computer sciences, psychology, and cognitive science. While the origins of the field may be traced as far back as to early philosophical inquiries into emotion, the more modern branch of computer science originated with Rosalind Picard's 1995 paper on affective computing. A motivation for the research is the ability to simulate empathy. The machine should interpret the emotional state of humans and adapt its behaviour to them, giving an appropriate response for those emotions.

Emotion and social skills play two roles for an intelligent agent. First, it must be able to predict the actions of others, by understanding their motives and emotional states. (This involves elements of game theory, decision theory, as well as the ability to model human emotions and the perceptual skills to detect emotions.) Also, in an effort to facilitate human-computer interaction, an intelligent machine might want to be able to *display* emotions—even if it does not actually experience them itself—in order to appear sensitive to the emotional dynamics of human interaction.

Creativity

A sub-field of AI addresses creativity both theoretically (from a philosophical and psychological perspective) and practically (via specific implementations of systems that generate outputs that can be considered creative, or systems that identify and assess creativity). Related areas of computational research are Artificial intuition and Artificial thinking.

General Intelligence

Many researchers think that their work will eventually be incorporated into a machine with *general* intelligence (known as strong AI), combining all the skills above and exceeding human abilities at most or all of them. A few believe that anthropomorphic features like artificial consciousness or an artificial brain may be required for such a project.

Many of the problems above may require general intelligence to be considered solved. For example, even a straightforward, specific task like machine translation requires that the machine read and write in both languages (NLP), follow the author's argument (reason), know what is being talked about (knowledge), and faithfully reproduce the author's intention (social intelligence). A problem like machine translation is considered "AI-complete". In order to solve this particular problem, one must solve all the problems.

Approaches

There is no established unifying theory or paradigm that guides AI research. Researchers disagree about many issues. A few of the most long standing questions that have remained unanswered are these: should artificial intelligence simulate natural intelligence by studying psychology or neurology? Or is human biology as irrelevant to AI research as bird biology is to aeronautical engineering? Can intelligent behavior be described using simple, elegant principles (such as logic or optimization)? Or does it necessarily require solving a large number of completely unrelated problems? Can intelligence be reproduced using high-level symbols, similar to words and ideas? Or does it require "sub-symbolic" processing? John Haugeland, who coined the term GOFAI (Good Old-Fashioned Artificial Intelligence), also proposed that AI should more properly be referred to as synthetic intelligence, a term which has since been adopted by some non-GOFAI researchers.

Cybernetics and Brain Simulation

In the 1940s and 1950s, a number of researchers explored the connection between neurology, information theory, and cybernetics. Some of them built machines that used electronic networks to exhibit rudimentary intelligence, such as W. Grey Walter's turtles and the Johns Hopkins Beast. Many of these researchers gathered for meetings of the Teleological Society at Princeton University and the Ratio Club in England. By 1960, this approach was largely abandoned, although elements of it would be revived in the 1980s.

Symbolic

When access to digital computers became possible in the middle 1950s, AI research began to explore the possibility that human intelligence could be reduced to symbol manipulation. The research was centered in three institutions: Carnegie Mellon University, Stanford and MIT, and each one developed its own style of research. John Haugeland named these approaches to AI "good old fashioned AI" or "GOFAI". During the 1960s, symbolic approaches had achieved great success at simulating high-level thinking in small demonstration programs. Approaches based on cybernetics or neural networks were abandoned or pushed into the background. Researchers in the 1960s and the 1970s were convinced that symbolic approaches would eventually succeed in creating a machine with artificial general intelligence and considered this the goal of their field.

Cognitive simulation

> Economist Herbert Simon and Allen Newell studied human problem-solving skills and attempted to formalize them, and their work laid the foundations of the field of artificial intelligence, as well as cognitive science, operations research and management science. Their research team used the results of psychological experiments to develop programs that simulated the techniques that people used to solve problems. This tradition, centered at Carnegie Mellon University would eventually culminate in the development of the Soar architecture in the middle 1980s.

Logic-based

> Unlike Newell and Simon, John McCarthy felt that machines did not need to simulate human thought, but should instead try to find the essence of abstract reasoning and problem solving, regardless of whether people used the same algorithms. His laboratory at Stanford (SAIL) focused on using formal logic to solve a wide variety of problems, including knowledge representation, planning and learning. Logic was also the focus of the work at the University of Edinburgh and elsewhere in Europe which led to the development of the programming language Prolog and the science of logic programming.

"Anti-logic" or "scruffy"

> Researchers at MIT (such as Marvin Minsky and Seymour Papert) found that solving difficult problems in vision and natural language processing required ad-hoc solutions – they argued that there was no simple and general principle (like logic) that would capture all the aspects of intelligent behavior. Roger Schank described their "anti-logic" approaches as "scruffy" (as opposed to the "neat" paradigms at CMU and Stanford). Commonsense knowledge bases (such as Doug Lenat's Cyc) are an example of "scruffy" AI, since they must be built by hand, one complicated concept at a time.

Knowledge-based

> When computers with large memories became available around 1970, researchers from all three traditions began to build knowledge into AI applications. This "knowledge revolution" led to the development and deployment of expert sys-

tems (introduced by Edward Feigenbaum), the first truly successful form of AI software. The knowledge revolution was also driven by the realization that enormous amounts of knowledge would be required by many simple AI applications.

Sub-symbolic

By the 1980s progress in symbolic AI seemed to stall and many believed that symbolic systems would never be able to imitate all the processes of human cognition, especially perception, robotics, learning and pattern recognition. A number of researchers began to look into "sub-symbolic" approaches to specific AI problems. Sub-symbolic methods manage to approach intelligence without specific representations of knowledge.

Bottom-up, embodied, situated, behavior-based or nouvelle AI

> Researchers from the related field of robotics, such as Rodney Brooks, rejected symbolic AI and focused on the basic engineering problems that would allow robots to move and survive. Their work revived the non-symbolic viewpoint of the early cybernetics researchers of the 1950s and reintroduced the use of control theory in AI. This coincided with the development of the embodied mind thesis in the related field of cognitive science: the idea that aspects of the body (such as movement, perception and visualization) are required for higher intelligence.

Computational intelligence and soft computing

> Interest in neural networks and "connectionism" was revived by David Rumelhart and others in the middle 1980s. Neural networks are an example of soft computing --- they are solutions to problems which cannot be solved with complete logical certainty, and where an approximate solution is often enough. Other soft computing approaches to AI include fuzzy systems, evolutionary computation and many statistical tools. The application of soft computing to AI is studied collectively by the emerging discipline of computational intelligence.

Statistical

In the 1990s, AI researchers developed sophisticated mathematical tools to solve specific subproblems. These tools are truly scientific, in the sense that their results are both measurable and verifiable, and they have been responsible for many of AI's recent successes. The shared mathematical language has also permitted a high level of collaboration with more established fields (like mathematics, economics or operations research). Stuart Russell and Peter Norvig describe this movement as nothing less than a "revolution" and "the victory of the neats." Critics argue that these techniques (with few exceptions) are too focused on particular problems and have failed to address the long-term goal of general intelligence. There is an ongoing debate about the relevance and validity of statistical approaches in AI, exemplified in part by exchanges between Peter Norvig and Noam Chomsky.

Integrating the Approaches

Intelligent agent paradigm

An intelligent agent is a system that perceives its environment and takes actions which maximize its chances of success. The simplest intelligent agents are programs that solve specific problems. More complicated agents include human beings and organizations of human beings (such as firms). The paradigm gives researchers license to study isolated problems and find solutions that are both verifiable and useful, without agreeing on one single approach. An agent that solves a specific problem can use any approach that works – some agents are symbolic and logical, some are sub-symbolic neural networks and others may use new approaches. The paradigm also gives researchers a common language to communicate with other fields—such as decision theory and economics—that also use concepts of abstract agents. The intelligent agent paradigm became widely accepted during the 1990s.

Agent architectures and cognitive architectures

Researchers have designed systems to build intelligent systems out of interacting intelligent agents in a multi-agent system. A system with both symbolic and sub-symbolic components is a hybrid intelligent system, and the study of such systems is artificial intelligence systems integration. A hierarchical control system provides a bridge between sub-symbolic AI at its lowest, reactive levels and traditional symbolic AI at its highest levels, where relaxed time constraints permit planning and world modelling. Rodney Brooks' subsumption architecture was an early proposal for such a hierarchical system.

Tools

In the course of 50 years of research, AI has developed a large number of tools to solve the most difficult problems in computer science. A few of the most general of these methods are discussed below.

Search and Optimization

Many problems in AI can be solved in theory by intelligently searching through many possible solutions: Reasoning can be reduced to performing a search. For example, logical proof can be viewed as searching for a path that leads from premises to conclusions, where each step is the application of an inference rule. Planning algorithms search through trees of goals and subgoals, attempting to find a path to a target goal, a process called means-ends analysis. Robotics algorithms for moving limbs and grasping objects use local searches in configuration space. Many learning algorithms use search algorithms based on optimization.

Simple exhaustive searches are rarely sufficient for most real world problems: the search space (the number of places to search) quickly grows to astronomical numbers. The result is a search that is too slow or never completes. The solution, for many problems, is to use "heuristics" or "rules of thumb" that eliminate choices that are unlikely to lead to the goal (called "pruning the search tree"). Heuristics supply the program with a "best guess" for the path on which the solution lies. Heuristics limit the search for solutions into a smaller sample size.

A very different kind of search came to prominence in the 1990s, based on the mathematical theory of optimization. For many problems, it is possible to begin the search with some form of a guess and then refine the guess incrementally until no more refinements can be made. These algorithms can be visualized as blind hill climbing: we begin the search at a random point on the landscape, and then, by jumps or steps, we keep moving our guess uphill, until we reach the top. Other optimization algorithms are simulated annealing, beam search and random optimization.

Evolutionary computation uses a form of optimization search. For example, they may begin with a population of organisms (the guesses) and then allow them to mutate and recombine, selecting only the fittest to survive each generation (refining the guesses). Forms of evolutionary computation include swarm intelligence algorithms (such as ant colony or particle swarm optimization) and evolutionary algorithms (such as genetic algorithms, gene expression programming, and genetic programming).

Logic

Logic is used for knowledge representation and problem solving, but it can be applied to other problems as well. For example, the satplan algorithm uses logic for planning and inductive logic programming is a method for learning.

Several different forms of logic are used in AI research. Propositional or sentential logic is the logic of statements which can be true or false. First-order logic also allows the use of quantifiers and predicates, and can express facts about objects, their properties, and their relations with each other. Fuzzy logic, is a version of first-order logic which allows the truth of a statement to be represented as a value between 0 and 1, rather than simply True (1) or False (0). Fuzzy systems can be used for uncertain reasoning and have been widely used in modern industrial and consumer product control systems. Subjective logic models uncertainty in a different and more explicit manner than fuzzy-logic: a given binomial opinion satisfies belief + disbelief + uncertainty = 1 within a Beta distribution. By this method, ignorance can be distinguished from probabilistic statements that an agent makes with high confidence.

Default logics, non-monotonic logics and circumscription are forms of logic designed to help with default reasoning and the qualification problem. Several extensions of logic have been designed to handle specific domains of knowledge, such as: description logics; situation calculus, event calculus and fluent calculus (for representing events and time); causal calculus; belief calculus; and modal logics.

Probabilistic Methods for Uncertain Reasoning

Many problems in AI (in reasoning, planning, learning, perception and robotics) require the agent to operate with incomplete or uncertain information. AI researchers have devised a number of powerful tools to solve these problems using methods from probability theory and economics.

Bayesian networks are a very general tool that can be used for a large number of problems: reasoning (using the Bayesian inference algorithm), learning (using the expectation-maximization algorithm), planning (using decision networks) and perception (using dynamic Bayesian networks). Probabilistic algorithms can also be used for filtering, prediction, smoothing and finding explanations for streams of data, helping perception systems to analyze processes that occur over time (e.g., hidden Markov models or Kalman filters).

A key concept from the science of economics is "utility": a measure of how valuable something is to an intelligent agent. Precise mathematical tools have been developed that analyze how an agent can make choices and plan, using decision theory, decision analysis, and information value theory. These tools include models such as Markov decision processes, dynamic decision networks, game theory and mechanism design.

Classifiers and Statistical Learning Methods

The simplest AI applications can be divided into two types: classifiers ("if shiny then diamond") and controllers ("if shiny then pick up"). Controllers do, however, also classify conditions before inferring actions, and therefore classification forms a central part of many AI systems. Classifiers are functions that use pattern matching to determine a closest match. They can be tuned according to examples, making them very attractive for use in AI. These examples are known as observations or patterns. In supervised learning, each pattern belongs to a certain predefined class. A class can be seen as a decision that has to be made. All the observations combined with their class labels are known as a data set. When a new observation is received, that observation is classified based on previous experience.

A classifier can be trained in various ways; there are many statistical and machine learning approaches. The most widely used classifiers are the neural network, kernel methods such as the support vector machine, k-nearest neighbor algorithm, Gaussian mixture model, naive Bayes classifier, and decision tree. The performance of these classifiers have been compared over a wide range of tasks. Classifier performance depends greatly on the characteristics of the data to be classified. There is no single classifier that works best on all given problems; this is also referred to as the "no free lunch" theorem. Determining a suitable classifier for a given problem is still more an art than science.

Neural Networks

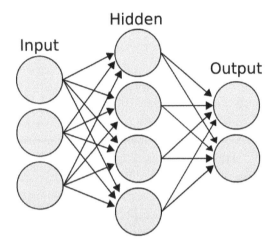

A neural network is an interconnected group of nodes, akin to the vast network of neurons in the human brain.

The study of non-learning artificial neural networks began in the decade before the field of AI research was founded, in the work of Walter Pitts and Warren McCullough. Frank Rosenblatt invented the perceptron, a learning network with a single layer, similar to the old concept of linear regression. Early pioneers also include Alexey Grigorevich Ivakhnenko, Teuvo Kohonen, Stephen Grossberg, Kunihiko Fukushima, Christoph von der Malsburg, David Willshaw, Shun-Ichi Amari, Bernard Widrow, John Hopfield, and others.

The main categories of networks are acyclic or feedforward neural networks (where the signal passes in only one direction) and recurrent neural networks (which allow feedback and short-term memories of previous input events). Among the most popular feedforward networks are perceptrons, multi-layer perceptrons and radial basis networks. Neural networks can be applied to the problem of intelligent control (for robotics) or learning, using such techniques as Hebbian learning, GMDH or competitive learning.

Today, neural networks are often trained by the backpropagation algorithm, which had been around since 1970 as the reverse mode of automatic differentiation published by Seppo Linnainmaa, and was introduced to neural networks by Paul Werbos.

Hierarchical temporal memory is an approach that models some of the structural and algorithmic properties of the neocortex.

Deep Feedforward Neural Networks

Deep learning in artificial neural networks with many layers has transformed many important subfields of artificial intelligence, including computer vision, speech recognition, natural language processing and others.

According to a survey, the expression "Deep Learning" was introduced to the Machine Learning community by Rina Dechter in 1986 and gained traction after Igor Aizenberg and colleagues introduced it to Artificial Neural Networks in 2000. The first functional Deep Learning networks were published by Alexey Grigorevich Ivakhnenko and V. G. Lapa in 1965. These networks are trained one layer at a time. Ivakhnenko's 1971 paper describes the learning of a deep feedforward multilayer perceptron with eight layers, already much deeper than many later networks. In 2006, a publication by Geoffrey Hinton and Ruslan Salakhutdinov introduced another way of pre-training many-layered feedforward neural networks (FNNs) one layer at a time, treating each layer in turn as an unsupervised restricted Boltzmann machine, then using supervised back-propagation for fine-tuning. Similar to shallow artificial neural networks, deep neural networks can model complex non-linear relationships. Over the last few years, advances in both machine learning algorithms and computer hardware have led to more efficient methods for training deep neural networks that contain many layers of non-linear hidden units and a very large output layer.

Deep learning often uses convolutional neural networks (CNNs), whose origins can be traced back to the Neocognitron introduced by Kunihiko Fukushima in 1980. In 1989, Yann LeCun and colleagues applied backpropagation to such an architecture. In the early 2000s, in an industrial application CNNs already processed an estimated 10% to 20% of all the checks written in the US. Since 2011, fast implementations of CNNs on GPUs have won many visual pattern recognition competitions.

Deep feedforward neural networks were used in conjunction with reinforcement learning by AlphaGo, Google Deepmind's program that was the first to beat a professional human player.

Deep Recurrent Neural Networks

Early on, deep learning was also applied to sequence learning with recurrent neural networks (RNNs) which are general computers and can run arbitrary programs to process arbitrary sequences of inputs. The depth of an RNN is unlimited and depends on the length of its input sequence. RNNs can be trained by gradient descent but suffer from the vanishing gradient problem. In 1992, it was shown that unsupervised pre-training of a stack of recurrent neural networks can speed up subsequent supervised learning of deep sequential problems.

Numerous researchers now use variants of a deep learning recurrent NN called the Long short term memory (LSTM) network published by Hochreiter & Schmidhuber in 1997. LSTM is often trained by Connectionist Temporal Classification (CTC). At Google, Microsoft and Baidu this approach has revolutionised speech recognition. For example, in 2015, Google's speech recognition experienced a dramatic performance jump of 49% through CTC-trained LSTM, which is now available through Google Voice to billions of smartphone users. Google also used LSTM to improve machine translation, Language Modeling and Multilingual Language Processing. LSTM combined with CNNs also improved automatic image captioning and a plethora of other applications.

Control Theory

Control theory, the grandchild of cybernetics, has many important applications, especially in robotics.

Languages

AI researchers have developed several specialized languages for AI research, including Lisp and Prolog.

Evaluating Progress

In 1950, Alan Turing proposed a general procedure to test the intelligence of an agent now known as the Turing test. This procedure allows almost all the major problems of artificial intelligence to be tested. However, it is a very difficult challenge and at present all agents fail.

Artificial intelligence can also be evaluated on specific problems such as small problems in chemistry, hand-writing recognition and game-playing. Such tests have been termed subject matter expert Turing tests. Smaller problems provide more achievable goals and there are an ever-increasing number of positive results.

One classification for outcomes of an AI test is:

1. Optimal: it is not possible to perform better.

2. Strong super-human: performs better than all humans.

3. Super-human: performs better than most humans.

4. Sub-human: performs worse than most humans.

For example, performance at draughts (i.e. checkers) is optimal, performance at chess is super-human and nearing strong super-human and performance at many everyday tasks (such as recognizing a face or crossing a room without bumping into something) is sub-human.

A quite different approach measures machine intelligence through tests which are developed from *mathematical* definitions of intelligence. Examples of these kinds of tests start in the late nineties devising intelligence tests using notions from Kolmogorov complexity and data compression. Two major advantages of mathematical definitions are their applicability to nonhuman intelligences and their absence of a requirement for human testers.

A derivative of the Turing test is the Completely Automated Public Turing test to tell Computers and Humans Apart (CAPTCHA). As the name implies, this helps to determine that a user is an actual person and not a computer posing as a human. In contrast to the standard Turing test, CAPTCHA administered by a machine and targeted to a human as opposed to being administered by a human and targeted to a machine. A computer asks a user to complete a simple test then generates a grade for that test. Computers are unable to solve the problem, so correct solutions are deemed to be the result of a person taking the test. A common type of CAPTCHA is the test that requires the typing of distorted letters, numbers or symbols that appear in an image undecipherable by a computer.

Applications

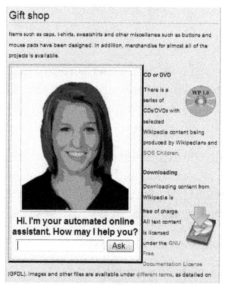

An automated online assistant providing customer service on a web page – one of many very primitive applications of artificial intelligence.

AI is relevant to any intellectual task. Modern artificial intelligence techniques are pervasive and are too numerous to list here. Frequently, when a technique reaches mainstream use, it is no longer considered artificial intelligence; this phenomenon is described as the AI effect.

High-profile examples of AI include autonomous vehicles (such as drones and self-driving cars), medical diagnosis, creating art (such as poetry), proving mathematical theorems, playing games (such as Chess or Go), search engines (such as Google search), online assistants (such as Siri), image recognition in photographs, spam filtering, and targeting online advertisements.

Competitions and Prizes

There are a number of competitions and prizes to promote research in artificial intelligence. The main areas promoted are: general machine intelligence, conversational behavior, data-mining, robotic cars, robot soccer and games.

Platforms

A platform (or "computing platform") is defined as "some sort of hardware architecture or software framework (including application frameworks), that allows software to run." As Rodney Brooks pointed out many years ago, it is not just the artificial intelligence software that defines the AI features of the platform, but rather the actual platform itself that affects the AI that results, i.e., there needs to be work in AI problems on real-world platforms rather than in isolation.

A wide variety of platforms has allowed different aspects of AI to develop, ranging from expert systems such as Cyc to deep-learning frameworks to robot platforms such as the Roomba with open interface. Recent advances in deep artificial neural networks and distributed computing have led to a proliferation of software libraries, including Deeplearning4j, TensorFlow, Theano and Torch.

Philosophy and Ethics

There are three philosophical questions related to AI:

1. Is artificial general intelligence possible? Can a machine solve any problem that a human being can solve using intelligence? Or are there hard limits to what a machine can accomplish?

2. Are intelligent machines dangerous? How can we ensure that machines behave ethically and that they are used ethically?

3. Can a machine have a mind, consciousness and mental states in exactly the same sense that human beings do? Can a machine be sentient, and thus deserve certain rights? Can a machine intentionally cause harm?

The Limits of artificial General Intelligence

Can a machine be intelligent? Can it "think"?

Turing's "polite convention"

> We need not decide if a machine can "think"; we need only decide if a machine can act as intelligently as a human being. This approach to the philosophical problems associated with artificial intelligence forms the basis of the Turing test.

The Dartmouth proposal

"Every aspect of learning or any other feature of intelligence can be so precisely described that a machine can be made to simulate it." This conjecture was printed in the proposal for the Dartmouth Conference of 1956, and represents the position of most working AI researchers.

Newell and Simon's physical symbol system hypothesis

"A physical symbol system has the necessary and sufficient means of general intelligent action." Newell and Simon argue that intelligence consists of formal operations on symbols. Hubert Dreyfus argued that, on the contrary, human expertise depends on unconscious instinct rather than conscious symbol manipulation and on having a "feel" for the situation rather than explicit symbolic knowledge.

Gödelian arguments

Gödel himself, John Lucas (in 1961) and Roger Penrose (in a more detailed argument from 1989 onwards) argued that humans are not reducible to Turing machines. The detailed arguments are complex, but in essence they derive from Kurt Gödel's 1931 proof in his first incompleteness theorem that it is always possible to create statements that a formal system could not prove. A human being, however, can (with some thought) see the truth of these "Gödel statements". Any Turing program designed to search for these statements can have its methods reduced to a formal system, and so will always have a "Gödel statement" derivable from its program which it can never discover. However, if humans are indeed capable of understanding mathematical truth, it doesn't seem possible that we could be limited in the same way. This is quite a general result, if accepted, since it can be shown that hardware neural nets, and computers based on random processes (e.g. annealing approaches) and quantum computers based on entangled qubits (so long as they involve no new physics) can all be reduced to Turing machines. All they do is reduce the complexity of the tasks, not permit new types of problems to be solved. Roger Penrose speculates that there may be new physics involved in our brain, perhaps at the intersection of gravity and quantum mechanics at the Planck scale. This argument, if accepted does not rule out the possibility of true artificial intelligence, but means it has to be biological in basis or based on new physical principles. The argument has been followed up by many counter arguments, and then Roger Penrose has replied to those with counter counter examples, and it is now an intricate complex debate.

The artificial brain argument

The brain can be simulated by machines and because brains are intelligent, simulated brains must also be intelligent; thus machines can be intelligent. Hans Moravec, Ray Kurzweil and others have argued that it is technologically feasible to copy the brain directly into hardware and software, and that such a simulation will be essentially identical to the original.

The AI effect

Machines are *already* intelligent, but observers have failed to recognize it. When Deep Blue beat Garry Kasparov in chess, the machine was acting intelligently. However, onlookers commonly discount the behavior of an artificial intelligence program by arguing that it is not "real" intelligence after all; thus "real" intelligence is whatever intelligent behavior people can do that machines still can not. This is known as the AI Effect: "AI is whatever hasn't been done yet."

Intelligent Behaviour and Machine Ethics

As a minimum, an AI system must be able to reproduce aspects of human intelligence. This raises the issue of how ethically the machine should behave towards both humans and other AI agents. This issue was addressed by Wendell Wallach in his book titled *Moral Machines* in which he introduced the concept of artificial moral agents (AMA). For Wallach, AMAs have become a part of the research landscape of artificial intelligence as guided by its two central questions which he identifies as "Does Humanity Want Computers Making Moral Decisions" and "Can (Ro)bots Really Be Moral". For Wallach the question is not centered on the issue of *whether* machines can demonstrate the equivalent of moral behavior in contrast to the *constraints* which society may place on the development of AMAs.

Machine Ethics

The field of machine ethics is concerned with giving machines ethical principles, or a procedure for discovering a way to resolve the ethical dilemmas they might encounter, enabling them to function in an ethically responsible manner through their own ethical decision making. The field was delineated in the AAAI Fall 2005 Symposium on Machine Ethics: "Past research concerning the relationship between technology and ethics has largely focused on responsible and irresponsible use of technology by human beings, with a few people being interested in how human beings ought to treat machines. In all cases, only human beings have engaged in ethical reasoning. The time has come for adding an ethical dimension to at least some machines. Recognition of the ethical ramifications of behavior involving machines, as well as recent and potential developments in machine autonomy, necessitate this. In contrast to computer hacking, software property issues, privacy issues and other topics normally ascribed to computer ethics, machine ethics is concerned with the behavior of machines towards human users and other machines. Research in machine ethics is key to alleviating concerns with autonomous systems—it could be argued that the notion of autonomous machines without such a dimension is at the root of all fear concerning machine intelligence. Further, investigation of machine ethics could enable the discovery of problems with current ethical theories, advancing our thinking about Ethics." Machine ethics is sometimes referred to as machine morality, computational ethics or computational morality. A variety of perspectives of this nascent field can be found in the collected edition "Machine Ethics" that stems from the AAAI Fall 2005 Symposium on Machine Ethics. Some suggest that to ensure that AI-equipped machines (sometimes called "smart machines") will act ethically requires a new kind of AI. This AI would be able to monitor, supervise, and if need be, correct the first order AI.

Malevolent and Friendly AI

Political scientist Charles T. Rubin believes that AI can be neither designed nor guaranteed to be benevolent. He argues that "any sufficiently advanced benevolence may be indistinguishable from malevolence." Humans should not assume machines or robots would treat us favorably, because there is no *a priori* reason to believe that they would be sympathetic to our system of morality, which has evolved along with our particular biology (which AIs would not share). Hyper-intelligent software may not necessarily decide to support the continued existence of mankind, and would be extremely difficult to stop. This topic has also recently begun to be discussed in academic publications as a real source of risks to civilization, humans, and planet Earth.

Physicist Stephen Hawking, Microsoft founder Bill Gates and SpaceX founder Elon Musk have expressed concerns about the possibility that AI could evolve to the point that humans could not control it, with Hawking theorizing that this could "spell the end of the human race".

One proposal to deal with this is to ensure that the first generally intelligent AI is 'Friendly AI', and will then be able to control subsequently developed AIs. Some question whether this kind of check could really remain in place.

Leading AI researcher Rodney Brooks writes, "I think it is a mistake to be worrying about us developing malevolent AI anytime in the next few hundred years. I think the worry stems from a fundamental error in not distinguishing the difference between the very real recent advances in a particular aspect of AI, and the enormity and complexity of building sentient volitional intelligence."

Devaluation of Humanity

Joseph Weizenbaum wrote that AI applications can not, by definition, successfully simulate genuine human empathy and that the use of AI technology in fields such as customer service or psychotherapy was deeply misguided. Weizenbaum was also bothered that AI researchers (and some philosophers) were willing to view the human mind as nothing more than a computer program (a position now known as computationalism). To Weizenbaum these points suggest that AI research devalues human life.

Decrease in Demand for Human Labor

Martin Ford, author of *The Lights in the Tunnel: Automation, Accelerating Technology and the Economy of the Future*, and others argue that specialized artificial intelligence applications, robotics and other forms of automation will ultimately result in significant unemployment as machines begin to match and exceed the capability of workers to perform most routine and repetitive jobs. Ford predicts that many knowledge-based occupations—and in particular entry level jobs—will be increasingly susceptible to automation via expert systems, machine learning and other AI-enhanced applications. AI-based applications may also be used to amplify the capabilities of low-wage offshore workers, making it more feasible to outsource knowledge work.

Machine Consciousness, Sentience and Mind

If an AI system replicates all key aspects of human intelligence, will that system also be sentient – will it have a mind which has conscious experiences? This question is closely related to the philosophical problem as to the nature of human consciousness, generally referred to as the hard problem of consciousness.

Computationalism

Computationalism is the position in the philosophy of mind that the human mind or the human brain (or both) is an information processing system and that thinking is a form of computing. Computationalism argues that the relationship between mind and body is similar or identical to the relationship between software and hardware and thus may be a solution to the mind-body problem. This philosophical position was inspired by the work of AI researchers and cognitive scientists in the 1960s and was originally proposed by philosophers Jerry Fodor and Hillary Putnam.

Strong AI Hypothesis

Searle's strong AI hypothesis states that "The appropriately programmed computer with the right inputs and outputs would thereby have a mind in exactly the same sense human beings have minds." John Searle counters this assertion with his Chinese room argument, which asks us to look *inside* the computer and try to find where the "mind" might be.

Robot Rights

Mary Shelley's *Frankenstein* considers a key issue in the ethics of artificial intelligence: if a machine can be created that has intelligence, could it also *feel*? If it can feel, does it have the same rights as a human? The idea also appears in modern science fiction, such as the film *A.I.: Artificial Intelligence*, in which humanoid machines have the ability to feel emotions. This issue, now known as "robot rights", is currently being considered by, for example, California's Institute for the Future, although many critics believe that the discussion is premature. The subject is profoundly discussed in the 2010 documentary film *Plug & Pray*.

Superintelligence

Are there limits to how intelligent machines – or human-machine hybrids – can be? A superintelligence, hyperintelligence, or superhuman intelligence is a hypothetical agent that would possess intelligence far surpassing that of the brightest and most gifted human mind. "Superintelligence" may also refer to the form or degree of intelligence possessed by such an agent.

Technological Singularity

If research into Strong AI produced sufficiently intelligent software, it might be able to reprogram and improve itself. The improved software would be even better at improving itself, leading to recursive self-improvement. The new intelligence could thus increase exponentially and dramatically surpass humans. Science fiction writer Vernor Vinge named this scenario "singularity". Technological singularity is when accelerating progress in technologies will cause a runaway effect wherein artificial intelligence will exceed human intellectual capacity and control, thus radically changing or even ending civilization. Because the capabilities of such an intelligence may be impossible to comprehend, the technological singularity is an occurrence beyond which events are unpredictable or even unfathomable.

Ray Kurzweil has used Moore's law (which describes the relentless exponential improvement in digital technology) to calculate that desktop computers will have the same processing power as human brains by the year 2029, and predicts that the singularity will occur in 2045.

Transhumanism

You awake one morning to find your brain has another lobe functioning. Invisible, this auxiliary lobe answers your questions with information beyond the realm of your own memory, suggests plausible courses of action, and asks questions that help bring out relevant facts. You quickly come to rely on the new lobe so much that you stop wondering how it works. You just use it. This is the dream of artificial intelligence.

—BYTE, April 1985

Robot designer Hans Moravec, cyberneticist Kevin Warwick and inventor Ray Kurzweil have predicted that humans and machines will merge in the future into cyborgs that are more capable and powerful than either. This idea, called transhumanism, which has roots in Aldous Huxley and Robert Ettinger, has been illustrated in fiction as well, for example in the manga *Ghost in the Shell* and the science-fiction series *Dune*.

In the 1980s artist Hajime Sorayama's Sexy Robots series were painted and published in Japan depicting the actual organic human form with lifelike muscular metallic skins and later "the Gynoids" book followed that was used by or influenced movie makers including George Lucas and other creatives. Sorayama never considered these organic robots to be real part of nature but always unnatural product of the human mind, a fantasy existing in the mind even when realized in actual form.

Edward Fredkin argues that "artificial intelligence is the next stage in evolution", an idea first proposed by Samuel Butler's "Darwin among the Machines" (1863), and expanded upon by George Dyson in his book of the same name in 1998.

Existential Risk

The development of full artificial intelligence could spell the end of the human race. Once humans develop artificial intelligence, it will take off on its own and redesign itself at an ever-increasing rate. Humans, who are limited by slow biological evolution, couldn't compete and would be superseded.

—Stephen Hawking

A common concern about the development of artificial intelligence is the potential threat it could pose to mankind. This concern has recently gained attention after mentions by celebrities including Stephen Hawking, Bill Gates, and Elon Musk. A group of prominent tech titans including Peter Thiel, Amazon Web Services and Musk have committed $1billion to OpenAI a nonprofit company aimed at championing responsible AI development. The opinion of experts within the field of artificial intelligence is mixed, with sizable fractions both concerned and unconcerned by risk from eventual superhumanly-capable AI.

In his book *Superintelligence*, Nick Bostrom provides an argument that artificial intelligence will pose a threat to mankind. He argues that sufficiently intelligent AI, if it chooses actions based on achieving some goal, will exhibit convergent behavior such as acquiring resources or protecting itself from being shut down. If this AI's goals do not reflect humanity's - one example is an AI told to compute as many digits of pi as possible - it might harm humanity in order to acquire more resources or prevent itself from being shut down, ultimately to better achieve its goal.

For this danger to be realized, the hypothetical AI would have to overpower or out-think all of humanity, which a minority of experts argue is a possibility far enough in the future to not be worth researching. Other counterarguments revolve around humans being either intrinsically or convergently valuable from the perspective of an artificial intelligence.

Concern over risk from artificial intelligence has led to some high-profile donations and investments. In January 2015, Elon Musk donated ten million dollars to the Future of Life Institute to fund research on understanding AI decision making. The goal of the institute is to "grow wisdom with which we manage" the growing power of technology. Musk also funds companies developing artificial intelligence such as Google DeepMind and Vicarious to "just keep an eye on what's going on with artificial intelligence. I think there is potentially a dangerous outcome there."

Development of militarized artificial intelligence is a related concern. Currently, 50+ countries are researching battlefield robots, including the United States, China, Russia, and the United Kingdom. Many people concerned about risk from superintelligent AI also want to limit the use of artificial soldiers.

Moral Decision-making

To keep AI ethical, some have suggested teaching new technologies equipped with AI, such as driver-less cars, to render moral decisions on their own. Others argued that these technologies could learn to act ethically the way children do—by interacting with adults, in particular, with ethicists. Still others suggest these smart technologies can determine the moral preferences of those who use them (just the way one learns about consumer preferences) and then be programmed to heed these preferences.

In Fiction

The implications of artificial intelligence have been a persistent theme in science fiction. Early stories typically revolved around intelligent robots. The word "robot" itself was coined by Karel Čapek in his 1921 play *R.U.R.*, the title standing for "Rossum's Universal Robots". Later, the SF writer Isaac Asimov developed the Three Laws of Robotics which he subsequently explored in a long series of robot stories. These laws have since gained some traction in genuine AI research.

Other influential fictional intelligences include HAL, the computer in charge of the spaceship in *2001: A Space Odyssey*, released as both a film and a book in 1968 and written by Arthur C. Clarke.

AI has since become firmly rooted in popular culture and is in many films, such as *The Terminator* (1984) and *A.I. Artificial Intelligence* (2001).

Robotics

Robotics is the branch of mechanical engineering, electrical engineering and computer science that deals with the design, construction, operation, and application of robots, as well as computer systems for their control, sensory feedback, and information processing.

The Shadow robot hand system

These technologies deal with automated machines (robots for short) that can take the place of humans in dangerous environments or manufacturing processes, or resemble humans in appearance, behaviour, and or cognition. Many of today's robots are inspired by nature, contributing to the field of bio-inspired robotics.

The concept of creating machines that can operate autonomously dates back to classical times, but research into the functionality and potential uses of robots did not grow substantially until the 20th century. Throughout history, it has been frequently assumed that robots will one day be able to mimic human behavior and manage tasks in a human-like fashion. Today, robotics is a rapidly growing field, as technological advances continue; researching, designing, and building new robots serve various practical purposes, whether domestically, commercially, or militarily. Many robots are built to do jobs that are hazardous to people such as defusing bombs, finding survivors in unstable ruins, and exploring mines and shipwrecks. Robotics is also used in STEM (Science, Technology, Engineering, and Mathematics) as a teaching aid.

Etymology

The word *robotics* was derived from the word *robot*, which was introduced to the public by Czech writer Karel Čapek in his play *R.U.R. (Rossum's Universal Robots)*, which was published in 1920. The word *robot* comes from the Slavic word *robota*, which means labour. The play begins in a factory that makes artificial people called *robots*, creatures who can be mistaken for humans – very similar to the modern ideas of androids. Karel Čapek himself did not coin the word. He wrote a short letter in reference to an etymology in the *Oxford English Dictionary* in which he named his brother Josef Čapek as its actual originator.

According to the *Oxford English Dictionary*, the word *robotics* was first used in print by Isaac Asimov, in his science fiction short story "Liar!", published in May 1941 in *Astounding Science Fiction*. Asimov was unaware that he was coining the term; since the science and technology of electrical devices is *electronics*, he assumed *robotics* already referred to the science and technology of robots. In some of Asimov's other works, he states that the first use of the word *robotics* was in his short story *Runaround* (Astounding Science Fiction, March 1942). However, the original publication of "Liar!" predates that of "Runaround" by ten months, so the former is generally cited as the word's origin.

History of Robotics

In 1942 the science fiction writer Isaac Asimov created his Three Laws of Robotics.

In 1948 Norbert Wiener formulated the principles of cybernetics, the basis of practical robotics.

Fully autonomous robots only appeared in the second half of the 20th century. The first digitally operated and programmable robot, the Unimate, was installed in 1961 to lift hot pieces of metal from a die casting machine and stack them. Commercial and industrial robots are widespread today and used to perform jobs more cheaply, more accurately and more reliably, than humans. They are also employed in some jobs which are too dirty, dangerous, or dull to be suitable for humans. Robots are widely used in manufacturing, assembly, packing and packaging, transport, earth and space exploration, surgery, weaponry, laboratory research, safety, and the mass production of consumer and industrial goods.

Date	Significance	Robot Name	Inventor
7000 BC	In Mohanjo-daro, the Dravidian civilization was using bow drills for dentistry. The recent unearthing of the fossil also opens up questions why early Tamils (Thamizh People) needed dentistry. The answer could be the starch, from the cooked ground flour-based food they were consuming.	Dentist bow driller	Early Tamils
Third century B.C. and earlier	One of the earliest descriptions of automata appears in the *Lie Zi* text, on a much earlier encounter between King Mu of Zhou (1023–957 BC) and a mechanical engineer known as Yan Shi, an 'artificer'. The latter allegedly presented the king with a life-size, human-shaped figure of his mechanical handiwork.		Yan Shi (Chinese: 偃師)

First century A.D. and earlier	Descriptions of more than 100 machines and automata, including a fire engine, a wind organ, a coin-operated machine, and a steam-powered engine, in *Pneumatica* and *Automata* by Heron of Alexandria		Ctesibius, Philo of Byzantium, Heron of Alexandria, and others
c. 420 B.C.E	A wooden, steam propelled bird, which was able to fly		Archytas of Tarentum
1206	Created early humanoid automata, programmable automaton band	Robot band, hand-washing automaton, automated moving peacocks	Al-Jazari
1495	Designs for a humanoid robot	Mechanical Knight	Leonardo da Vinci
1738	Mechanical duck that was able to eat, flap its wings, and excrete	Digesting Duck	Jacques de Vaucanson
1898	Nikola Tesla demonstrates first radio-controlled vessel.	Teleautomaton	Nikola Tesla
1921	First fictional automatons called "robots" appear in the play *R.U.R.*	Rossum's Universal Robots	Karel Čapek
1930s	Humanoid robot exhibited at the 1939 and 1940 World's Fairs	Elektro	Westinghouse Electric Corporation
1946	First general-purpose digital computer	Whirlwind	Multiple people
1948	Simple robots exhibiting biological behaviors	Elsie and Elmer	William Grey Walter
1956	First commercial robot, from the Unimation company founded by George Devol and Joseph Engelberger, based on Devol's patents	Unimate	George Devol
1961	First installed industrial robot.	Unimate	George Devol
1973	First industrial robot with six electromechanically driven axes	Famulus	KUKA Robot Group
1974	The world's first microcomputer controlled electric industrial robot, IRB 6 from ASEA, was delivered to a small mechanical engineering company in southern Sweden. The design of this robot had been patented already 1972.	IRB 6	ABB Robot Group
1975	Programmable universal manipulation arm, a Unimation product	PUMA	Victor Scheinman

Robotic Aspects

Robotic construction

Electrical aspect

```
// Dev-C++ 4.9.9.2
// Project Type: Win32 GUI
// Window: Window Header
#include <Windows.h>
#include "resource.h"
// Window: Window Name
#ifdef NULL
#undef NULL
#define NULL 0
#endif
#define Wnd_Class "WIN_CHK"
#define Wnd_Title "預設視窗"
// Window: Window Parameters
static UINT WndPos_X = 0, WndPos_Y = 0;
// 400 x 300
static UINT WndPos_Width = 400, WndPos_Height = 300;
static HWND hwndWnd = 0;
static HINSTANCE hinstWnd = 0;
LRESULT CALLBACK WndProc(HWND, UINT, WPARAM, LPARAM);
BOOL ProcMsg(void);
BOOL BuildWnd( const char*, const char*);
void InitWindow_PositionCenter( UINT&, UINT&, UINT, UINT, BOOL);
// Window: Window Entry
int WINAPI WinMain(HINSTANCE hInstance, HINSTANCE hPrevInstance,
                    LPSTR lpCmdLine, int nShowCmd)
{
    //==START of WinMain==//
    if ( (hwndWnd = ::FindWindow( Wnd_Class, Wnd_Title)) != NULL )
    {
        ::SetForegroundWindow(hwndWnd);
        return NULL;
    }
    if ( BuildWnd( Wnd_Class, Wnd_Title) == TRUE )
    {
        while ( ProcMsg() == TRUE );
    }
    //==END of WinMain==//
    return NULL;
}
```

A level of programming

There are many types of robots; they are used in many different environments and for many different uses, although being very diverse in application and form they all share three basic similarities when it comes to their construction:

1. Robots all have some kind of mechanical construction, a frame, form or shape designed to achieve a particular task. For example, a robot designed to travel across heavy dirt or mud, might use caterpillar tracks. The mechanical aspect is mostly the creator's solution to completing the assigned task and dealing with the physics of the environment around it. Form follows function.

2. Robots have electrical components which power and control the machinery. For example, the robot with caterpillar tracks would need some kind of power to move the tracker treads. That power comes in the form of electricity, which will have to travel through a wire and originate from a battery, a basic electrical circuit. Even petrol powered machines that get their power mainly from petrol still require an electric current to start the combustion process which is why most petrol powered machines like cars, have batteries. The electrical aspect of robots is used for movement (through motors), sensing (where electrical signals are used to measure things like heat, sound, position, and energy status) and operation (robots need some level of electrical energy supplied to their motors and sensors in order to activate and perform basic operations)

3. All robots contain some level of computer programming code. A program is how a robot decides when or how to do something. In the caterpillar track example, a robot that needs to move across a muddy road may have the correct mechanical construction, and receive the correct amount of power from its battery, but would not go anywhere without a program telling it to move. Programs are the core essence of a robot, it could have excellent mechanical and electrical construction, but if its program is poorly constructed its performance will be very poor (or it may not perform at all). There are three different types of robotic programs: remote control, artificial intelligence and hybrid. A robot with remote control programing has a preexisting set of commands that it will only perform if and when it receives a signal from a control source, typically a human being with a remote control. It is perhaps more appropriate to view devices controlled primarily by human commands as falling in the discipline of automation rather than robotics. Robots that use artificial intelligence interact with their environment on their own without a control source, and can determine reactions to objects and problems they encounter using their preexisting programming. Hybrid is a form of programming that incorporates both AI and RC functions.

Applications

As more and more robots are designed for specific tasks this method of classification becomes more relevant. For example, many robots are designed for assembly work, which may not be readily adaptable for other applications. They are termed as "assembly robots". For seam welding, some suppliers provide complete welding systems with the robot i.e. the welding equipment along with other material handling facilities like turntables etc. as an integrated unit. Such an integrated robotic system is called a "welding robot" even though its discrete manipulator unit could be adapted to a variety of tasks. Some robots are specifically designed for heavy load manipulation, and are labelled as "heavy duty robots."

Current and potential applications include:

- Military robots

- Caterpillar plans to develop remote controlled machines and expects to develop fully autonomous heavy robots by 2021. Some cranes already are remote controlled.

- It was demonstrated that a robot can perform a herding task.

- Robots are increasingly used in manufacturing (since the 1960s). In the auto industry they can amount for more than half of the "labor". There are even "lights off" factories such as an IBM keyboard manufacturing factory in Texas that is 100% automated.

- Robots such as HOSPI are used as couriers in hospitals (hospital robot). Other hospital tasks performed by robots are receptionists, guides and porters helpers,

- Robots can serve as waiters and cooks., also at home. Boris is a robot that can load a dishwasher.

- Robot combat for sport – hobby or sport event where two or more robots fight in an arena to disable each other. This has developed from a hobby in the 1990s to several TV series worldwide.

- Cleanup of contaminated areas, such as toxic waste or nuclear facilities.

- Agricultural robots (AgRobots,).

- Domestic robots, cleaning and caring for the elderly

- Medical robots performing low-invasive surgery

- Household robots with full use.

- Nanorobots

Components

Power Source

At present mostly (lead–acid) batteries are used as a power source. Many different types of batteries can be used as a power source for robots. They range from lead–acid batteries, which are safe and have relatively long shelf lives but are rather heavy compared to silver–cadmium batteries that are much smaller in volume and are currently much more expensive. Designing a battery-powered robot needs to take into account factors such as safety, cycle lifetime and weight. Generators, often some type of internal combustion engine, can also be used. However, such designs are often mechanically complex and need fuel, require heat dissipation and are relatively heavy. A tether connecting the robot to a power supply would remove the power supply from the robot entirely. This has the advantage of saving weight and space by moving all power generation and storage components elsewhere. However, this design does come with the drawback of constantly having a cable connected to the robot, which can be difficult to manage. Potential power sources could be:

- pneumatic (compressed gases)

- Solar power (using the sun's energy and converting it into electrical power)

- hydraulics (liquids)

- flywheel energy storage

- organic garbage (through anaerobic digestion)

- nuclear

Actuation

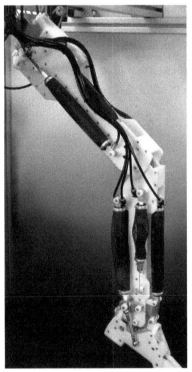

A robotic leg powered by air muscles

Actuators are the "muscles" of a robot, the parts which convert stored energy into movement. By far the most popular actuators are electric motors that rotate a wheel or gear, and linear actuators that control industrial robots in factories. There are some recent advances in alternative types of actuators, powered by electricity, chemicals, or compressed air.

Electric Motors

The vast majority of robots use electric motors, often brushed and brushless DC motors in portable robots or AC motors in industrial robots and CNC machines. These motors are often preferred in systems with lighter loads, and where the predominant form of motion is rotational.

Linear Actuators

Various types of linear actuators move in and out instead of by spinning, and often have quicker direction changes, particularly when very large forces are needed such as with industrial robotics. They are typically powered by compressed air (pneumatic actuator) or an oil (hydraulic actuator).

Series Elastic Actuators

A spring can be designed as part of the motor actuator, to allow improved force control. It has been used in various robots, particularly walking humanoid robots.

Air Muscles

Pneumatic artificial muscles, also known as air muscles, are special tubes that expand(-typically up to 40%) when air is forced inside them. They are used in some robot applications.

Muscle Wire

Muscle wire, also known as shape memory alloy, Nitinol® or Flexinol® wire, is a material which contracts (under 5%) when electricity is applied. They have been used for some small robot applications.

Electroactive Polymers

EAPs or EPAMs are a new plastic material that can contract substantially (up to 380% activation strain) from electricity, and have been used in facial muscles and arms of humanoid robots, and to enable new robots to float, fly, swim or walk.

Piezo Motors

Recent alternatives to DC motors are piezo motors or ultrasonic motors. These work on a fundamentally different principle, whereby tiny piezoceramic elements, vibrating many thousands of times per second, cause linear or rotary motion. There are different mechanisms of operation; one type uses the vibration of the piezo elements to step the motor in a circle or a straight line. Another type uses the piezo elements to cause a nut to vibrate or to drive a screw. The advantages of these motors are nanometer resolution, speed, and available force for their size. These motors are already available commercially, and being used on some robots.

Elastic Nanotubes

Elastic nanotubes are a promising artificial muscle technology in early-stage experimental development. The absence of defects in carbon nanotubes enables these filaments to deform elastically by several percent, with energy storage levels of perhaps 10 J/cm³ for metal nanotubes. Human biceps could be replaced with an 8 mm diameter wire of this material. Such compact "muscle" might allow future robots to outrun and outjump humans.

Sensing

Sensors allow robots to receive information about a certain measurement of the environment, or internal components. This is essential for robots to perform their tasks, and act upon any changes in the environment to calculate the appropriate response. They are used for various forms of measurements, to give the robots warnings about safety or malfunctions, and to provide real time information of the task it is performing.

Touch

Current robotic and prosthetic hands receive far less tactile information than the human hand. Recent research has developed a tactile sensor array that mimics the mechanical properties and touch receptors of human fingertips. The sensor array is constructed as a rigid core surrounded by conductive fluid contained by an elastomeric skin. Electrodes are mounted on the surface of the rigid core and are connected to an impedance-measuring device within the core. When the artificial skin touches an object the fluid path around the electrodes is deformed, producing impedance changes that map the forces received from the object. The researchers expect that an important function of such artificial fingertips will be adjusting robotic grip on held objects.

Scientists from several European countries and Israel developed a prosthetic hand in 2009, called SmartHand, which functions like a real one—allowing patients to write with it, type on a keyboard, play piano and perform other fine movements. The prosthesis has sensors which enable the patient to sense real feeling in its fingertips.

Vision

Computer vision is the science and technology of machines that see. As a scientific discipline, computer vision is concerned with the theory behind artificial systems that extract information from images. The image data can take many forms, such as video sequences and views from cameras.

In most practical computer vision applications, the computers are pre-programmed to solve a particular task, but methods based on learning are now becoming increasingly common.

Computer vision systems rely on image sensors which detect electromagnetic radiation which is typically in the form of either visible light or infra-red light. The sensors are designed using solid-state physics. The process by which light propagates and reflects off surfaces is explained using optics. Sophisticated image sensors even require quantum mechanics to provide a complete understanding of the image formation process. Robots can also be equipped with multiple vision sensors to be better able to compute the sense of depth in the environment. Like human eyes, robots' "eyes" must also be able to focus on a particular area of interest, and also adjust to variations in light intensities.

There is a subfield within computer vision where artificial systems are designed to mimic the processing and behavior of biological system, at different levels of complexity. Also, some of the learning-based methods developed within computer vision have their background in biology.

Other

Other common forms of sensing in robotics use lidar, radar and sonar.

Manipulation

Robots need to manipulate objects; pick up, modify, destroy, or otherwise have an effect. Thus the "hands" of a robot are often referred to as *end effectors*, while the "arm" is referred to as a *manipulator*. Most robot arms have replaceable effectors, each allowing them to perform some small range of tasks. Some have a fixed manipulator which cannot be replaced, while a few have one very general purpose manipulator, for example a humanoid hand. Learning how to manipulate a robot often requires a close feedback between human to the robot, although there are several methods for remote manipulation of robots.

KUKA industrial robot operating in a foundry

Puma, one of the first industrial robots

Baxter, a modern and versatile industrial robot developed by Rodney Brooks

Mechanical Grippers

One of the most common effectors is the gripper. In its simplest manifestation it consists of just two fingers which can open and close to pick up and let go of a range of small objects. Fingers can for example be made of a chain with a metal wire run through it. Hands that resemble and work more like a human hand include the Shadow Hand and the Robonaut hand. Hands that are of a mid-level complexity include the Delft hand. Mechanical grippers can come in various types, including friction and encompassing jaws. Friction jaws use all the force of the gripper to hold the object in place using friction. Encompassing jaws cradle the object in place, using less friction.

Vacuum Grippers

Vacuum grippers are very simple astrictive devices, but can hold very large loads provided the prehension surface is smooth enough to ensure suction.

Pick and place robots for electronic components and for large objects like car windscreens, often use very simple vacuum grippers.

General Purpose Effectors

Some advanced robots are beginning to use fully humanoid hands, like the Shadow Hand, MANUS, and the Schunk hand. These are highly dexterous manipulators, with as many as 20 degrees of freedom and hundreds of tactile sensors.

Rolling Robots

Segway in the Robot museum in Nagoya

For simplicity most mobile robots have four wheels or a number of continuous tracks. Some researchers have tried to create more complex wheeled robots with only one or two wheels. These can have certain advantages such as greater efficiency and reduced parts, as well as allowing a robot to navigate in confined places that a four-wheeled robot would not be able to.

Two-wheeled Balancing Robots

Balancing robots generally use a gyroscope to detect how much a robot is falling and then drive the wheels proportionally in the same direction, to counterbalance the fall at hundreds of times per second, based on the dynamics of an inverted pendulum. Many different balancing robots have been designed. While the Segway is not commonly thought of as a robot, it can be thought of as a component of a robot, when used as such Segway refer to them as RMP (Robotic Mobility Platform). An example of this use has been as NASA's Robonaut that has been mounted on a Segway.

One-wheeled Balancing Robots

A one-wheeled balancing robot is an extension of a two-wheeled balancing robot so that it can move in any 2D direction using a round ball as its only wheel. Several one-wheeled balancing robots have been designed recently, such as Carnegie Mellon University's "Ballbot" that is the approximate height and width of a person, and Tohoku Gakuin University's "BallIP". Because of the long, thin shape and ability to maneuver in tight spaces, they have the potential to function better than other robots in environments with people.

Spherical Orb Robots

Several attempts have been made in robots that are completely inside a spherical ball, either by spinning a weight inside the ball, or by rotating the outer shells of the sphere. These have also been referred to as an orb bot or a ball bot.

Six-wheeled Robots

Using six wheels instead of four wheels can give better traction or grip in outdoor terrain such as on rocky dirt or grass.

Tracked Robots

TALON military robots used by the United States Army

Tank tracks provide even more traction than a six-wheeled robot. Tracked wheels behave as if they were made of hundreds of wheels, therefore are very common for outdoor and military robots, where the robot must drive on very rough terrain. However, they are difficult to use indoors such as on carpets and smooth floors. Examples include NASA's Urban Robot "Urbie".

Walking Applied to Robots

Walking is a difficult and dynamic problem to solve. Several robots have been made which can walk reliably on two legs, however none have yet been made which are as robust as a human. There has been much study on human inspired walking, such as AMBER lab which was established in 2008 by the Mechanical Engineering Department at Texas A&M University. Many other robots have been built that walk on more than two legs, due to these robots being significantly easier to construct. Walking robots can be used for uneven terrains, which would provide better mobility and energy efficiency than other locomotion methods. Hybrids too have been proposed in movies such as I, Robot, where they walk on 2 legs and switch to 4 (arms+legs) when going to a sprint. Typically, robots on 2 legs can walk well on flat floors and can occasionally walk up stairs. None can walk over rocky, uneven terrain. Some of the methods which have been tried are:

Zmp Technique

The Zero Moment Point (ZMP) is the algorithm used by robots such as Honda's ASIMO. The robot's onboard computer tries to keep the total inertial forces (the combination of Earth's gravity and the acceleration and deceleration of walking), exactly opposed by the floor reaction force (the force of the floor pushing back on the robot's foot). In this way, the two forces cancel out, leaving no moment (force causing the robot to rotate and fall over). However, this is not exactly how a human walks, and the difference is obvious to human observers, some of whom have pointed out that ASIMO walks as if it needs the lavatory. ASIMO's walking algorithm is not static, and some dynamic balancing is used. However, it still requires a smooth surface to walk on.

Hopping

Several robots, built in the 1980s by Marc Raibert at the MIT Leg Laboratory, successfully demonstrated very dynamic walking. Initially, a robot with only one leg, and a very small foot, could stay upright simply by hopping. The movement is the same as that of a person on a pogo stick. As the robot falls to one side, it would jump slightly in that direction, in order to catch itself. Soon, the algorithm was generalised to two and four legs. A bipedal robot was demonstrated running and even performing somersaults. A quadruped was also demonstrated which could trot, run, pace, and bound.

Dynamic Balancing (Controlled Falling)

A more advanced way for a robot to walk is by using a dynamic balancing algorithm, which is potentially more robust than the Zero Moment Point technique, as it constantly monitors the robot's motion, and places the feet in order to maintain stability. This technique was recently demonstrated by Anybots' Dexter Robot, which is so stable, it can even jump. Another example is the TU Delft Flame.

Passive Dynamics

Perhaps the most promising approach utilizes passive dynamics where the momentum of swinging limbs is used for greater efficiency. It has been shown that totally unpowered humanoid mechanisms can walk down a gentle slope, using only gravity to propel themselves. Using this technique, a robot need only supply a small amount of motor power to walk along a flat surface or a little more to walk up a hill. This technique promises to make walking robots at least ten times more efficient than ZMP walkers, like ASIMO.

Other Methods of Locomotion

Flying

Two robot snakes. Left one has 64 motors (with 2 degrees of freedom per segment), the right one 10.

A modern passenger airliner is essentially a flying robot, with two humans to manage it. The autopilot can control the plane for each stage of the journey, including takeoff, normal flight, and even landing. Other flying robots are uninhabited, and are known as unmanned aerial vehicles (UAVs). They can be smaller and lighter without a human pilot on board, and fly into dangerous territory for military surveillance missions. Some can even fire on targets under command. UAVs are also being developed which can fire on targets automatically, without the need for a command from a human. Other flying robots include cruise missiles, the Entomopter, and the Epson micro helicopter robot. Robots such as the Air Penguin, Air Ray, and Air Jelly have lighter-than-air bodies, propelled by paddles, and guided by sonar.

Snaking

Several snake robots have been successfully developed. Mimicking the way real snakes move, these robots can navigate very confined spaces, meaning they may one day be used to search for people trapped in collapsed buildings. The Japanese ACM-R5 snake robot can even navigate both on land and in water.

Skating

A small number of skating robots have been developed, one of which is a multi-mode walking and skating device. It has four legs, with unpowered wheels, which can either step or roll. Another robot, Plen, can use a miniature skateboard or roller-skates, and skate across a desktop.

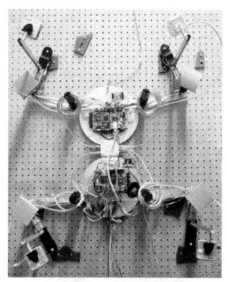

Capuchin, a climbing robot

Climbing

Grasping is a central issue when climbing a vertical surface. Nevertheless, even when grasping is straightforward real time climbing avoiding obstacles may still be a complex task,. An example for the centrality of the grasping task would be Capuchin, built by Dr. Ruixiang Zhang at Stanford University, California. Another approach uses the specialized toe pad method of wall-climbing geckoes, which can run on smooth surfaces such as vertical glass. Examples of this approach include Wallbot and Stickybot. China's *Technology Daily* reported on November 15, 2008 that Dr. Li Hiu Yeung and his research group of New Concept Aircraft (Zhuhai) Co., Ltd. had successfully developed a bionic gecko robot named "Speedy Freelander". According to Dr. Li, the gecko robot could rapidly climb up and down a variety of building walls, navigate through ground and wall fissures, and walk upside-down on the ceiling. It was also able to adapt to the surfaces of smooth glass, rough, sticky or dusty walls as well as various types of metallic materials. It could also identify and circumvent obstacles automatically. Its flexibility and speed were comparable to a natural gecko. A third approach is to mimic the motion of a snake climbing a pole.. Lastly one may mimic the movements of a human climber on a wall with protrusions; adjusting the center of mass and moving each limb in turn to gain leverage.

Swimming (Piscine)

It is calculated that when swimming some fish can achieve a propulsive efficiency greater than 90%. Furthermore, they can accelerate and maneuver far better than any man-made boat or submarine, and produce less noise and water disturbance. Therefore, many researchers studying underwater robots would like to copy this type of locomotion. Notable examples are the Essex University Computer Science Robotic Fish G9, and the Robot Tuna built by the Institute of Field Robotics, to analyze and mathematically model thunniform motion. The Aqua Penguin, designed and built by Festo of Germany, copies the streamlined shape and propulsion by front "flippers" of penguins. Festo have also built the Aqua Ray and Aqua Jelly, which emulate the locomotion of manta ray, and jellyfish, respectively.

Robotic Fish: *iSplash*-II

In 2014 *iSplash*-II was developed by R.J Clapham PhD at Essex University. It was the first robotic fish capable of outperforming real carangiform fish in terms of average maximum velocity (measured in body lengths/ second) and endurance, the duration that top speed is maintained. This build attained swimming speeds of 11.6BL/s (i.e. 3.7 m/s). The first build, *iSplash*-I (2014) was the first robotic platform to apply a full-body length carangiform swimming motion which was found to increase swimming speed by 27% over the traditional approach of a posterior confined wave form.

Sailing

The autonomous sailboat robot *Vaimos*

Sailboat robots have also been developed in order to make measurements at the surface of the ocean. A typical sailboat robot is *Vaimos* built by IFREMER and ENS-TA-Bretagne. Since the propulsion of sailboat robots uses the wind, the energy of the batteries is only used for the computer, for the communication and for the actuators (to tune the rudder and the sail). If the robot is equipped with solar panels, the robot could theoretically navigate forever. The two main competitions of sailboat robots are WRSC, which takes place every year in Europe, and Sailbot.

Environmental Interaction and Navigation

Radar, GPS, and lidar, are all combined to provide proper navigation and obstacle avoidance (vehicle developed for 2007 DARPA Urban Challenge)

Though a significant percentage of robots in commission today are either human controlled, or operate in a static environment, there is an increasing interest in robots that can operate autonomously in a dynamic environment. These robots require some combination of navigation hardware and software in order to traverse their environment. In particular unforeseen events (e.g. people and other obstacles that are not stationary) can cause problems or collisions. Some highly advanced robots such as ASIMO, and Meinü robot have particularly good robot navigation hardware and software. Also, self-controlled cars, Ernst Dickmanns' driverless car, and the entries in the DARPA Grand Challenge, are capable of sensing the environment well and subsequently making navigational decisions based on this information. Most of these robots employ a GPS navigation device with waypoints, along with radar, sometimes combined with other sensory data such as lidar, video cameras, and inertial guidance systems for better navigation between waypoints.

Human-robot Interaction

The state of the art in sensory intelligence for robots will have to progress through several orders of magnitude if we want the robots working in our homes to go beyond vacuum-cleaning the floors. If robots are to work effectively in homes and other non-industrial environments, the way they are instructed to perform their jobs, and especially how they will be told to stop will be of critical importance. The people who interact with them may have little or no training in robotics, and so any interface will need to be extremely intuitive. Science fiction authors also typically assume that robots will eventually be capable of communicating with humans through speech, gestures, and facial expressions, rather than a command-line interface. Although speech would be the most natural way for the human to communicate, it is unnatural for the robot. It will probably be a long time before robots interact as naturally as the fictional C-3PO, or Data of Star Trek, Next Generation.

Kismet can produce a range of facial expressions.

Speech Recognition

Interpreting the continuous flow of sounds coming from a human, in real time, is a difficult task for a computer, mostly because of the great variability of speech. The same word, spoken by the same person may sound different depending on local acoustics, volume, the previous word, whether or not the speaker has a cold, etc.. It becomes even harder when the speaker has a different accent. Nevertheless, great strides have been made in the field since Davis, Biddulph, and Balashek designed the first "voice input system" which recognized "ten digits spoken by a single user with 100% accuracy" in 1952. Currently, the best systems can recognize continuous, natural speech, up to 160 words per minute, with an accuracy of 95%.

Robotic Voice

Other hurdles exist when allowing the robot to use voice for interacting with humans. For social reasons, synthetic voice proves suboptimal as a communication medium, making it necessary to develop the emotional component of robotic voice through various techniques.

Gestures

One can imagine, in the future, explaining to a robot chef how to make a pastry, or asking directions from a robot police officer. In both of these cases, making hand gestures would aid the verbal descriptions. In the first case, the robot would be recognizing gestures made by the human, and perhaps repeating them for confirmation. In the second case, the robot police officer would gesture to indicate "down the road, then turn right".

It is likely that gestures will make up a part of the interaction between humans and robots. A great many systems have been developed to recognize human hand gestures.

Facial Expression

Facial expressions can provide rapid feedback on the progress of a dialog between two humans, and soon may be able to do the same for humans and robots. Robotic faces have been constructed by Hanson Robotics using their elastic polymer called Frubber, allowing a large number of facial expressions due to the elasticity of the rubber facial coating and embedded subsurface motors (servos). The coating and servos are built on a metal skull. A robot should know how to approach a human, judging by their facial expression and body language. Whether the person is happy, frightened, or crazy-looking affects the type of interaction expected of the robot. Likewise, robots like Kismet and the more recent addition, Nexi can produce a range of facial expressions, allowing it to have meaningful social exchanges with humans.

Artificial Emotions

Artificial emotions can also be generated, composed of a sequence of facial expressions and/or gestures. As can be seen from the movie Final Fantasy: The Spirits Within, the programming of these artificial emotions is complex and requires a large amount of human observation. To simplify this programming in the movie, presets were created together with a special software program. This decreased the amount of time needed to make the film. These presets could possibly be transferred for use in real-life robots.

Personality

Many of the robots of science fiction have a personality, something which may or may not be desirable in the commercial robots of the future. Nevertheless, researchers are trying to create robots which appear to have a personality: i.e. they use sounds, facial expressions, and body language to try to convey an internal state, which may be joy, sadness, or fear. One commercial example is Pleo, a toy robot dinosaur, which can exhibit several apparent emotions.

Social Intelligence

The Socially Intelligent Machines Lab of the Georgia Institute of Technology researches new concepts of guided teaching interaction with robots. Aim of the projects is a social robot learns task goals from human demonstrations without prior knowledge of high-level concepts. These new concepts are grounded from low-level continuous sensor data through unsupervised learning, and task goals are subsequently learned using a Bayesian approach. These concepts can be used to transfer knowledge to future tasks, resulting in faster learning of those tasks. The results are demonstrated by the robot *Curi* who can scoop some pasta from a pot onto a plate and serve the sauce on top.

Control

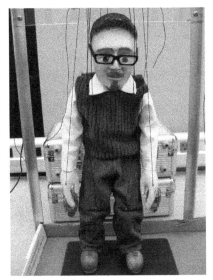

Puppet Magnus, a robot-manipulated marionette with complex control systems

RuBot II can resolve manually Rubik cubes

The mechanical structure of a robot must be controlled to perform tasks. The control of a robot involves three distinct phases – perception, processing, and action (robotic paradigms). Sensors give information about the environment or the robot itself (e.g. the position of its joints or its end effector). This information is then processed to be stored or transmitted, and to calculate the appropriate signals to the actuators (motors) which move the mechanical.

The processing phase can range in complexity. At a reactive level, it may translate raw sensor information directly into actuator commands. Sensor fusion may first be used to estimate parameters of interest (e.g. the position of the robot's gripper) from noisy sensor data. An immediate task (such as moving the gripper in a certain direction) is inferred from these estimates. Techniques from control theory convert the task into commands that drive the actuators.

At longer time scales or with more sophisticated tasks, the robot may need to build and reason with a "cognitive" model. Cognitive models try to represent the robot, the world, and how they interact. Pattern recognition and computer vision can be used to track objects. Mapping techniques can be used to build maps of the world. Finally, motion planning and other artificial intelligence techniques may be used to figure out how to act. For example, a planner may figure out how to achieve a task without hitting obstacles, falling over, etc.

Autonomy Levels

TOPIO, a humanoid robot, played ping pong at Tokyo IREX 2009.

Control systems may also have varying levels of autonomy.

1. Direct interaction is used for haptic or tele-operated devices, and the human has nearly complete control over the robot's motion.

2. Operator-assist modes have the operator commanding medium-to-high-level tasks, with the robot automatically figuring out how to achieve them.

3. An autonomous robot may go for extended periods of time without human interaction. Higher levels of autonomy do not necessarily require more complex cognitive capabilities. For example, robots in assembly plants are completely autonomous, but operate in a fixed pattern.

Another classification takes into account the interaction between human control and the machine motions.

1. Teleoperation. A human controls each movement, each machine actuator change is specified by the operator.

2. Supervisory. A human specifies general moves or position changes and the machine decides specific movements of its actuators.

3. Task-level autonomy. The operator specifies only the task and the robot manages itself to complete it.

4. Full autonomy. The machine will create and complete all its tasks without human interaction.

Robotics Research

Much of the research in robotics focuses not on specific industrial tasks, but on investigations into new types of robots, alternative ways to think about or design robots, and new ways to manufacture them but other investigations, such as MIT's cyberflora project, are almost wholly academic.

A first particular new innovation in robot design is the opensourcing of robot-projects. To describe the level of advancement of a robot, the term "Generation Robots" can be used. This term is coined by Professor Hans Moravec, Principal Research Scientist at the Carnegie Mellon University Robotics Institute in describing the near future evolution of robot technology. *First generation* robots, Moravec predicted in 1997, should have an intellectual capacity comparable to perhaps a lizard and should become available by 2010. Because the *first generation* robot would be incapable of learning, however, Moravec predicts that the *second generation* robot would be an improvement over the *first* and become available by 2020, with the intelligence maybe comparable to that of a mouse. The *third generation* robot should have the intelligence comparable to that of a monkey. Though *fourth generation* robots, robots with human intelligence, professor Moravec predicts, would become possible, he does not predict this happening before around 2040 or 2050.

The second is evolutionary robots. This is a methodology that uses evolutionary computation to help design robots, especially the body form, or motion and behavior controllers. In a similar way to natural evolution, a large population of robots is allowed to compete in some way, or their ability to perform a task is measured using a fitness function. Those that perform worst are removed from the population, and replaced by a new set, which have new behaviors based on those of the winners. Over time the population improves, and eventually a satisfactory robot may appear. This happens without any direct programming of the robots by the researchers. Researchers use this method both to create better robots, and to explore the nature of evolution. Because the process often requires many generations of robots to be simulated, this technique may be run entirely or mostly in simulation, then tested on real robots once the evolved algorithms are good enough. Currently, there are about 10 million industrial robots toiling around the world, and Japan is the top country having high density of utilizing robots in its manufacturing industry.

Dynamics and Kinematics

The study of motion can be divided into kinematics and dynamics. Direct kinematics refers to the calculation of end effector position, orientation, velocity, and acceleration when the corresponding joint values are known. Inverse kinematics refers to the opposite case in which required joint values are calculated for given end effector values, as done in path planning. Some special aspects of kinematics include handling of redundancy (different possibilities of performing the same movement), collision avoidance, and singularity avoidance. Once all relevant positions, velocities, and accelerations have been calculated using kinematics, methods from the field of dynamics are used to study the effect of forces upon these movements. Direct dynamics refers to the calculation of accelerations in the robot once the applied forces are known. Direct dynamics is used in computer simulations of the robot. Inverse dynamics refers to the calculation of the actuator forces necessary to create a prescribed end effector acceleration. This information can be used to improve the control algorithms of a robot.

In each area mentioned above, researchers strive to develop new concepts and strategies, improve existing ones, and improve the interaction between these areas. To do this, criteria for "optimal" performance and ways to optimize design, structure, and control of robots must be developed and implemented.

Bionics and Biomimetics

Bionics and biomimetics apply the physiology and methods of locomotion of animals to the design of robots. For example, the design of BionicKangaroo was based on the way kangaroos jump.

Non Rigid Robots

One can distinguish two robot types with regards to their backbone structure:

- Soft robotics deals with mechanisms that possess a compressible flexible backbone. Examples are scarce. A notable example for this type of robots was introduced by Shepherd et al. A robot built only from elastic polymers moves as a four-legged mechanism with the ability to actuate each leg individually in a one-axis bending motion. This motion is achieved by small air pockets placed on the top of one side of the leg's elastic backbone. When compressed with air, the air pockets bend the leg as a result of volume change. Despite the simple mechanism, compressed air (or fluid) must be delivered constantly for locomotion and thus a second system is forced, which the robot needs to carry. On the other hand, electronic-free soft mechanisms have the advantages of water resistance and crush sustainability,both which are essential for rescue missions. Another soft "crushable mechanism" was designed by Sangbae et al. - A soft robot actuated with NiTi wires. The researchers have fabricated a mechanism capable of crawling like an earthworm using peristaltic motion.

- "Flexible robots" possess a non-compressible flexible backbone. Medina et al. introduced an Actuated Flexible Manifold - a two-dimensional hyper-redundant grid surface mechanism which can be manipulated into any continuous smooth function. Recent years show an increased interest in flexible robots due to their efficiency in hard and unknown terrain.

Education and Training

Robotics engineers design robots, maintain them, develop new applications for them, and conduct research to expand the potential of robotics. Robots have become a popular educational tool in some middle and high schools, particularly in parts of the USA, as well as in numerous youth summer camps, raising interest in programming, artificial intelligence and robotics among students. First-year computer science courses at some universities now include programming of a robot in addition to traditional software engineering-based coursework.

Career Training

Universities offer bachelors, masters, and doctoral degrees in the field of robotics. Vocational schools offer robotics training aimed at careers in robotics.

Certification

The Robotics Certification Standards Alliance (RCSA) is an international robotics certification authority that confers various industry- and educational-related robotics certifications.

Summer Robotics Camp

Several national summer camp programs include robotics as part of their core curriculum, including Digital Media Academy, RoboTech, and Cybercamps. In addition, youth summer robotics programs are frequently offered by celebrated museums such as the American Museum of Natural History and The Tech Museum of Innovation in Silicon Valley, CA, just to name a few. An educational robotics lab also exists at the IE & mgmnt Faculty of the Technion. It was created by Dr. Jacob Rubinovitz.

Some examples of summer camps are: EdTech, the Robotics Camp-Montreal, After-Four-Toronto, Exceed Robotics-Thornhill, among many others.

All this camps offers:

- Practical ideas for using technology in your classroom.

- A small, collaborative, hands-on learning environment.

- Sixteen+ hours of learning in a relaxed and picturesque setting.

- Develop a repertoire of new tools and tactics to effectively integrate technology into your lessons.

Robotics Competitions

There are lots of competitions all around the globe. One of the most important competitions is the FLL or FIRST Lego League. The idea of this specific competition is that kids start developing knowledge and getting into robotics while playing with Legos since they are 9 years old. This competition is associated with Ni or National Instruments.

Robotics Afterschool Programs

Many schools across the country are beginning to add robotics programs to their after school curriculum. Some major programs for afterschool robotics include FIRST Robotics Competition, Botball and B.E.S.T. Robotics. Robotics competitions often include aspects of business and marketing as well as engineering and design.

The Lego company began a program for children to learn and get excited about robotics at a young age.

Employment

A robot technician builds small all-terrain robots. (Courtesy: MobileRobots Inc)

Robotics is an essential component in many modern manufacturing environments. As factories increase their use of robots, the number of robotics–related jobs grow and have been observed to be steadily rising. The employment of robots in industries has increased productivity and efficiency savings and is typically seen as a long term investment for benefactors.

Occupational Safety and Health Implications of Robotics

A discussion paper drawn up by EU-OSHA highlights how the spread of robotics presents both opportunities and challenges for occupational safety and health (OSH).

The greatest OSH benefits stemming from the wider use of robotics should be substitution for people working in unhealthy or dangerous environments. In space, defence, security, or the nuclear industry, but also in logistics, maintenance and inspection, autonomous robots are particularly useful in replacing human workers performing dirty, dull or unsafe tasks, thus avoiding workers' exposures to hazardous agents and conditions and reducing physical, ergonomic and psychosocial risks. For example, robots are already used to perform repetitive and monotonous tasks, to handle radioactive material or to work in explosive atmospheres. In the future, many other highly repetitive, risky or unpleasant tasks will be performed by robots in a variety of sectors like agriculture, construction, transport, healthcare, firefighting or cleaning services.

Despite these advances, there are certain skills to which humans will be better suited than machines for some time to come and the question is how to achieve the best combination of human and robot skills. The advantages of robotics include heavy-duty jobs with precision and repeatability, whereas the advantages of humans include creativity, decision-making, flexibility and adaptability. This need to combine optimal skills has resulted in collaborative robots and humans sharing a common workspace more closely and led to the development of new approaches and standards to guarantee the safety of the "man-robot merger". Some European countries are including robotics in their national programmes and trying to promote a safe and flexible co-operation between robots and operators to achieve better productivity. For example, the German Federal Institute for Occupational Safety and Health (BAuA) organises annual workshops on the topic "human-robot collaboration".

In future, co-operation between robots and humans will be diversified, with robots increasing their autonomy and human-robot collaboration reaching completely new forms. Current approaches and technical standards aiming to protect employees from the risk of working with collaborative robots will have to be revised.

Systems Development Life Cycle

The systems development life cycle (SDLC), also referred to as the application development life-cycle, is a term used in systems engineering, information systems and software engineering to describe a process for planning, creating, testing, and deploying an information system. The systems development life-cycle concept applies to a range of hardware and software configurations, as a system can be composed of hardware only, software only, or a combination of both.

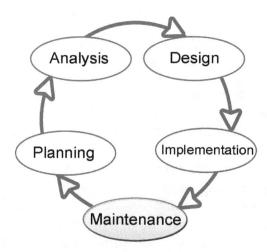

Model of the systems development life cycle, highlighting the maintenance phase.

Overview

A systems development life cycle is composed of a number of clearly defined and distinct work phases which are used by systems engineers and systems developers to plan for, design, build, test, and deliver information systems. Like anything that is manufactured on an assembly line, an SDLC aims to produce high quality systems that meet or exceed customer expectations, based on customer requirements, by delivering systems which move through each clearly defined phase, within scheduled time-frames and cost estimates. Computer systems are complex and often (especially with the recent rise of service-oriented architecture) link multiple traditional systems potentially supplied by different software vendors. To manage this level of complexity, a number of SDLC models or methodologies have been created, such as "waterfall"; "spiral"; "Agile software development"; "rapid prototyping"; "incremental"; and "synchronize and stabilize".

SDLC can be described along a spectrum of agile to iterative to sequential. Agile methodologies, such as XP and Scrum, focus on lightweight processes which allow for rapid changes (without necessarily following the pattern of SDLC approach) along the development cycle. Iterative methodologies, such as Rational Unified Process and dynamic systems development method, focus on limited project scope and expanding or improving products by multiple iterations. Sequential or big-design-up-front (BDUF) models, such as waterfall, focus on complete and correct planning to guide large projects and risks to successful and predictable results. Other models, such as anamorphic development, tend to focus on a form of development that is guided by project scope and adaptive iterations of feature development.

In project management a project can be defined both with a project life cycle (PLC) and an SDLC, during which slightly different activities occur. According to Taylor (2004) "the project life cycle encompasses all the activities of the project, while the systems development life cycle focuses on realizing the product requirements".

SDLC is used during the development of an IT project, it describes the different stages involved in the project from the drawing board, through the completion of the project.

History and Details

The product life cycle describes the process for building information systems in a very deliberate, structured and methodical way, reiterating each stage of the product's life. The systems development life cycle, according to Elliott & Strachan & Radford (2004), "originated in the 1960s, to develop large scale functional business systems in an age of large scale business conglomerates. Information systems activities revolved around heavy data processing and number crunching routines".

Several systems development frameworks have been partly based on SDLC, such as the structured systems analysis and design method (SSADM) produced for the UK government Office of Government Commerce in the 1980s. Ever since, according to Elliott (2004), "the traditional life cycle approaches to systems development have been increasingly replaced with alternative approaches and frameworks, which attempted to overcome some of the inherent deficiencies of the traditional SDLC".

Phases

The system development life cycle framework provides a sequence of activities for system designers and developers to follow. It consists of a set of steps or phases in which each phase of the SDLC uses the results of the previous one.

The SDLC adheres to important phases that are essential for developers, such as planning, analysis, design, and implementation, and are explained in the section below. It includes evaluation of present system, information gathering, feasibility study and request approval. A number of SDLC models have been created: waterfall, fountain, spiral, build and fix, rapid prototyping, incremental, synchronize and stabilize. The oldest of these, and the best known, is the waterfall model: a sequence of stages in which the output of each stage becomes the input for the next. These stages can be characterized and divided up in different ways, including the following:

- Preliminary analysis: The objective of phase 1 is to conduct a preliminary analysis, propose alternative solutions, describe costs and benefits and submit a preliminary plan with recommendations.

  Conduct the preliminary analysis: in this step, you need to find out the organization's objectives and the nature and scope of the problem under study. Even if a problem refers only to a small segment of the organization itself then you need to find out what the objectives of the organization itself are. Then you need to see how the problem being studied fits in with them.

  Propose alternative solutions: In digging into the organization's objectives and specific problems, you may have already covered some solutions. Alternate proposals may come from interviewing employees, clients, suppliers, and/or consultants. You can also study what competitors are doing. With this data, you will have three choices: leave the system as is, improve it, or develop a new system.

Describe the costs and benefits.

- **Systems analysis, requirements definition**: Defines project goals into defined functions and operation of the intended application. It is the process of gathering and interpreting facts, diagnosing problems and recommending improvements to the system. Analyzes end-user information needs and also removes any inconsistencies and incompleteness in these requirements.

A series of steps followed by the developer are:

1. Collection of Facts: End user requirements are obtained through documentation, client interviews, observation and questionnaires,

2. Scrutiny of the existing system: Identify pros and cons of the current system in-place, so as to carry forward the pros and avoid the cons in the new system.

3. Analyzing the proposed system: Solutions to the shortcomings in step two are found and any specific user proposals are used to prepare the specifications.

- Systems design: Describes desired features and operations in detail, including screen layouts, business rules, process diagrams, pseudocode and other documentation.

- Development: The real code is written here.

- Integration and testing: Brings all the pieces together into a special testing environment, then checks for errors, bugs and interoperability.

- Acceptance, installation, deployment: The final stage of initial development, where the software is put into production and runs actual business.

- Maintenance: During the maintenance stage of the SDLC, the system is assessed to ensure it does not become obsolete. This is also where changes are made to initial software. It involves continuous evaluation of the system in terms of its performance.

- Evaluation: Some companies do not view this as an official stage of the SDLC, while others consider it to be an extension of the maintenance stage, and may be referred to in some circles as post-implementation review. This is where the system that was developed, as well as the entire process, is evaluated. Some of the questions that need to be answered include: does the newly implemented system meet the initial business requirements and objectives? Is the system reliable and fault-tolerant? Does the system function according to the approved functional requirements? In addition to evaluating the software that was released, it is important to assess the effectiveness of the development process. If there are any aspects of the entire process, or certain stages, that management is not satisfied with, this is the time to improve. Evaluation and assessment is a difficult issue. However, the company must reflect on the process and address weaknesses.

- Disposal: In this phase, plans are developed for discarding system information, hardware and software in making the transition to a new system. The purpose here is to properly move, archive, discard or destroy information, hardware and software that is being replaced, in a manner that prevents any possibility of unauthorized disclosure of sensitive data. The disposal activities ensure proper migration to a new system. Particular emphasis is given to proper preservation and archival of data processed by the previous system. All of this should be done in accordance with the organization's security requirements.

In the following example (see picture) these stages of the systems development life cycle are divided in ten steps from definition to creation and modification of IT work products:

Systems Development Life Cycle (SDLC)
Life-Cycle Phases

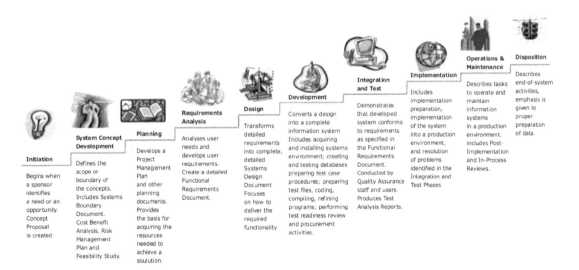

The tenth phase occurs when the system is disposed of and the task performed is either eliminated or transferred to other systems. The tasks and work products for each phase are described in subsequent chapters.

Not every project will require that the phases be sequentially executed. However, the phases are interdependent. Depending upon the size and complexity of the project, phases may be combined or may overlap.

System investigation

The system investigates the IT proposal. During this step, we must consider all current priorities that would be affected and how they should be handled. Before any system planning is done, a feasibility study should be conducted to determine if creating a new or improved system is a viable solution. This will help to determine the costs, benefits, resource requirements, and specific user needs required for completion. The development process can only continue once management approves of the recommendations from the feasibility study.

Following are different components of the feasibility study:

- Operational feasibility

- Economic feasibility

- Technical feasibility

- Human factors feasibility

- Legal/Political feasibility

System Analysis

The goal of system analysis is to determine where the problem is, in an attempt to fix the system. This step involves breaking down the system in different pieces to analyze the situation, analyzing project goals, breaking down what needs to be created and attempting to engage users so that definite requirements can be defined.

Design

In systems design, the design functions and operations are described in detail, including screen layouts, business rules, process diagrams and other documentation. The output of this stage will describe the new system as a collection of modules or subsystems.

The design stage takes as its initial input the requirements identified in the approved requirements document. For each requirement, a set of one or more design elements will be produced as a result of interviews, workshops, and/or prototype efforts.

Design elements describe the desired system features in detail, and generally include functional hierarchy diagrams, screen layout diagrams, tables of business rules, business process diagrams, pseudo-code, and a complete entity-relationship diagram with a full data dictionary. These design elements are intended to describe the system in sufficient detail, such that skilled developers and engineers may develop and deliver the system with minimal additional input design.

Environments

Environments are controlled areas where systems developers can build, distribute, install, configure, test, and execute systems that move through the SDLC. Each environment is aligned with different areas of the SDLC and is intended to have specific purposes. Examples of such environments include the:

- *Development environment*, where developers can work independently of each other before trying to merge their work with the work of others,

- *Common build environment*, where merged work can be built, together, as a combined system,

- *Systems integration testing environment*, where basic testing of a system's integration points to other upstream or downstream systems can be tested,

- *User acceptance testing environment*, where business stakeholders can test against their original business requirements,

- *Production environment*, where systems finally get deployed to, for final use by their intended end users.

Testing

The code is tested at various levels in software testing. Unit, system and user acceptance testings are often performed. This is a grey area as many different opinions exist as to what the stages of testing are and how much, if any iteration occurs. Iteration is not generally part of the waterfall model, but the means to rectify defects and validate fixes prior to deployment is incorporated into this phase.

The following are types of testing that may be relevant, depending on the type of system under development:

- *Defect testing* the failed scenarios, including defect tracking

- Path testing

- Data set testing

- Unit testing

- System testing

- Integration testing

- Black-box testing

- White-box testing

- Regression testing

- Automation testing
- User acceptance testing
- Software performance testing

Training and Transition

Once a system has been stabilized through adequate testing, the SDLC ensures that proper training on the system is performed or documented before transitioning the system to its support staff and end users.

Training usually covers operational training for those people who will be responsible for supporting the system as well as training for those end users who will be using the system after its delivery to a production operating environment.

After training has been successfully completed, systems engineers and developers transition the system to its final production environment, where it is intended to be used by its end users and supported by its support and operations staff.

Operations and Maintenance

The deployment of the system includes changes and enhancements before the decommissioning or sunset of the system. Maintaining the system is an important aspect of SDLC. As key personnel change positions in the organization, new changes will be implemented. There are two approaches to system development; there is the traditional approach (structured) and object oriented. Information Engineering includes the traditional system approach, which is also called the structured analysis and design technique. The object oriented approach views the information system as a collection of objects that are integrated with each other to make a full and complete information system.

Evaluation

The final phase of the SDLC is to measure the effectiveness of the system and evaluate potential enhancements.

Systems Analysis and Design

The systems analysis and design (SAD) is the process of developing information systems (IS) that effectively use hardware, software, data, processes, and people to support the company's businesses objectives. System analysis and design can be considered the meta-development activity, which serves to set the stage and bound the problem. SAD can be leveraged to set the correct balance among competing high-level requirements in the functional and non-functional analysis domains. System analysis and design interacts strongly with distributed enterprise architecture, enterprise I.T. Architecture, and business architecture, and relies heavily on concepts such as partitioning, interfaces, personae and roles, and deployment/operational modeling to arrive at a high-level system description. This high level description is then further broken down into the components and modules which can be analyzed, designed, and constructed separately and integrated to accomplish the business goal. SDLC and SAD are cornerstones of full life cycle product and system planning.

Object-Oriented Analysis

Object-oriented analysis (OOA) is the process of analyzing a task (also known as a problem domain), to develop a conceptual model that can then be used to complete the task. A typical OOA model would describe computer software that could be used to satisfy a set of customer-defined requirements. During the analysis phase of problem-solving, a programmer might consider a written requirements statement, a formal vision document, or interviews with stakeholders or other interested parties. The task to be addressed might be divided into several subtasks (or domains), each representing a different business, technological, or other areas of interest. Each subtask would be analyzed separately. Implementation constraints, (e.g., concurrency, distribution, persistence, or how the system is to be built) are not considered during the analysis phase; rather, they are addressed during object-oriented design (OOD).

The conceptual model that results from OOA will typically consist of a set of use cases, one or more UML class diagrams, and a number of interaction diagrams. It may also include some kind of user interface mock-up.

The input for object-oriented design is provided by the output of object-oriented analysis. Realize that an output artifact does not need to be completely developed to serve as input of object-oriented design; analysis and design may occur in parallel, and in practice the results of one activity can feed the other in a short feedback cycle through an iterative process. Both analysis and design can be performed incrementally, and the artifacts can be continuously grown instead of completely developed in one shot.

Some typical (but common to all types of design analysis) input artifacts for object-oriented:

- Conceptual model: Conceptual model is the result of object-oriented analysis, it captures concepts in the problem domain. The conceptual model is explicitly chosen to be independent of implementation details, such as concurrency or data storage.

- Use case: Use case is a description of sequences of events that, taken together, lead to a system doing something useful. Each use case provides one or more scenarios that convey how the system should interact with the users called actors to achieve a specific business goal or function. Use case actors may be end users or other systems. In many circumstances use cases are further elaborated into use case diagrams. Use case diagrams are used to identify the actor (users or other systems) and the processes they perform.

- System Sequence Diagram: System Sequence diagram (SSD) is a picture that shows, for a particular scenario of a use case, the events that external actors generate, their order, and possible inter-system events.

- User interface documentations (if applicable): Document that shows and describes the look and feel of the end product's user interface. It is not mandatory to have this, but it helps to visualize the end-product and therefore helps the designer.

- Relational data model (if applicable): A data model is an abstract model that describes how data is represented and used. If an object database is not used, the relational data model should usually be created before the design, since the strategy chosen for object-relational mapping is an output of the OO design process. However, it is possible to develop the relational data model and the object-oriented design artifacts in parallel, and the growth of an artifact can stimulate the refinement of other artifacts.

Life Cycle

Management and Control

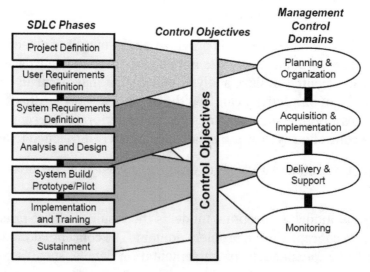

SPIU phases related to management controls.

The SDLC phases serve as a programmatic guide to project activity and provide a flexible but consistent way to conduct projects to a depth matching the scope of the project. Each of the SDLC phase objectives are described in this section with key deliverables, a description of recommended tasks, and a summary of related control objectives for effective management. It is critical for the project manager to establish and monitor control objectives during each SDLC phase while executing projects. Control objectives help to provide a clear statement of the desired result or purpose and should be used throughout the entire SDLC process. Control objectives can be grouped into major categories (domains), and relate to the SDLC phases as shown in the figure.

To manage and control any SDLC initiative, each project will be required to establish some degree of a work breakdown structure (WBS) to capture and schedule the work necessary to complete the project. The WBS and all programmatic material should be kept in the "project description" section of the project notebook. The WBS format is mostly left to the project manager to establish in a way that best describes the project work.

There are some key areas that must be defined in the WBS as part of the SDLC policy. The following diagram describes three key areas that will be addressed in the WBS in a manner established by the project manager. The diagram shows coverage spans numerous phases of the SDLC but the associated MCD has a subset of primary mappings to the SDLC phases. For example, Analysis and Design is primarily performed as part of the Acquisition and Implementation Domain and System Build and Prototype is primarily performed as part of delivery and support.

Work Breakdown Structured Organization

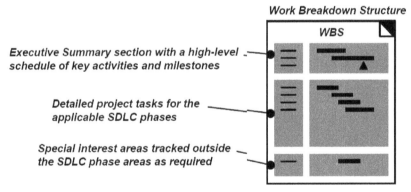

Work breakdown structure.

The upper section of the work breakdown structure (WBS) should identify the major phases and milestones of the project in a summary fashion. In addition, the upper section should provide an overview of the full scope and timeline of the project and will be part of the initial project description effort leading to project approval. The middle section of the WBS is based on the seven systems development life cycle phases as a guide for WBS task development. The WBS elements should consist of milestones and "tasks" as opposed to "activities" and have a definitive period (usually two weeks or more). Each task must have a measurable output (e.x. document, decision, or analysis). A WBS task may rely on one or more activities (e.g. software engineering, systems engineering) and may require close coordination with other tasks, either internal or external to the project. Any part of the project needing support from contractors should have a statement of work (SOW) written to include the appropriate tasks from the SDLC phases. The development of a SOW does not occur during a specific phase of SDLC but is developed to include the work from the SDLC process that may be conducted by external resources such as contractors.

Baselines

Baselines are an important part of the systems development life cycle. These baselines are established after four of the five phases of the SDLC and are critical to the iterative nature of the model . Each baseline is considered as a milestone in the SDLC.

- functional baseline: established after the conceptual design phase.

- allocated baseline: established after the preliminary design phase.

- product baseline: established after the detail design and development phase.

- updated product baseline: established after the production construction phase.

Complementary Methodologies

Complementary software development methods to systems development life cycle are:

- Software prototyping

- Joint applications development (JAD)

- Rapid application development (RAD)

- Extreme programming (XP);

- Open-source development

- End-user development

- Object-oriented programming

Comparison of Methodology Approaches (Post, & Anderson 2006)							
	SDLC	**RAD**	**Open source**	**Objects**	**JAD**	**Prototyping**	**End User**
Control	Formal	MIS	Weak	Standards	Joint	User	User
Time frame	Long	Short	Medium	Any	Medium	Short	Short –
Users	Many	Few	Few	Varies	Few	One or two	One
MIS staff	Many	Few	Hundreds	Split	Few	One or two	None
Transaction/DSS	Transaction	Both	Both	Both	DSS	DSS	DSS
Interface	Minimal	Minimal	Weak	Windows	Crucial	Crucial	Crucial

Documentation and training	Vital	Limited	Internal	In Objects	Limited	Weak	None
Integrity and security	Vital	Vital	Unknown	In Objects	Limited	Weak	Weak
Reusability	Limited	Some	Maybe	Vital	Limited	Weak	None

Strengths and Weaknesses

Few people in the modern computing world would use a strict waterfall model for their SDLC as many modern methodologies have superseded this thinking. Some will argue that the SDLC no longer applies to models like Agile computing, but it is still a term widely in use in technology circles. The SDLC practice has advantages in traditional models of systems development, that lends itself more to a structured environment. The disadvantages to using the SDLC methodology is when there is need for iterative development or (i.e. web development or e-commerce) where stakeholders need to review on a regular basis the software being designed. Instead of viewing SDLC from a strength or weakness perspective, it is far more important to take the best practices from the SDLC model and apply it to whatever may be most appropriate for the software being designed.

A comparison of the strengths and weaknesses of SDLC:

Strength and Weaknesses of SDLC	
Strengths	**Weaknesses**
Control.	Increased development time.
Monitor large projects.	Increased development cost.
Detailed steps.	Systems must be defined up front.
Evaluate costs and completion targets.	Rigidity.
Documentation.	Hard to estimate costs, project overruns.
Well defined user input.	User input is sometimes limited.
Ease of maintenance.	
Development and design standards.	
Tolerates changes in MIS staffing.	

An alternative to the SDLC is rapid application development, which combines prototyping, joint application development and implementation of CASE tools. The advantages of RAD are speed, reduced development cost, and active user involvement in the development process.

References

* Luger, George; Stubblefield, William (2004). Artificial Intelligence: Structures and Strategies for Complex Problem Solving (5th ed.). Benjamin/Cummings. ISBN 0-8053-4780-1.

- Neapolitan, Richard; Jiang, Xia (2012). Contemporary Artificial Intelligence. Chapman & Hall/CRC. ISBN 978-1-4398-4469-4.

- Russell, Stuart J.; Norvig, Peter (2003), Artificial Intelligence: A Modern Approach (2nd ed.), Upper Saddle River, New Jersey: Prentice Hall, ISBN 0-13-790395-2.

- Poole, David; Mackworth, Alan; Goebel, Randy (1998). Computational Intelligence: A Logical Approach. New York: Oxford University Press. ISBN 0-19-510270-3.

- Raphael, Bertram (1976). The Thinking Computer,Mind Inside Matter. W.H.Freeman and Company. ISBN 0-7167-0722-5.

- Crevier, Daniel (1993), AI: The Tumultuous Search for Artificial Intelligence, New York, NY: BasicBooks, ISBN 0-465-02997-3.

- McCorduck, Pamela (2004), Machines Who Think (2nd ed.), Natick, MA: A. K. Peters, Ltd., ISBN 1-56881-205-1.

- Newquist, HP (1994). The Brain Makers: Genius, Ego, And Greed In The Quest For Machines That Think. New York: Macmillan/SAMS. ISBN 0-672-30412-0.

- Nilsson, Nils (2009). The Quest for Artificial Intelligence: A History of Ideas and Achievements. New York: Cambridge University Press. ISBN 978-0-521-12293-1.

- Dreyfus, Hubert; Dreyfus, Stuart (1986). Mind over Machine: The Power of Human Intuition and Expertise in the Era of the Computer. Oxford, UK: Blackwell. ISBN 0-02-908060-6.

- Fearn, Nicholas (2007). The Latest Answers to the Oldest Questions: A Philosophical Adventure with the World's Greatest Thinkers. New York: Grove Press. ISBN 0-8021-1839-9.

- Kahneman, Daniel; Slovic, D.; Tversky, Amos (1982). Judgment under uncertainty: Heuristics and biases. New York: Cambridge University Press. ISBN 0-521-28414-7.

- Koza, John R. (1992). Genetic Programming (On the Programming of Computers by Means of Natural Selection). MIT Press. ISBN 0-262-11170-5.

- Shapiro, Stuart C. (1992). "Artificial Intelligence". In Shapiro, Stuart C. Encyclopedia of Artificial Intelligence (PDF) (2nd ed.). New York: John Wiley. pp. 54–57. ISBN 0-471-50306-1.

- Weizenbaum, Joseph (1976). Computer Power and Human Reason. San Francisco: W.H. Freeman & Company. ISBN 0-7167-0464-1.

- Crane, Carl D.; Joseph Duffy (1998). Kinematic Analysis of Robot Manipulators. Cambridge University Press. ISBN 0-521-57063-8. Retrieved 2007-10-16.

- Marakas, James A. O'Brien, George M. (2010). Management information systems (10th ed.). New York: McGraw-Hill/Irwin. pp. 485–489. ISBN 0073376817.

- Bach, Joscha (2008). "Seven Principles of Synthetic Intelligence". In Wang, Pei; Goertzel, Ben; Franklin, Stan. Artificial General Intelligence, 2008: Proceedings of the First AGI Conference. IOS Press. pp. 63–74. ISBN 978-1-58603-833-5.

- Hutter, M. (2012). "One Decade of Universal Artificial Intelligence". Theoretical Foundations of Artificial General Intelligence. Atlantis Thinking Machines 4. doi:10.2991/978-94-91216-62-6_5. ISBN 978-94-91216-61-9.

- Katz, Yarden (1 November 2012). "Noam Chomsky on Where Artificial Intelligence Went Wrong". The Atlantic. Retrieved 26 October 2014.

Permissions

Index

www.ingramcontent.com/pod-product-compliance
Lightning Source LLC
Jackson TN
JSHW052155130125
77033JS00004B/181

* 9 7 8 1 6 3 5 4 9 1 5 0 0 *